# How to Actively Engage Our Students in the Language Classes

Edited by

**Carmela B. Scala**

Rutgers University

**Series in Education**

**VERNON PRESS**

www.vernonpress.com

*In the Americas:*
Vernon Press
1000 N West Street, Suite 1200
Wilmington, Delaware, 19801
United States

*In the rest of the world:*
Vernon Press
C/Sancti Espiritu 17,
Malaga, 29006
Spain

Series in Education

Library of Congress Control Number: 2022943139

ISBN: 978-1-64889-702-3

Also available: 978-1-64889-522-7 [Hardback]; 978-1-64889-583-8 [PDF, E-Book]

# Table of Contents

# List of Figures

# List of Tables

# Foreword

This volume was inspired by a presentation I gave at a conference a few years ago.

I presented a paper on how to engage our generation of students and how to make learning and precisely make learning a language more relevant to them.

In a world that moves at a speed that only a few years ago seemed impossible to achieve, our students are used to having the universe at their fingertips and breathing technology. As educators in the twenty-first century, we need to understand its impact on society and especially on our student's learning experience and find a way to make it work to our, and most importantly, their — our students'— advantage.

Personally, I have been experimenting with several active learning strategies to promote a student-centered learning environment where learners get the chance to engage with the professor, the course material, and their peers on a deeper level. They get to share what they learn and have an opportunity to confront their understanding with peers and practice 'freely' (with no pressure) what they have learned via different media. However, I was eager to know what other colleagues around the world had been doing on the matter. That is why I decided to send out a call for articles on engaging students in the classroom (both in-person and online). The response I got was overwhelming, and I carefully selected the more innovative and thought-provoking articles.

This edited volume presents some inspiring research in second language acquisition, focusing on active learning, cooperative and collaborative approach, and other innovative strategies to engage the students and promote learning. I sincerely hope you enjoy reading it as much as I did, and I hope you can find some valuable advice and inspiration in it.

**Carmela B. Scala**

**Editor**

Chapter 1

# Incorporating *Last Week Tonight* into an ESL/EFL Active Learning Classroom

Jon Bakos
*Indiana State University*

**Abstract:** When teaching a writing course, it can be daunting to include active learning - one of the main things the students should be doing is writing, which is inherently not very social. However, in many Composition classes, one of the primary skills being acquired is argumentation, and this can be very social indeed. This chapter presents an approach for using episodes of the HBO show *Last Week Tonight* as a frame for modeling argumentation, followed by a simulation roleplay that requires active debate and discussion for the students. Although I present this as mainly a writing lesson, it can easily incorporate all the traditional four skills of reading, writing, speaking and listening. Further, while the lesson described focuses the classroom discussion around the topic of lotteries, the chapter is intended as a template that could be applied to many other topics investigated by the show.

**Keywords:** Active learning, argumentative writing, ESL, role-playing, simulations.

\*\*\*

## Intended Audience

This is a lesson template intended for adult learners and would work best in a Writing/Composition course or four-skills ESL course. I have used these lessons at Indiana State University in our ESL 103A and B courses, which are intended to prepare for college-level Introductory Composition. As such, the students have tested into the university with sufficient English to take college courses, but have been found to need enough writing support that they don't go straight into native-speaking writing courses. 103A (and B especially) are modeled after Composition and feature similar assignments, such as Compare and Contrast and Argumentative essays. Thus, the lessons here focus on analyzing argumentation and rhetorical appeals and are intended for advanced learners of English. Neither the topics nor the register of language is appropriate for children, although they might be fitting for high schoolers.

### Active Learning and Simulations

Felder and Brent define *active learning* as "anything course-related that all students in a class session are called upon to do other than simply watching, listening and taking notes" (Felder and Brent 2009, 2). With that in mind, this chapter aims to incorporate active learning methods into an ESL writing curriculum, with a focus on simulations. There is strong scholarly evidence that active learning classroom practices are beneficial to students – to the point that a meta-study of 225 papers on active learning had this to say:

> If the experiments analyzed here had been conducted as randomized controlled trials of medical interventions, they may have been stopped for benefit—meaning that enrolling patients in the control condition might be discontinued because the treatment being tested was clearly more beneficial. (Freeman et al. 2014, 8413).

Freeman et al. point to improved scores on tests as specific benefits of an active learning classroom, and Allsop, Young, Nelson, Piatt, and Knapp point to additional benefits in their own work to assess the benefits of active learning, commenting:

> The results of this study support previous research demonstrating that increases in student engagement, participation and learning are firmly established benefits of active learning. The findings also identified four additional active learning classroom benefits: communication and interactivity, community and connectedness, satisfaction, and flexibility. (Allsop et al. 2020, 423).

There are many ways to employ active learning strategies, from games to debates to simulations, but they must be consciously be made part of the pedagogy. How, then, can ESL instructors create this environment, and what might a set of lessons look like?

This chapter uses an example simulation from the text *English Composition Simulations* by Gene Halleck (Halleck 2013), and so I'll spend some time discussing the book as well as some of its premises which relate to simulations in general. Simulations are unscripted role-plays in which the participants act out a scenario, usually with some sort of intended goal or outcome at the conclusion. Many examples of this style of activity can be seen in popular culture, such as party games like murder mysteries, *Werewolf* or *Mafia,* or the recently-trendy *Among Us* video game. In the latter examples, the players are asked to work as a group to determine who among them is a double-agent or 'Imposter,' who is working to undermine the team.

While I'm a great fan of using these games in a teaching setting, a key element of them is that the players have almost no actual information to work with, because there are very few mechanics to definitively learn another player's role. They must base nearly everything on intuition and reading mannerisms. While this can make for great fun and speculation, the players have little concrete evidence to form arguments with. Many of the simulations in *English Composition Simulations*, however (such as the one discussed here), require prior research on the students' part in order to carry out effectively. This can make them more suited to a Composition classroom, as the students will need to plan their own arguments, as well as be ready for possible counter-arguments from other teams.

Although this chapter's simulation is similar in style to a debate, it is important to notice the role-playing component of it. Beyond just arguing a pro or con position, the students are encouraged to take on named roles (in this case, a family deciding how to spend lottery winnings). There are a few reasons for this – one, providing a backstory and character dynamics can make for a more engaging activity with more rigorous (and fun) debate. But in addition, it allows some mental space and distance between the students and their roles. Students that may be more reluctant to speak in class are sometimes willing to be more vocal and direct if they are playing a role rather than being themselves. A crucial element of the role-play, however, is the distraction from language provided by playing the game. Discussions during the simulation can be animated, intense, and most importantly, spontaneous. While the students will have had time to prepare and research their positions, the actual argumentation and discussion will be unscripted, and they will need quick responses. Wanting to win and to perform their role becomes the primary goal, and they will not have time to carefully plan and conjugate every sentence. A simulation such as this thus provides an excellent balance for skills in the classroom – some initial scaffolding and planning time to learn vocabulary and form arguments, a time to actively debate and speak off the cuff, and a debriefing time afterward to reflect. Halleck emphasizes the importance of this last piece, commenting:

> Each simulation in this book includes recommendations for debriefing. We consider debriefing to be an integral part of each simulation and hope that when you introduce a simulation in class that you remember to allocate time for participants to debrief at the end. (Halleck 2013, vi)

## Last Week Tonight

As background, the news satire series *Last Week Tonight with John Oliver* (Carvell et al. 2014-2022) has been airing on HBO since 2014, and as of this writing, has been renewed for three more seasons, to continue at least through 2023. The show airs as a 30-minute episode hosted by John Oliver on Sunday nights at 11pm, and most often consists of some shorter segments that frame a single-topic monologue by Oliver. Its format has been compared to Comedy Central's *The Daily Show*, on which Oliver was a correspondent, but it is notably different with its longer deep-dives on issues rather than being a series of short segments. The topics vary weekly and have included discussion of lotteries, tobacco, and government goings-on. Some topics have recurred, such as multiple episodes addressing Net Neutrality, and corruption within the FIFA sports organization.

Oliver's main discussion generally lasts around twenty minutes, and these clips are uploaded weekly by HBO to YouTube, allowing them to be used as a no-cost classroom resource. His examinations of a topic are always argumentative, using a mix of comedy and news to make and substantiate his points. As such, I have found his clips to be of great value for a college-aged audience – his topics are relevant and current, and the use of humor keeps them from being dry or boring to the students. At the same time, a 15-20-minute runtime for clips works well for a classroom discussion – the clip can be shown at the beginning of a class with ample time available afterwards for activities and follow-up or assigned as homework without a student needing to block off hours for screening.

The organization of the clips is also well-suited to teaching argumentative writing – Oliver typically has a central argument that he reinforces with two or three central premises. For example, in his "Tobacco" segment (Oliver 2015), he argues that tobacco companies are unethical bullies, and supports this by focusing on three central issues – their desire to market to children, their dubious litigation attempts to overturn plain-packaging laws, and their threats to bankrupt small countries that impose any sorts of limitations on smoking. During a classroom discussion, all of these can be analyzed in further detail. For a rhetoric-minded course, an instructor could draw attention to Oliver's ethos appeals (a company shouldn't be able to overturn the laws of a sovereign nation), while also noting the effect of his use humor, at one point trotting out 'Jeff the Diseased Lung' as a proposed new mascot for Marlboro.

In this chapter, I'll focus on adapting one episode in particular – *The Lottery*, (Oliver 2014a) to an active classroom discussion, but I want to emphasize that I see a central value of the program as being the diversity of its topics – its episodes could easily be adapted to any number of lessons. The format of the show itself can also generate strong discussion, such as examining the situated ethos of Oliver himself as a non-expert speaking with authority, or what the structure of the show reveals about its intended audiences (for example, the fact that it airs on a pay-cable channel implies a more well-to-do viewership, and its late airing time (and liberal swearing) suggests a show not intended for children).

## Main Lesson

This lesson combines an Oliver clip (*The Lottery* – [Oliver 2014a]) with a simulation from Halleck – in this case the *Lottery: Money Changes Everything* simulation by Galena Shleykina (Shleykina 2013). Both relate to lotteries, and I'll walk through the main points and takeaways of the activities, and also include ways to add additional exercises and expand upon them if so desired. For addressing the Oliver clip, I suggest roughly an hour to view and discuss it, and for the Halleck simulation I recommend at least an hour or more for students to prepare for it, an hour for the simulation itself, and some time afterward to debrief.

## The Lottery

This clip is 14:35 minutes, and Oliver begins the clip by describing it as "the second-best use of markers on ping-pong balls after Kermit the Frog's eyes." He then starts his discussion by introducing a major Mega Millions winner, but with the advice that if the viewer themselves hasn't won, they'll have plenty of other chances to play. Showing a map that depicts the 44 states of the US that hold lotteries, he emphasizes that state-run lotteries are extremely prevalent in the United States, and also have a long history. This is part of why I've used this particular clip for this assignment, as learners in nearly all of the US will be getting exposure to American lotteries.

From here, he addresses lotteries as major money-makers for states, who thus obviously have a huge incentive to run them, as they bring in $68 billion annually. He comments that the idea of state-run gambling businesses is a bit odd but has been propped up by treating the gambling more as charity. The money is justified by three main points, and attacking them forms the basis for the rest of the clip:

1) They're essentially harmless fun for those who lose

2) Lotteries provide big benefits to those who win

3) The money raised by them goes to good causes within their states, often education funding

At 2:55 he makes the points explicit, saying "So let's take a look at those slogans – 'Everybody wins,' 'The lottery does good things,' and 'It's game-changing, life-changing fun. Is it, does it, and do they?" For an instructor, this is a nicely visible way to lay out both his main thesis ('lotteries are harmful'), while also presenting three clear threads of argument to reinforce the argument. Notice that such a layout also fits nicely with teaching five-paragraph essays or other shorter writing/presenting work, in which the student will likely have space to address two or three central points. Breaking down the clip with the students in the class essentially models outlining for them.

To address the first point, Oliver points to studies of who spends on the lottery and observes that players are primarily those with low incomes, and do not have much money to spend. He points to ads that depict aspirational spending for winners like paying for their children's college or whimsical things like taking a penguin hang-gliding so it can fly. However, he shows clips that discuss how incredibly unlikely winning the lottery is, and then the discussion darkens further as he presents data showing that state-run gambling such as video poker machines are extremely addictive, with players losing on average over $2,500 a year. He plays a news interview with a woman who spent their family's available grocery money on video poker coming home with no money and no groceries. If you are using a more rhetoric-focused discussion in the classroom, it's worth noting that these points reinforce Oliver's position with several appeals – using Logos to show data of significant financial loss, using Pathos to evoke sympathy for the woman's plight, and using Ethos to argue that the job of the state is not to be causing harm to its own citizens. He punctuates this last point by showing a Google hit for 'lottery intervention,' which, instead of offering support for problem gambling, is in fact an ad for Washington DC's lottery.

In addressing the point that lotteries benefit their winners, he makes similar moves, presenting a montage of headlines such as 'Lottery Winner Blows Through $27 million,' 'Lottery Winner Found Dead in Bed,' and 'Brother Hired Hit Man Over $16 Million Jackpot Win.' He then shows lottery winners in Israel wearing masks to protect their identities, along with a man from Gaza collecting his money with a bag over his head. This section receives by far the least discussion and is the weakest of three points, which again is a teachable moment – the other two points receive multiple minutes of discussion, whereas possible harm for winners is extremely brief. The class could address the fact that while risks are certainly possible, they're likely not the norm, and thus part of why Oliver spends little time with them.

Oliver spends much more time addressing his final point – after showing the harms that can be caused by lotteries, he asks 'Why do state lawmakers keep approving lotteries?' To answer this, he walks through some history, showing a clip from the first New Hampshire state lottery's founding in 1964. In it, a woman buys a ticket and remarks "I feel that it is for a very good cause – education." He quips that funding education indirectly like this is inefficient, and there are better ways to do so, such as "sales tax, bake sales, or simply putting cash into an envelope, writing 'SCHOOL' on the front of it, and mailing it." Beyond inefficiency, however, he moves on to point out that the money allocated for education from lotteries often never makes it there.

He shows a news clip that investigates 24 states that fund education with lotteries and finds that 21 of the states have either flat or lower spending on education since before the lotteries started. "How is this possible?" he asks, moving into a look at North Carolina specifically. He presents another clip describing how North Carolina essentially reallocated money after its 'North Carolina Education Lottery' went live – taking money away from education and moving it to construction and then replacing (not even all!) the loss with lottery funds. Notice again a paired approach of rhetorical appeals – Logos to show dollar figures and evidence that the money-shifting took place, followed by an Ethos appeal that this is unethical, or at the very least not in the spirit that the lottery had been initially marketed as.

He concludes with the following summation:

> As I think we've seen by now, lotteries are bad for losers, often bad for winners, and a pretty compromising way to assist state budgets. Think about it this way – gambling is a little like alcohol. Most people like it, some are addicted to it, and it's not like the state can or should outlaw it altogether. But it would be a little strange if the state was in the liquor business, advertising it by claiming that every shot of vodka you drink helps schoolchildren learn.

As you can see, Oliver's clip thus mirrors very well what a student is expected to do in an argumentative piece – lays out a clear thesis, presents three central positions that support the thesis using a variety of rhetorical appeals, and concisely finishes with a conclusion that draws from all of the main points. Though not every piece of his has its structure wrapped up quite so nicely in a bow, a great many clips of his address relevant, topical issues that make for good discussion in a writing class. While an in-class breakdown of a *Last Week Tonight* monologue can make for an excellent activity on its own, it can also be used as scaffolding for further class periods on the same topic.

## Lottery: Money Changes Everything

As an example of a way to employ active learning after a *Last Week Tonight Clip*, I will walk through an example simulation from *English Composition*

*Simulations* (Shleykina 2013, 131-146), also on the topic of lotteries. The simulation itself includes its own scaffolding, asking students to listen to an NPR clip entitled *Economic Woes Won't Stop Spain's Lottery Dreams* (Frayer 2012) and answer a few short comprehension questions. The clip addresses El Gordo, Spain's massive yearly Christmas lottery. Worth noting is that this clip, like most on NPR, is great for a language-teaching classroom, as it includes both an audio file and a written transcript, allowing the instructor to reinforce whichever language skills they wish. And, of course, if the instructor desires a more recent clip on the subject, El Gordo will receive fresh coverage every year.

The simulation also includes questions responding to a 2012 piece from the *Wall Street Journal* by Robert Frank, entitled *Will Winning the Lottery Ruin Your Life?* (Frank 2012) which obviously pairs well with the themes addressed in Oliver's segment. And like El Gordo, if the instructor desires more recent material on the theme, there are many options (Canales 2019; Witt 2018; York 2019). Also included are a pair of short, fictional articles written on the topic that include prompts to give opinions or respond to questions. Suffice it to say, the materials allow for a high degree of customization on the amount of scaffolding and support for the unit in a class. Between Oliver and the other media, multiple class sessions could be spent on the topic of lotteries, teaching vocabulary if needed, addressing controversies, and doing anything else necessary to prepare students for the simulation itself.

In the simulation, the students are asked to roleplay as members of the Rogers family, who have recently won $500,000 in the lottery. The family is torn on how to spend the money and has to pick from one of several options, such as buying a house or sending a child to college (because in many areas, it would be possible to do more than one option with the winnings, I've usually lowered the payout to something more like $50,000 or $100,000 – enough of a windfall to make options feasible but not so much that the teams could realistically just divide up the money). The five full teams provided have the following main goals:

1) Buy a house for the family
2) Take the entire family on a once-in-a-lifetime world tour
3) Sending a gifted daughter in the family to a prestigious college
4) Donating the money to charity
5) Paying back another family (The Woes) who gave them money in the past and are now in dire need

With these in mind, you can see why I recommend lowering the payout – blowing a full $500,000 on travel is a bit ludicrous, but taking a dozen or so people on a world tour for $50,000 could realistically spend the lot. And while

$50,000 would not pay for a house or for college, it could be established that it would be enough for a down payment or to otherwise make those options feasible.

Along these lines, since the simulation doesn't stipulate, I strongly recommend setting ground conditions for the family's pre-win lifestyle so that the class is all on the same page. Students on Team House, for example, will tend to dream up the family living in squalor if allowed, and so setting some opening conditions is valuable. In general, I suggest having the family in a tolerable-but-not-great financial state – for example, renting a small house instead of owning a larger one, or being able to afford community college for the gifted daughter, but not more than that. A modest income should be decided on as well. The amount of help the Woes gave should also be addressed, although it should have been a gift and not a loan.

The simulation provides named roles for up to fifteen people plus up to two judges to make the final decision, but the arrangement of it is very flexible – a student per team is the bare minimum needed, although having them in groups allows for much more engaging strategizing and planning. With a low number of students, I'd likely opt to remove some of the teams rather than split them down to singletons. The judges are intended to mingle with the teams and structure the debate, as well as make the decision on who wins, but I've found this to work poorly with students in the role – apart from some initial discussion at the beginning, they basically have nothing to do. Instead, I recommend that the instructor take this role, or most ideally, outside judges (such as other instructors) be brought in to moderate. Having to convince people that the students may not know well adds some rigor to the exercise.

The simulation materials recommend five class periods to run it, but I've found that students generally need two class periods to prepare, with one for the actual debate, followed by some time in another session to debrief (possibly with a written reflection). The research time is essential, as each time will need to develop their own position, as well as prepare for the possible arguments of the other groups. Examples include:

1) House

Research real estate, prices, and mortgages – they will need to present a case that the house they pick would be good for the family – for example, large enough that everyone could fit under one roof, accommodate older parents, etc.

This is generally one of the most solid positions, as the arguers can frame the house as an investment for the family and something that they'll all benefit from, although the College team will usually point out that the children will soon be leaving home, and a large house may not be needed.

2) Travel

Consider possible itineraries and destinations and draw up a budget.

Of the five teams, this is arguably the one with the weakest position, as they're basically locked into purely Pathos appeals of enjoyment and relaxation, and perhaps Ethos appeals of expanding one's horizons and cultural knowledge. They could take the tack of the trips being educational for the children or a final opportunity for older members of the family. In my experience, this group is also incentivized to go negative, forced to argue flaws of other teams rather than their own strengths. This may be problematic (and warrant cutting this team), but their strategies can be an excellent point to address during debriefing.

3)  College

This team will benefit the most from researching college costs, as well as the likely future rewards of graduating from a prestigious school. They most often need to defend against the other teams alleging that the daughter is the sole beneficiary of the money or suggesting that she might not make it through her degree. This team will often argue that the daughter will pay the money back with the wealth she earns after graduation, although savvy opponents can counter that this will take considerable time.

4)  Charity

Although giving away the money may seem like a doomed proposition, it can be a surprisingly strong stance. This team generally does the best when they research charitable causes in detail, showing exactly what the tangible benefits of the gift would be. This is also part of why I recommend having the family not be destitute pre-winnings – they should be in a position where giving away the money wouldn't be a crippling loss. This team (and the next) can also draw from the materials above that show the dangers of winning the lottery, and further research on that front can aid them.

5)  Giving Back

In this case, the arguers must primarily lean on ethos appeals – researching the costs of cancer treatments and then insisting that the lottery winners pay them back for help given in the past. They can take a similar tack to the charity team, arguing that rather than by being harmed by holding onto the money, they can apply it toward a tangible benefit. And of course, they can appeal to a sense of duty and integrity of the family for having helped them out in the past.

As far as running the actual debate itself, I've found it works well to give each team an uninterrupted opening and closing speech, followed by a more open-ended discussion moderated by the judges. With five teams, the moderation is essential, to ensure that the teams aren't talking over each other, or that a few teams don't monopolize the discussion. Depending on the amount of structure desired, the judges can have pre-written questions that they ask the teams, or simply let the groups respond and rebut after their opening statements. When the judges make a final decision, they should be encouraged to give detail as to how they arrived at their conclusions, and what swayed them the most.

## Debriefing

When the debate has been resolved and a winner declared, you should include some time for students to discuss the debate afterwards. Some questions to consider regarding each team, but also for the simulation as a whole:

1)  Which arguments did the teams find the most compelling and why?

2)  Which points seemed to be the most thoroughly researched, and how could they tell?

3)  Were there arguments from the other teams that the students hadn't planned for?

4)  Was there a team that they thought had the best starting position, or that they were most concerned about responding to?

5)  Beyond their own team, which team did they think should have won and why?

As the instructor, I recommend keeping track of arguments made by the teams as they are doing their research and debating so that you can revisit those points during the discussion. It can be beneficial to zero in on individual points and strategies made during the simulation and analyze their effectiveness. And of course, if teaching a rhetoric-focused class, address the rhetorical appeals made. If Team Woe or Charity has won, for example, they have probably done so through Ethos appeals. Debriefing can be done by full classroom discussion, but a short written individual reflection response can also be valuable, giving the students a chance to assemble their own thoughts on the activity.

## Conclusion

My hope is that you are able to use this activity directly in your own teaching or to use it as a template for your own activity that incorporates simulations in active learning. As of this writing, there are nine seasons of *Last Week Tonight*, allowing for a great number of possible topics to draw from, some of which directly match simulations from *English Composition Simulations*, such as Oliver's July 2021 episode on housing discrimination and African American reparations and the *"Repairing" Past Injustices* simulation by Jon Smythe

(Smythe 2013), and the *Arizona Immigration Law* simulation (Codita 2013), which could be paired with any of Oliver's several features on immigration and seeking political asylum (Oliver 2015, 2018, 2019, 2020). Other *Last Week Tonight* topics could easily lend themselves to additional simulation or debate activities, such as the legalization of marijuana (Oliver 2017), and the rampant use of sugar in American food (Oliver 2014b). (This last clip can pair very well with Jamie Oliver's TED talk on the overuse of sugar in school lunches (Oliver 2010), which I also like to present with Sam Cel Roman's blog post *Hey Jamie Oliver, Go Fuck Yourself* (Roman 2014) as a counterpoint. The variability of the topics means that there are many options to choose from, and you can select based on your students' interests, or pick something topical at the moment.

Similarly, while the Halleck book includes many other simulations, you can also devise your own to match the topic of an Oliver segment. His discussion of sugar could for example be matched with a simulation on reducing junk food in school lunches, with roles devised for concerned parents, industry/government representatives, and possibly the students themselves. If creating your own simulation, the primary concern should be that all the possible sides have plausible paths to winning the debate. But regardless of the topic you choose, the archetype for the lesson arc remains the same:

1) Scaffolding that consists of an Oliver clip and other realia as needed

2) A simulation that allows students to engage with the scaffolded material

3) A debriefing assignment that synthesizes the core elements of all the activities

With this, you have a flexible, adaptable tool that can be part of a writing class, or more general four skills class, with the leeway to emphasize the skills most appropriate and desired.

## Bibliography

Allsop, Jared, Sarah J. Young, Erik J. Nelson, Jennifer Piatt, and Dough Knapp. 2020. "Examining the Benefits Associated with Implementing an Active Learning Classroom among Undergraduate Students." *International Journal of Teaching and Learning in Higher Education* 32, (3): 418-426.

Canales, Katie. 2019. "Disappointing Stories Reveal What It's Really Like to Win the Lottery." *Business Insider*, March 2. https://www.businessinsider.com/winning-lottery-downsides-2018-12

Carvell, Tim, John Oliver, Liz Stanton, James Taylor, and Jon Thoday. 2014-2022. *Last Week Tonight with John Oliver*. Avalon Television.

Codita, Ana. 2013. "Arizona Immigration Law." In *English Composition Simulations* edited by Gene Halleck, 101-116. Dubuque: Kendall Hunt Publishing.

Felder, Richard. M., and Rebecca Brent. 2009. "Active learning: An Introduction." *ASQ Higher Education Brief, 2* (4): 1-6.

Frank, Robert. 2012. "Will Winning the Lottery Ruin Your Life?" *The Wall Street Journal,* March 30. https://www.wsj.com/articles/BL-WHB-5052

Frayer, Lauren. 2012. "Economic Woes Won't Stop Spain's Lottery Dreams." *NPR Weekend Edition Saturday,* December 22. https://www.npr.org/2012/12/22/167861447/economic-woes-dont-stop-spains-lottery-dreams

Freeman, Scott, Sarah L. Eddy, Miles McDonough, Michelle K. Smith, Nnadozie Okoroafor, Hannah Jordt and Mary Pat Wenderoth. 2014. "Active Learning Increases Student Performance in Science, Engineering, and Mathematics." *Proceedings of the National Academy of Sciences of the United States of America* 111 (23): 8410-8415.

Halleck, Gene. 2013. *English Composition Simulations.* Dubuque: Kendall Hunt Publishing.

Oliver, Jamie. 2010. "Teach Every Child about Food." YouTube. TED, February 12. https://www.youtube.com/watch?v=go_QOzc79Uc

Oliver, John. 2014. "The Lottery: Last Week Tonight with John Oliver (HBO)." YouTube. HBO, November 9. https://www.youtube.com/watch?v=9PK-netuhHA

———. 2014. "Sugar: Last Week Tonight with John Oliver (HBO)." YouTube. HBO, October 26. https://www.youtube.com/watch?v=MepXBJjsNxs

———. 2015. "Tobacco: Last Week Tonight with John Oliver (HBO)." YouTube. HBO, February 15. https://www.youtube.com/watch?v=6UsHHOCH4q8

———. 2017. "Marijuana: Last Week Tonight with John Oliver (HBO)." YouTube. HBO, April 2. https://www.youtube.com/watch?v=BcR_Wg42dv8

———. 2018. "Family Separation: Last Week Tonight with John Oliver (HBO)." YouTube. HBO, November 5. https://www.youtube.com/watch?v=ygVX1z6tDGI

———. 2019. "Legal Immigration: Last Week Tonight with John Oliver (HBO)." YouTube. HBO, September 16. https://www.youtube.com/watch?v=tXqnRMU1fTs

———. 2020. "Asylum: Last Week Tonight with John Oliver (HBO)." YouTube. HBO, October 25. https://www.youtube.com/watch?v=xtdU5RPDZqI

Roman, Sam Cel. 2014. "Hey Jamie Oliver, Go Fuck Yourself." All Things Romania, October 26. https://kingofromania.com/2014/10/26/hey-jamie-oliver-go-fuck-yourself/comment-page-8/

Shleykina, Galina. 2013. "Lottery: Money Changes Everything." In *English Composition Simulations* edited by Gene Halleck, 131-146. Dubuque: Kendall Hunt Publishing.

Smythe, Jon. 2013. "Repairing' Past Injustices." In *English Composition Simulations* edited by Gene Halleck, 201-212. Dubuque: Kendall Hunt Publishing.

Witt, April. 2018. "He Won Powerball's $314 Million Jackpot. It Ruined His Life." *The Washington Post,* October 23. https://www.washingtonpost.com/history/2018/10/24/jack-whittaker-powerball-lottery-winners-life-was-ruined-after-m-jackpot/

York, Chris. 2019. "8 Times the Lottery Ruined Someone's Life." *The Huffington Post,* September 10. https://www.huffingtonpost.co.uk/entry/lottery-winners-no-happy-ending_uk_5c2f6c40e4b08aaf7a98a41a

Chapter 2

# Online Teaching of Chinese as a Second Language in an Extended COVID-19 Situation: How to Engage Students in Active Learning

Valentina Ornaghi

*Italian Institute of Oriental Studies (ISO), University "La Sapienza"*

Ching-Yi Amy Juan

*University of Milan*

**Abstract**: Due to the continued Covid-19 epidemic, the Italian universities courses carried out face-to-face had to remain online with a severe impact for language courses, where classroom interaction has an essential role for language acquisition.

In order to enhance interaction and students' participation, the teachers chose a mix of asynchronous and synchronous teaching tools to engage students in language activities, with a focus on synchronous activities. This chapter analyses the use of asynchronous and synchronous tools to promote students' active language learning, including the use of video-lessons and other materials to promote students' self-learning, the assignment of real-life tasks to stimulate students' production and the use of synchronous communication platforms, virtual classrooms and chatrooms to enable student-teacher and peer-to-peer interaction.

The choice of teaching methods was based on the existing literature. This chapter covers their application and presents some findings and final remarks based on teaching experience and on questionnaires filled out by students.

**Keywords**: Online teaching, emergency remote teaching, active language learning, Chinese language teaching, blended learning

*** 

## Introduction

Due to the continued Covid-19 epidemic, the Italian universities courses once carried out face-to-face had to be shifted and carried out online for two consecutive semesters, with a severe impact for language learning, where classroom interaction has an essential role for language acquisition. This chapter focuses on "online teaching in an emergency situation" and on the subsequent moves taken in order to improve online courses for three Chinese language degree classes, in two state universities in the Lombardy region of Italy. Two classes are from a postgraduate master's degree course (herein named as M1 and M2) and one class is from a first-year undergraduate course (B1).

In order to enhance interaction and student participation, the teachers chose a mix of asynchronous and synchronous teaching tools to engage students in language activities, with a particular focus on synchronous activities. This chapter, therefore, analyses the use of asynchronous and synchronous tools to promote students' active language learning, including the use of video-lessons and other materials to promote self-learning, the assignment of group work tasks to stimulate students' production and the use of synchronous communication platforms, virtual classrooms and chatrooms to enable student-teacher and student-student interaction.

The choice of teaching methods was based on the existing literature. This chapter covers their application and presents some findings and final remarks based on teaching experience and on questionnaires filled out by students.

## Background Literature

In general terms, the development of online courses essentially draws on the theories of constructivism and connectivism (Lin and Zhang 2014). Constructivism views learning as a process in which the learner actively engages in new ideas through collaborative group activities. With respect to online teaching, one of the main theories is online collaborative learning theory (OCL) proposed by Harasim (2012). Connectivism, a fairly new theory, takes into account that the learning content available on the web and the internet platforms are frequently changing. In addition, it highlights importance of networking and self-organization to navigate the complex digital environment (Siemens 2005).

In practical aspects, designing an online course requires many resources, not only teachers but also other professionals for designing and planning content (Laici 2005; Weerasinghe et al. 2009). An online course therefore should be carefully planned in advance.

Weerasinghe et al. (2009) suggest applying the following course structure: 1) display the learning outcomes at the beginning of the course and display the related learning objectives at the beginning of the section; 2) order the learning content according to the syllabus; 3) add activities to each unit of the learning content; 4) add at least one quiz to the end of each section of a course to let students evaluate their learning achievements after completing a section of the course; 5) add discussion forums and chat rooms.

One of the main issues with online courses is to ensure interaction, teacher presence and social presence, which are key points in avoiding high drop-out rates (Hua 2018; Kaplan and Haenlein 2016; Means et al. 2014; Panagiotidis 2019). This is even more true in the case of language learning, which cannot be compared to other subjects, as language teaching requires a high degree of interaction between speakers and multiple mental tasks (Panagiotidis 2019).

Vygotsky (1986) explains that humans learn through interaction. In an asynchronous course, such interaction can be achieved through discussion threads and wikis, which require cooperation and mutual work, being a shared space in which participants can write and edit at the same time (Lin and Zhang 2014). In order to solve the problem of student-teacher interaction, some teachers can dedicate time online to meet students or use synchronous tools such as Google Hangouts to hold online conversations and answer their questions (Yaden 2019). Chatrooms are also an appreciated tool for written synchronous interaction, through which students can receive immediate feedback. They also facilitate those students who tend to be shy and do not participate actively in face-to-face classes (Payne and Whitney 2002; Wang and Bellassen 2017). Other tools for synchronous online interaction include role-playing in real time, virtual office hours, online guest lecturers, amongst other examples (Lin and Zhang 2014). "Active learning" activities such as role-playing can be carried out in small groups: group work may be the answer to speaking and writing exercises, and it has demonstrated a positive outcome in other Chinese language courses (Sun 2011). Another important aspect of moving classes away from the classroom is that students' minds wander more frequently during online learning (Szpunar et al. 2013). A good length for an online lecture to introduce active learning, via intermittent quizzing and group activities, is between 15 and 20 minutes as reported by Prunuske et al. (2012). Plans for short online "instructional" lectures and actively engaging students with activities should be able to maintain interest and create a lively classroom atmosphere.

This active learning approach is in line with the suggestion from Burgerova and Cimermanova (2014) to have small groups collaborate, engage students, and make activities more authentic. Their suggestion is a blended approach, that is a mix of synchronous and asynchronous, such as uploading texts to present theoretical material, animated presentations, wiki and threads for asynchronous discussion and chats for synchronous communication.

The most recent approach suggests the use of the flipped classroom to enhance interaction and to ensure active learning (Hua 2018; Schaffhauser 2016; Trentin 2020; Yaden 2019). In the flipped classroom pattern of teaching and learning, mini lectures through videos or other materials are given to the students to learn before class. Hua (2018) states that, "In the class, students and teachers are mainly involved in the activities of analyzing key points, doing exercises, researching on projects, and taking part in group discussion, etc.". Moreover, breaking the on-length teaching in the class by using this flipped pattern brings benefits such as "promising integration of online learning, offline learning, self-learning, group learning and investigative learning" (Hua 2018, 164).

### How to engage students in active learning

#### The experience during the first semester

Due to the Covid-19 lockdown, starting from February 2020 Italian universities took up remote teaching to avoid the discontinuity of education. Courses that had previously been carried out face-to-face had to be shifted online within two weeks of notice. Due to this short notice, there was no time for systematic training of how to structure teaching online, although there were some short introductions to the use of platforms.

Before the lockdown, the language courses involved in this study took place in classrooms which had two pieces of basic hardware for teaching: a computer connected to the internet and a video projector. During lessons, teachers usually used one main textbook combined with additional lecture notes. Often PowerPoint presentations (PPT) were projected to help students catch the key content and maintain a smooth flow of the lecture. Teachers and students also had the textbook on hand to refer to when further details or exercises were required. Any other related material from the internet, such as YouTube videos, could be found through the computer in the classroom and showed to students to make the lesson content more varied and interesting. All these different materials - textbook, lecture notes, PPT and internet links - complemented each other during the lesson. Moreover, classroom teaching involved interactions amongst teachers and students.

In addition to the traditional teaching activities, a Learning Management System (LMS) which served as an asynchronous teaching platform was used merely in support of classroom teaching. The platform provided teachers with a space where some supplementary materials for students, such as further reading, as well as classroom notices could be uploaded. There was also a forum where students could ask and reply to questions.

The lockdown coincided with the break between the first and second semester and teachers decided to continue with the already selected textbooks, adapting them to online teaching. Initially, part of the materials was switched to video-lessons, which were made with PPT and voice recordings uploaded to the LMS for students' self-study, which is in line with previous research (Yaden 2019). The platform did not have a function to support online teaching synchronously.

Later, Microsoft Teams was provided to all teachers in order to deliver synchronous online classes and to keep them as similar as possible to in-class lessons. However, due to intermittent internet connectivity, it was not possible to have the same amount of oral and visual interaction as in the classroom which frequently had over 20, 30 and 50 participants in the three classes in this study. As a consequence, screen sharing and PPT were relied on to explain the lesson in order to offer students a visual aid.

Part of the interaction that could not be done orally was then carried out via synchronous chat. Microsoft Teams allows participants to interact both orally and through the chatroom. Many students used the synchronous chat to propose their solutions to the teachers' questions. Some synchronous online lessons were also recorded and made available with the teaching materials on Teams, in order to help students review and to catch up with the lesson in their own time. This also helped those students who had experienced technical issues to follow the recorded synchronous lesson.

In order to gather data on students' satisfaction, all students from the three classes were asked to fill out an anonymous questionnaire via internet during the last lesson of the academic year. The questionnaire was divided in two sections. The first part of the questionnaire aimed to gain an overview by asking questions on a 5-point scale focused on students' experiences using Microsoft Teams in language acquisition:

q1)  Is the platform practical and simple to use?

q2)  Can you easily follow the teachers' explanation?

q3)  Can you interact with the teachers?

q4)  Can you exercise speaking?

q5)  Can you practice writing?

q6)  Are the materials shared by the teachers clearly displayed?

q7)  Would you take another online course? (Yes/No)

The answers to the first six questions were classed on a 5-point scale:

a)   strongly agree

b)   agree

c)   neither agree nor disagree

d)   disagree

e)   strongly disagree

The second part of the questionnaire included three main themes: difficulties and advantages of online learning, and suggestions for improvements, which aimed to gain more insightful information in order to help the teachers to plan better future online teaching activities. Students could vote for more than one item from a list of answers on each of the three themes. The questions are illustrated in Figure 2.2.

In total, 33 students out of 50 from the first-year Chinese course (M1), 26 students out of 30 from the second-year Chinese course (M2) of the master's degree course and 20 students out of 30 from the first-year bachelor's degree course (B1) filled out the questionnaire.

The dominant answers for questions on ease of use of the platform, access to materials, teachers' explanations, and the possibility of interacting with the teachers were: a) "strongly agree" and b) "agree". At least 85% of participants gave positive feedback on these four questions.

When students were asked whether they would follow another online course, the positive answers (greater than 75%) received from all three classes, confirm the substantially positive opinion on the platform and course delivery.

The feedback regarding the possibility to interact in the speaking and writing exercises is, however, not as positive compared to the previous questions noted above, as can be seen in Tables 2.1 and 2.2.

**Table 2.1**. Feedback on speaking exercise

| Can you exercise speaking? | M1 n=33 | M2 n=26 | B1 n=20 |
|---|---|---|---|
| a: strongly agree | 6% | 8% | 20% |
| b: agree | 39.5% | 28% | 40% |
| c: neither agree nor disagree | 36.5% | 48% | 35% |
| d:disagree | 15% | 12% | 5% |
| e:strongly disagree | 3% | 4% | 0 |

The values shown are the percentages of the total number of replies.

**Table 2.2.** Feedback on writing exercise

| Can you practice writing? | M1 n=33 | M2 n=26 | B1 n=20 |
|---|---|---|---|
| a: strongly agree | 9% | 0% | 10% |
| b: agree | 12% | 24% | 35% |
| c: neither agree nor disagree | 33.5% | 44% | 35% |
| d:disagree | 36.5% | 32% | 20% |
| e:strongly disagree | 9% | 0 | 0 |

The values shown are the percentages of the total number of replies.

For speaking exercises, most answers fall in b) "agree" and c) "neither agree nor disagree". The general feedback of students is in the neutral to positive range. The answers with c) "neither agree nor disagree" has a slightly higher number of responses. In the wider prospective of "agree", that is the summing up "strongly agree" and "agree", 46%, 36%, and 60% of the M1, M2 and B1 students, respectively, felt they were given enough opportunity to practice speaking. The visual effect of this summing up is illustrated in Figure 2.1.

**Figure 2.1.** Speaking and writing a+b

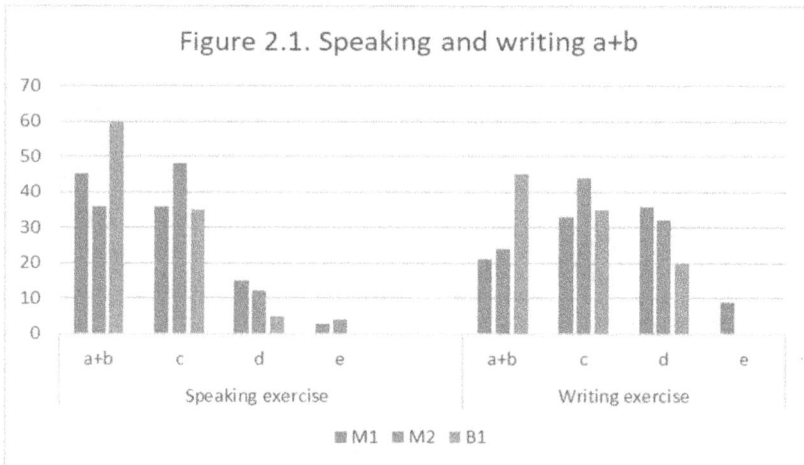

This figure shows the percentage of replies, grouping together positive replies (strongly agree and agree).

With regards to writing exercises, the reply c) also has a higher percentage of responses. However, the number of replies of d) "disagree" (36.5%, 32% and 20%) is more significant than for the question on speaking. It is at least double compared to the reply d) in the speaking exercise, as presented in Table 2.2. In classes M1 and M2, the negative replies of d) and e) are more significant compared to the positive answers. Instead, the class B1 students show a stronger positive feedback on the writing exercise being positive over the negative ones.

The second part of the questionnaire included questions on three areas: difficulties (d1 to d8), advantages (a1 to a8) and suggestions for improvements (s1 to s6). The students could vote for more than one option in each section. The votes are presented in Figure 2.2.

**Figure 2.2.** Questionnaire on difficulties, advantages and suggestions

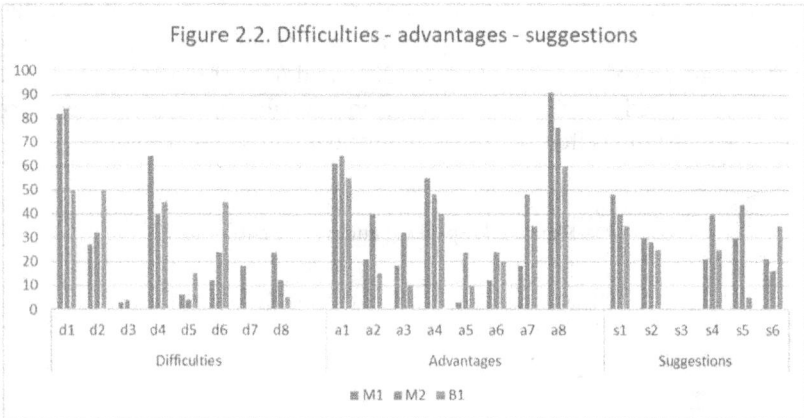

Figure 2.2. Difficulties - advantages - suggestions

| d1 | Internet connection problems |
|----|------------------------------|
| d2 | little chance to interact |
| d3 | unclear materials |
| d4 | little opportunity to practice writing |
| d5 | difficult to follow the teacher's explanation |
| d6 | little chance of speaking orally |
| d7 | materials not suitable for an online course |
| d8 | little exercise in the classroom |

| a1 | lesson from home is more comfortable |

a2      less embarrassed

a3      writing exercises are easier at the computer

a4      possible to answer the exercises via chat

a5      additional materials for self-study

a6      I can concentrate more and follow the teacher's explanations better

a7      screen sharing of materials and PPT makes it easier to follow the lesson

a8      can record and review the lesson


s1      provide more self-learning materials, such as readings, videos, listening exercises

s2      produce multiple PPTs with recorded voice or video-lessons in support of synchronous lessons

s3      during the lesson, the teacher should devote more time to explanations with PPT

s4      during the lesson, the teacher should devote more time to oral interaction with students

s5      during the lesson dedicate more time to writing exercises, also using chat

s6      assign multiple tasks or intermediate tests to monitor the level of learning


The most noted difficulty encountered was d1 (poor internet connections) with 59 votes coming from over 80% of students in M1 and M2 and 50% of class B1. The second difficulty was d4 (little opportunity to practice writing) with a total of 40 votes across the three courses. The third difficulty was the d2 (little opportunity to interact with teachers and students) followed by d6 (little chance of speaking orally).

As for the advantages, the students noted that a8 (can record and review the lesson) with 62 votes was the most welcomed factor of the online course. The second popular advantage was a1 (lesson from home is more comfortable) with 48 votes followed by a4 (it is possible to answer the exercises via chat) with 38 votes.

The suggestions did not show any significant preference by the students apart from s1 (provide more self-learning materials) with 34 votes. Suggestions s2 (produce multiple PPTs with recorded voice), s4 (during the lesson the teacher should devote more time to oral interaction with the students) and s5 (during the lesson, devote more time to the writing exercises, also using chat) show 23, 22, 19 votes, respectively.

Based on these results, teachers decided to increase active learning and small-group activities in order to enable students to engage in more active speaking and writing practice.

## Planning the new semester

This first investigation showed that the transfer of Chinese language lessons online during the Covid-19 pandemic met its goal of continuing the education, as a remote emergency measure, ensuring the minimum possible discontinuity in teaching.

However, the fact that it was a sudden change inevitably meant there were occasional shortcomings and mistakes during the transition. The feedback from the students gave an opportunity for improvement.

First of all, on the basis of the findings, the most noted difficulty is the internet connection. The high responses on suggestions for "more self-learning materials" (s1) and "multiple PPTs with recorded voice or video lessons" (s2) are interrelated with this limitation of internet connectivity and bandwidth. It should be mentioned here that the high number of responses on s1 and s2 can also be linked with answers on the advantages of online teaching. Students appreciated the comfort of being at home (a1), which saved commuting time to university every day. They also welcomed the possibility to review the recorded-lessons (a8) allowing them to study at their own pace. These are in line with the major literature on the topic, which highlights that fewer restrictions on location and time enable students to learn independently at their own pace without the requirement to follow a fixed schedule (Kaplan and Haenlein 2016; Piras et al. 2020; Sun 2011).

Secondly, the important teaching activities of speaking and writing need to be enhanced to fit the online education as the degree of satisfaction of both activities during the first lockdown was lower compared to the general course delivery. In addition, students also requested to have more oral and written exercises (s4 and s5). Student-teacher interaction is a key element in these two activities. The face-to-face lessons can provide a direct student-teacher environment, whereas online teaching has limited opportunities for direct contact. An alternative method needed to be found so to maintain similar levels as in face-to-face lessons.

The practice of "active learning" in small groups was thought be the answer to speaking and writing exercises, as it could direct students to take part together with other course members in the learning process. This approach with group activities would not only promote the student-centered active learning, but also help form a student online learning community in substitution for the campus. Teachers decided to adopt this method for the new semester. It was believed that these group activities could increase the sense of community as a third difficulty, "little chance to interact with the teacher and other students", was also found in the survey.

**Active speaking exercises.** The speaking exercise was redesigned to be more task-based and interactive. In order to ensure truly functional active learning, the following "who-what-when-how and assessment" elements were implemented:

1) groups of two to four students (who)

2) clearly defined and achievable oral presentation assignments (what)

3) regular and frequent submitting with set deadlines (when)

4) using software or available platforms to record a podcast presentation (how)

5) the exercise is part of course assessment leading to the final marks (assessment).

As an example of such exercises, students were given assignments which required recording of audio/video or to present "live" online a group roleplay as a means to exercise their oral language skill. It has been shown to be effective even when synchronous interaction is limited due to high numbers (Sun, 2011). In addition to acquiring the speaking ability, the absence of campus learning and interaction between students can be replaced in part by these group activities. That is, in preparation for a group assignment, students need to know each other and actively collaborate through constant communication, which can also be achieved through social media, which allows learners to easily talk to one another virtually, which is useful for online courses or hybrid courses. Learners can work together outside the classroom synchronously using video-conferencing tools (Skype, Google Hangout, Zoom), and real-time editing applications such as Google Docs.

**Active writing exercises.** The active learning method with the "who-what-when-how and assessment" elements mentioned for the "speaking exercise" was also applied to improve and consolidate students' writing skills. This was done by integrating speaking with writing. That is, students prepared written PPT presentations to accompany their oral presentations. Besides the group activities, the individual writing assignment was considered an effective method. Again, regular and frequent submitting were key to a successful outcome. Therefore, teachers also decided to use the LMS platform provided by the University to post written assignments for students.

### Carrying out the new activities and collecting data

During the first semester of the academic year 2020-2021, all lessons were still held online. Therefore, the following experiment was conducted with students from the second-year master's degree course, the previous M1 class. Teaching materials focused on two case studies of two foreign companies and their entrance and growth in the Chinese market. One approach was to adopt the flipped classroom pattern. Students were asked to preview explanations of new vocabulary and texts individually and then work on them either in groups from home or together in class. Alternatively, they were divided in small groups using Teams channels as breakout rooms, which has been reported in the literature (Schaffhauser 2016). This type of assignment or group activity took place periodically and it made teachers' explanations quicker, allowing more time for practice during class. When group work was carried out at home, students sent their work to teachers via email and the results were presented and analyzed together in class the following week. Students were also assigned individual written compositions to send to the teachers via email, following the example of previous research (Yaden 2019). Finally, for the end of the semester they were assigned the following type of group work: preparing a presentation on the strategies for a foreign company to enter the Italian market and presenting it to the class in turns using a PPT. The aim was to practice both active speaking by doing oral presentations in small groups and active writing, by preparing a written presentation. At the end of the semester, all students were asked again to fill out an anonymous questionnaire via internet. The questionnaire was completed by 39 out of 41 students.

As can be seen by the above figures, in the first questionnaire M1 students mainly noted the scarce writing practice and required more oral interaction as well as more self-learning materials and assignments to monitor the level of learning. Therefore, it was decided to prepare a new anonymous questionnaire focusing on the main criticalities encountered in the previous semester, with the aim of understanding if the new teaching methods were helpful in overcoming such shortcomings.

Questions on speaking and writing practice (the two main shortcomings) were maintained, while some questions focusing on the new teaching methods were added, as follows:

q1) Was it possible to have more speaking practice compared to the previous semester?

q2) Was it possible to have more writing practice compared to the previous semester?

q3) Did student-teacher interaction improve?

q4) Did group work improve student-student interaction?

q5) Did periodical homework assignment help you keep a constant learning pace and monitor the level of learning?

q6) Was it easier to prepare for the exam?

q7) How much on the Likert scale has this new phase been an improvement, compared to the previous online emergency teaching?

The answers to the questions were classed on a 5-point scale:

a) strongly agree

b) agree

c) neither agree nor disagree

d) disagree

e) strongly disagree

It was also decided to maintain the last multiple-choice question on suggestions, to monitor if the new teaching methods affected these.

### Results from experimenting active teaching and learning

As can be seen in Figure 2.3 students' responses on the first seven questions are all highly positive. This is even more evident by looking at Table 2.3, which illustrates the number of answers for each question.

**Table 2.3.** Students' answers about the new semester's improvements (N)

| | Q1 | Q2 | Q3 | Q4 | Q5 | Q6 | Q7 |
|---|---|---|---|---|---|---|---|
| a: strongly agree | 8 | 5 | 9 | 17 | 14 | 5 | 10 |
| b: agree | 22 | 21 | 23 | 21 | 18 | 20 | 24 |
| c: neither agree nor disagree | 7 | 8 | 6 | 0 | 4 | 10 | 5 |
| d:disagree | 2 | 5 | 1 | 1 | 3 | 3 | 0 |
| e:strongly disagree | 0 | 0 | 0 | 0 | 0 | 1 | 0 |

The values shown are the total number of replies.

**Figure 2.3.** Students' opinions on the new semester's improvements (%)

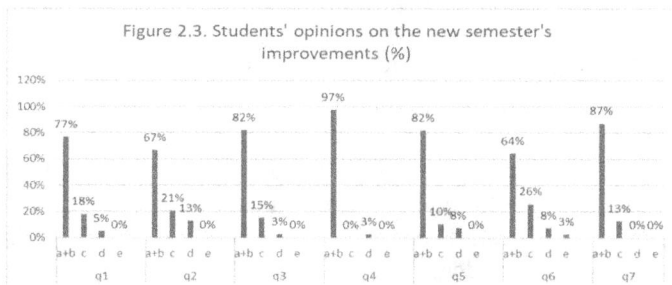

Figure 2.3. Students' opinions on the new semester's improvements (%)

The values shown are the percentage of replies.

Questions q1 to q6 regard some specific aspects such as speaking, writing and preparation for the exam, as well as the new teaching methods (group work and homework assignments), while question q7 is more general, asking an opinion on the overall improvement compared to the previous semester. This section starts by analyzing the first 6 questions.

Questions q3, q4 and q5 showed highly positive replies (a+b between 82% and 97%). In particular, question q4 (Did group work improve student-student interaction?) had 38 positive responses (a+b) out of 39 and only one negative response, which demonstrated that group work activities actually enhanced student-student interaction. Also question q3 (Did student-teacher interaction improve?) had a positive response: 82% of the students (32 out of 39) believe there was an improvement, while 6 were undecided. Only one student gave a negative answer.

As for questions q1, q2 and q6, responses were still positive, even though less markedly than the previous ones: a+b=77% (30 out of 39) for q1, a+b=67% (26 out of 39) for q2 and a+b=64% (25 out of 39) for q6. All of this shows that students felt a significant improvement in terms of increased interaction and of the greater possibility of keeping a constant learning pace and monitoring the level of learning through periodical homework assignments. There has been also an improvement about speaking and writing practice and exam preparation, even though less marked.

As for the last question q7 (How much on the Likert scale has this new phase been an improvement, compared to the previous online emergency teaching?), it also registered positive responses (87%), which confirms that students felt an overall improvement compared to the previous semester.

Figure 2.4 shows students' responses on the second part of the questionnaire covering suggestions.

The main suggestions remain s1 (provide more self-learning materials, such as readings, videos, listening exercises) and s2 (produce multiple PPTs with recorded voice or video-lessons in support of synchronous lessons), but with an inverted proportion compared to the first time. Now s2 has become the main suggestion. The course mainly focused on synchronous interaction and group work, while a small number of video-lessons prepared by the two teachers were uploaded on the online platform. It is possible that, while students enjoyed the increased interaction, they would have appreciated more video-lessons. So, students could follow them at their own pace and integrate teachers' synchronous explanations. As we have seen, having no time and space restrictions is one of the advantages of online asynchronous courses (Kaplan and Haenlein 2016; Piras et al. 2020; Sun 2011). As for other self-learning materials, even though it is still one of the main suggestions, it shows a decrease compared to the previous semester. This is probably due to the fact that teachers uploaded a larger number of extra learning materials, especially multimedia such as YouTube videos, compared to the previous semester. Students probably appreciated this and would wish for more.

**Figure 2.4.** Changes in students' suggestions

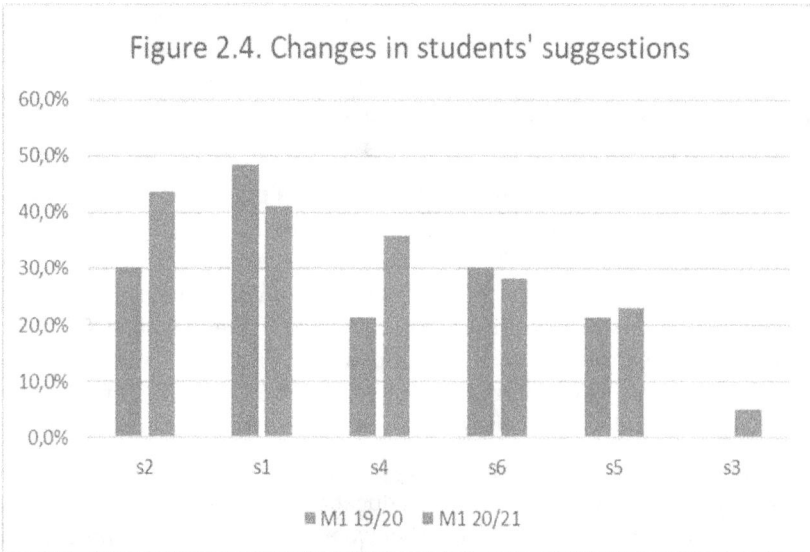

This figure compares M1 class suggestions for the last semester of the academic year 2019-2020 and the first semester of the academic year 2020-2021.

Another main variation can be noted for suggestion s4 (During the lesson, the teacher should devote more time to oral interaction with students), which shows an increase. This might seem to be in contradiction with question q3 (Did student-teacher interaction improve?), which showed highly positive responses. There could be two possible explanations for this. Either students enjoyed student-teacher interaction and would like to have more, or even though they noted an improvement in interaction compared to the emergency phase, they still require a greater effort in this sense. This would suggest more work is needed in order to get as close as possible to typical onsite lessons, which they have been used to for the most part of their academic career.

### Conclusions

Based on the findings of the two surveys and reflections of the teachers, not only the first phase of emergency remote teaching met its goal of ensuring the minimum disruption to teaching, but also the implementation of new activities in the second phase, flipped classroom as well as periodical group work and assignments, all have successfully guided students towards their goal of acquiring key language skills. The authors recognize that the sample of students in the questionnaires is relatively modest. However, it is considered a good method for monitoring and then applying the best teaching practices in this period of change. That said, there were some teaching aspects which still needed improvement, especially speaking and writing practice and interaction among students and between students and teachers. The main aspect that remains not to be overlooked is the need for more self-learning materials, especially asynchronous video-lessons, to integrate what is being done synchronously.

One should bear in mind that the online classes presented in this chapter were not the predesigned well-organized "conventional" online courses, such as Open University in the UK. All the approaches taken were to ensure that students met their goal of studying. The comparison of M1 course in the two different semesters shows the course delivered in the extended Covid-19 situation received positive feedback and was welcomed by students. This demonstrates that an emergency course can be "fruitful" through the planning and learning from the experience of well-established online courses.

Another general outcome from the worldwide COVID crisis, is that the internet-based economy (not only education, but also commerce and entertainment) has made a giant leap equivalent to years of development in a period of a few months. This may drive a development of education to more diverse online based platforms and delivery methods. Such changes will require a significant investment in resources and developers, compared to an attempt by the course teachers only, for a temporary fix to an emergency.

## Authorship

This chapter is the result of the close collaboration between the two authors. Specifically, Valentina Ornaghi takes responsibility for Sections 1, 2, 3.3 and 4, whereas Ching-Yi Amy Juan takes responsibility for Sections 3.1, 3.2 and 5.

## Bibliography

Burgerova, Jana, and Ivana Cimermanova. 2014. "Creating a Sense of Presence in Online Learning Environment". *DIVAI 2014: The 10th International Scientific Conference in Distance Learning in Applied Informatics*: 275-284.

Harasim, Linda. 2012. *Learning theory and online technologies*. New York: Routledge/Taylor & Francis.

Hua, Lu. 2018. "Construction of SPOC-based Learning Model and Its Application in Linguistics Teaching." *iJET* 13 (2): 157-169. https://doi.org/10.3991/ijet.v13i02.7929.

Kaplan, Andreas M., and Michael Haenlein. 2016. "Higher Education and the Digital Revolution. About MOOCs, SPOCs, Social Media, and the Cookie Monster." *Business Horizons* (59): 441-450. https://doi.org/10.1016/j.bushor.2016.03.00.

Laici, Chiara. 2005. "Le figure professionali dell'e-learning". In *E-learning. Aspetti pedagogici e didattici*, edited by Floriana Falcinelli, 19-63. Perugia: Morlacchi.

Lin, Chin-His, and Yining Zhang. 2014. "慕课与对外汉语教学 Muke yu duiwai hanyu jiaoxue (MOOCs and Chinese Language Education)". *Journal of Technology and Chinese Language Teaching* 5 (2): 49-65.

Means, Barbara, Marianne Bakia, and Robert Murphy. 2014. *Learning Online. What Research Tells Us About Whether, When and How*. New York: Routledge.

Panagiotidis, Panos. 2019. "MOOCs for Language Learning. Reality and Prospects". *SITE 2019*: 286-292.

Payne, Scott, and Paul Whitney. 2002. "Developing L2 Oral Proficiency through Synchronous CMC: Output, Working Memory, and Interlanguage Development". *CALICO Journal* 20, (1): 7-32.

Piras, Valeria, Maria Cecilia Reyes, and Guglielmo Trentin. 2020. *Come disegnare un corso online. Criteri di progettazione didattica e della comunicazione*. Milano: Franco Angeli.

Prunuske, Amy. Janet Batzlin, Evelyn Howell, Sarah Miller. 2012. "Using Online Lectures to Make Time for Active Learning". *Genetics* 192 (1): 67-72. https://doi.org/10.1534/genetics.112.141754

Schaffauser, Dian. 2016. "Teaching with Tech. A Balancing Act". *Campus Technology* 29 (8). Available at: https://pdf.1105media.com/CampusTech/2016/701920958/CAM_1608DG.pdf (Accessed 7 December 2020).

Siemens, George. 2005. "Connectivism: A Learning Theory for the Digital Age". *International Journal of Instructional Technology and Distance Learning* 2 (1). Available at: https://jotamac.typepad.com/jotamacs_weblog/files/Connectivism.pdf (Accessed 17 September 2020).

Sun, Susan Yue Hua. 2011. "Online Language Teaching. The Pedagogical Challenges". *Knowledge Management & E-Learning: An International Journal* 3 (3): 428-447.

Szpunar, Karl, Samuel Moulton, and Daniel Schacter. 2013. "Mind wandering and education: from the classroom to online learning". *Frontiers in Psychology* 4: 1-7. https://doi.org/10.3389/fpsyg.2013.00495

Trentin, Guglielmo. 2020. *Didattica con e nella rete. Dall'emergenza all'uso ordinario*. Milano: Franco Angeli.

Vygotsky, Lev Semënovič. 1986. *Thought and Language*. Cambridge: MIT Press.

Wang, Jue, and Joël Bellassen. 2017. "面向法语母语学习者的中文初阶慕课 Kit de contact en langue chinoise：设计，实施和发现 Mianxiang fayu muyu xuexizhe de zhongwen chujie muke Kit de contact en langue chinoise: sheji, shishi he faxian (Design, Implementation and Reflection on the Introductory Chinese

MOOC Kit de contact en langue chinoise)". *Journal of Modernization of Chinese language education* 6 (1): 31-41.

Weerasinghe, Thushani, Robert Ramberg, and Kamalanath Hewagamage. 2009. "Designing Online Learning Environments for Distance Learning". *International Journal of Instructional Technology and Distance Learning* 6 (3): 21-42.

Yaden, Bridget. 2019. "The Acquisition Environment for Instructed L2 Learners: Implementing Hybrid and Online Language Courses". In *L2 Grammatical Representation and Processing*, edited by Deborah Arteaga, 139-159. Bristol: Multilingual Matters.

Chapter 3

# Traveling from Italian to Chinese: An Interdisciplinary Course Design

Silvia Tiboni-Craft
*Wake Forest University*

Qiaona Yu
*Wake Forest University*

"We were born for cooperation, like feet, like hands, like eyelids, like the rows of upper and lower teeth. So to work in opposition to one another is against nature" (Marcus Aurelius *Med.* 2.1)

**Abstract:** This chapter introduces an innovative interdisciplinary cross-course design that blends learning of foreign languages, literature, history, culture, and business skills. Through a 360° map creation project, students from an Italian literature course and a business Chinese course virtually explored the Silk Road. First, we retrace the intriguing encounter between Italian literature and business Chinese to set the background of the study. Then, we illustrate the main steps students took for the project. In ITA 213, students first read excerpts from the book *The Travels of Marco Polo* to acquire the appropriate literary, cultural, and historical background. Students then designed a cultural and geographical virtual map, through which they recreated and experienced, by using virtual reality (VR), Marco Polo's journeys along the Silk Road during the Middle Ages. In CHI 255, students screened a CCTV documentary series on China's contemporary *Belt and Road Initiative* (BRI). Students then virtually mapped selected projects by the BRI, discussed the BRI from their own perspectives, and designed original business proposals targeting the market along the BRI route. Next, we reflect on challenges and shared takeaways at integrating VR in teaching and learning. Last, we examine how the project facilitated interdisciplinary learning including digital literacy development.

**Keywords:** Cross-course design, Digital Humanities, interdisciplinary Learning, language learning, VR.

\*\*\*

## Introduction

In recent years, educators at all levels around the United States have been engaged in a deep reflection on how to incorporate multiculturalism and cross-culturalism in teaching in order to better prepare students to navigate and understand the increasingly globalized world. Ladson-Billing (1995, 468) proposed the necessity to build a culturally relevant theory of education that would study cultures by bridging micro-perspectives and macro-perspectives instead of studying them separately. The approach proposed by Ladson-Billing invited educators to re-think how to mediate and interact with inclusive ways of introducing the material to students in order to teach the democracy of multiculturalism. Django Paris (2012) proposed substituting the word "relevant" with something more representative of contemporary society such as "sustaining". In line with this proposal, *the culturally sustaining pedagogy* intends to foster and therefore sustain "linguistic, literate, and cultural pluralism as part of the democratic project of schooling." This interdisciplinary project was born with the intent to show students how two different cultures, such as Italian and Chinese, can be profoundly connected. In addition, this project seeks to demonstrate to students that two different disciplines, such as literature and business, can dialogue and work together. The use of interdisciplinary collaborations is an effective tool to embrace a *culturally sustaining pedagogy* in order for students to appreciate the diversity that characterizes a multicultural pedagogical discourse. The idea of this project arose from campus-wide interdisciplinary work on the Silk Road and it aims to combine Italian literature with business Chinese by exploring the Silk Road from past to present. Students of both classes started by working separately, following detailed steps to explore the topic within their own field. In the end, they came together to virtually travel along the Silk Road from the Medieval time to contemporary days. This helped them elaborate on their works and ultimately interrogate themselves on the thread that links the two disciplines. The creation of a 360 map immersed students into a virtual and more engaging journey. In order to show properly all the steps of this project, the chapter is organized as follows. First, this chapter analyzes the topic from a micro-perspective by explaining what students have done in each individual class: Introduction to Italian Literature and Business Chinese. Then, it discusses the work that students did together by presenting their works and their results. Lastly, it examines the benefits and the challenges that students and instructors faced while working on the project, reflecting particularly on the use of technology in the creation of a 360° Virtual Reality Map along the Silk Road. The interdisciplinarity approach allows instructors to connect the classroom with the real world and to cross the barriers of each conventional discipline toward a more fluid way of teaching that may better connect with Generation Z.

### What is Interdisciplinary Teaching? Bridging Italian Literature and Business Chinese

As previously anticipated, the focus of this collaboration was to propose a more fluid and inclusive way of teaching with the intent of showing students how different disciplines can partner together to overcome the limits of studying them discretely. The interdisciplinary approach invites instructors to scaffold students' learning across disciplines in order to develop inter-connecting critical skills, to better prepare them for a multi-cultural dominated world. With this in mind, it is first necessary to define the term *interdisciplinary*. In an article which appeared in 1974 in the Journal of General Education, Tamara Swora and James L. Morrinson define it as:

> ... An adjective describing the *interaction* among two or more different disciplines. The interaction might range from simple communication of ideas to the mutual integration of organizing *concepts, methodologies, procedures, epistemologies, terminology, data* and *education* in a fairly large field [...]. (Swora and Morrison 1974, 45)

This approach therefore encourages interaction and integration among different disciplines, fosters inclusivity by exploring diverse methodologies, and develops a macro-perspective of topics that shifts the traditional vertical structure of discipline-oriented departments towards a more horizontal structure (Swora and Morrison 1974, 49). This more horizontal structure encourages collaboration among faculty with diverse expertise to find connections among different areas of study and foster a more inclusive way of teaching. This approach also brings about a reflection on and revision of the instructor-student relationship by shifting towards a less hierarchical dynamic that stimulates cooperation among teachers and pupils. Educators will continue to guide students but "no longer merely transmit knowledge" (Swora and Morrison 1974, 52). Rather, they accompany students toward their learning goals by encouraging them to share their own expertise, thereby assuming agency in the acquisition process. The collaboration among Italian

Literature and Business Chinese courses in this contribution demonstrates in practice how disciplines can join forces in a fruitful cooperation in which faculty and students are fully engaged in an analysis of the proposed topic through the macro-perspective lens of interdisciplinarity.

### Introduction to Italian Literature: A New Way of Reading and Analyzing the Literary Work *The Travels of Marco Polo*

When we started to develop this project, the instructor of ITA 213 Introduction to Italian Literature class took into consideration two essential aspects. The first required students to be exposed to complex literary texts in Italian after having had only three or four semesters of the language. It was therefore crucial to properly evaluate each student's level of proficiency. Students in the Italian Literature class were mostly at Intermediate High level on the ACTFL Proficiency Guidelines,[1] so this project presented sufficient challenges to pull students out of their comfort zone and toward the next level of learning.[2] In doing this, it was important to be aware that a project of mismatched difficulty could intimidate students. To avoid this potential risk, it was crucial to find an appropriate version of *The Travels of Marco Polo*, the book they had to read before working on the virtual tour along the Silk Road. This step was key to building the necessary scaffolding for the future steps of project.[3] After consulting several editions, a simplified version of the book that is typically used at the Middle School level in Italy was chosen. This version also had a small manual to accompany the main text that summarized each chapter with some interactive activities.[4] After assessing proficiency and choosing the text, the

---

[1] ACTFL Performance Descriptors for Language Learners https://www.actfl.org/sites/default/files/publications/ACTFLPerformance_Descriptors.pdf

[2] According to Vygotsky's sociocultural theory, students are able to reach higher levels of learning through the mediation of more knowledgeable members of the educational community such as the instructor. The mediator or instructor therefore leads students out of their comfort zones into their Zone of Proximal Development (ZPD) where they meet and overcome new challenges due to the presence of the mediator. Thus, they can successfully accomplish their new learning tasks.

[3] In 1967, the American Psychologist Jerome Bruner used for the first time the term *scaffolding* to refer to the series of activities and steps that an instructor creates in order to help students to reach a higher level of knowledge. According to Bruner, this mediation will increase a student's progress with his/her learning.

[4] Marco Polo, *Il Milione Traduzione e adattamento di Elena Frontaloni* (Monte San Vito, AN: Raffaello Libri, 2003). This textbook narrates the story of the journey of Marco Polo in a simplified manner where the protagonist tells the story of his travel in first person. It is divided into three parts. The first part covers Marco Polo's life in Venice until he

instructor constructed the other steps of the project. While the focus of the project was on building intercultural competences, it is important to acknowledge that the project also built digital literacy thanks to the use of the 360° map and the virtual reality (VR). This part will be in a later section.

The first step was for students to learn the appropriate historical background of the city of Venice at the time of Marco Polo in the thirteenth century. This initial step was introduced by presenting students with two maps, Italy during the Middle Ages and Italy today. Afterwards, they were tasked with comparing and contrasting what they observed. Such an activity served to help students understand that Italy was a fractured country before its unification in 1861 and the city of Venice was a Republic—information that would prove very relevant throughout the course of the project. It was also very important for students to actively participate and to take agency during the whole process such that, as James Paul Gee explained,[5] they could identify with the learning process and feel involved. The combination of taking agency and identification aided in the creation of a new student-instructor relationship, which was based on a collaboration throughout the learning processes. The whole introductory section was essentially a collaboration between the students and the instructor who served as a mediator[6] between learners and knowledge by providing students with the material to reflect and to analyze. Students learned about the social and political structures of the Republic of Venice by analyzing the figure of the Doge and the Dogess, the main holidays celebrated at the time, the organization of the everyday social life and the city itself, the importance of the Arsenal and the meaning of living in close contact with the water.

---

reaches China, the second part narrates Polo's life at Khan's Palace, and the last part covers Marco Polo's experience as an ambassador of the Khan. The activities in the workbook are very engaging and help students to navigate and understand the content of the readings.

[5] James Paul Gee applied his theory of identity and agency to the use of video games for educational purposes in the class setting. His theory explains the benefit of a student-centered class that empowered them by teaching them how to solve problems. For more information about his theory, see James Paul Gee, *Social Linguistics and Literacies: Ideology in Discourses* (London: Falmer Press, 1990) and James Paul Gee, "Good Video Games and Good Learning." *Phi Kappa Phi Forum* 85, no 2 (Summer 2005): 34–7.

[6] Refer to footnote 1.

The learning process centered around students acquiring the information by using another simplified introductory text,[7] and then coming to class ready to discuss and to present the information in small groups. This discussion was facilitated by questions previously prepared and assigned to the class to guide their readings. Students answered the questions in advance which prepared them to engage each other in conversations. It should be noted that the discussion and reflection in this first stage was about Venice being a portal city and therefore a city with fluid and open borders. This reflection immediately led students to understand the complexity of intercultural relationships that Venice had with the outside world and how living on the water was an invitation to explore and receive different cultures. Furthermore, the analysis allowed students to understand how the role of *mercanti*, the businessmen of the time, was involved in bringing diversity to the Republic of Venice. This therefore helped students to make connections between the Italian Literature class and the Business Chinese. The figure of the *mercanti*, embodied by Marco Polo, and the element of water were important subjects of the critical thinking needed used in developing Intercultural Learning competency which is defined as "a set of cognitive, affective, and behavioral skills and characteristics that support a student's understanding of people, events and processes from other cultures."[8] In this first micro-analysis, students worked on developing the cognitive, affective, and behavioral skills as pertain to Italian culture. Cognitive skills were developed as students explored the complexity of the history, politics, economy, and practices of the Italian culture through the example of the Republic of Venice. Affective skills were engaged and enhanced as students interpreted the multicultural experience of confronting their own culture with the Italian one. Then, they started to acquire behavioral skills by asking inquisitive questions on Italian culture. In the last stage of the project when students from both classes shared their works in a collaborative way, they were capable of extending their knowledge by connecting the two disciplines and therefore by understanding multiple worldwide perspectives.

---

[7] To facilitate this step, the instructor found it very helpful to consult a children's map entitled *Il viaggio di Marco Polo da Venezia alla Cina e ritorno* that gives some of the main information on the book *Travels of Marco Polo*. It uses a map so that students can easily identify the main steps and cultural discoveries of Polo's journey. Also, for introducing students to the structure of the Republic of Venice, it is worth mentioning another children's book called *Venezia nei Giorni fi Marco Polo* that recounts the life of Marco Polo in Venice.

[8] "Core Education Competencies /Rubrics", Wake Forest University Assessment of Students Learning https://assessment.college.wfu.edu/core-education-competenciesrubrics/

After the preliminary and introductory sessions on the history and structure of the Republic of Venice, students moved on to read, study, and analyze the book *The Travels of Marco Polo*. As previously stated, this was an easier version written in contemporary Italian and in a quite casual narrative style. After a brief introduction to Marco Polo, students were assigned chapters to read along with comprehension questions to guide their understanding of the main points. Students worked through additional exercises created to summarize each chapter. In addition, they were invited to reflect on the cultural experience that Marco Polo underwent during his journey along the Silk Road and also on the cultural exchange in which he participated and ultimately brought back with him to his native city. To help students internalize the material covered in the literary text, they used a map to identify the places visited by Marco Polo. Along with the visual representations, students discussed how each country's borders and political power changed along the Silk Road from the Middle Ages to the modern day. This was a critical part of the project as it segued into the construction of their own virtual 360° maps.

The reading of *The Travels of Marco Polo* offered many opportunities to reflect on the different cultural experiences that Marco Polo encountered along his travels. It was also a moment for students to reflect on their own cultural perspectives by interacting different cultures. Students compared the different historical time frames, past and present, and observed the different contexts of interpretation. Their initial micro-perspective analysis of the class project was starting to branch out into a macro-perspective analysis. The description of a fascinating and diverse world encountered by Marco Polo sparked several conversations and curiosities that were related to contemporary topics. One example is the conversation generated by the legend of *La città dei profumi* (The City of Scents) that portrays women as the cause of the God's punishments in the city.[9] This story was a moment of reflection on the depiction of women since antiquity and the

---

[9] The legend states that once upon a time there was a very rich and fruitful city that one day received the visit of a poor man who asked for shelter. All male inhabitants of the city welcomed him immediately, but the women did not want to help him and sent him away. Unfortunately, the poor old man was, in reality, a very vindictive god who became very angry and cast a spell making the once fertile soil and trees of the city unfruitful. The male inhabitants desperately sent the wiser old man to the god to ask for an explanation. In the end, the god offered the city a deal which stated that in order to expiate their mistakes they should let all women of the city welcome and engage with all the men who were visiting the city. They accepted, and from that day forward all the women pleased each wayfarer who visited the city.

perpetuation of the patriarchal mentality to contemporary days on the continuation of mirroring the image of angels or witches. This consideration of the legend was critical for students to see how a text from the thirteenth century can still communicate to them and be engaging and relevant in the twenty-first century.

### Encountering Business Chinese along the Contemporary Silk Road

The collaborator with the Italian literature class in this cross-course design was a Business Chinese class offered at the same university. The Business Chinese course focused on fostering students' Mandarin communicative competence in Chinese-speaking business contexts and practices. Students in this class had successfully completed third-year college-level Chinese language courses and ranged between Intermediate-Mid and Advanced-Low on the ACTFL Proficiency Guidelines.

In the Business Chinese class, students were guided through real-life cross-cultural experiences completing three modules of searching for a job using Chinese, working and socializing with coworkers of different language and cultural backgrounds, and team-designing transnational business proposals. The interdisciplinary Silk Road Project was part of Module Three. In Module Three, students surveyed and critiqued various marketing strategies employed by multinational incorporations to target the Chinese market. Informed with successful marketing strategies, students were then tasked with team-designing their own marketing proposals in the Silk Road Project. A CCTV documentary series on China's contemporary *Belt and Road Initiative* (BRI) was chosen as the main text. BRI is a global infrastructure development strategy adopted by the Chinese government in 2013. It has involved investment in nearly 70 countries and international organizations along the historical trade routes along overland and maritime Silk Road across Asia, Africa, and Europe. In class, students together screened Episode One. Realizing the difficulty of authentic materials, the instructor of the Business Chinese class primed students with background information. Same as the Italian Literature class, a global map of the BRI was presented to students for a macro-level analysis on its motive, scope, practice, and especially its impact locally and globally. Students were given scaffolding comprehension questions prior to watching Episode One in Chinese. After providing their answers, students then screened the English-translation dubbed version of the same episode to check their responses.

### Bridging the Cross-Course Collaboration on a Virtual Silk Road

The last part of the project was collaboratively conducted by both the Italian Literature and Business Chinese courses. Students created a virtual 360° map that combined the work from both classes. In order to build this map, we provided students with the technical tools that consisted of a subscription to a virtual map creating program *Thinglink*,[10] VR headsets, and 360° cameras to film the videos. To purchase the material, we applied for and received a grant offered by the Center for the Advancement of Teaching at our institution who greatly supported this interdisciplinary project. After providing the equipment and software to the classes, we started to work on the last part of the project; first individually and then with students together to navigate each other's virtual projects. The process of developing the 360° map created a very interactive teamwork dynamic not only among students but also between the instructor and the students, since the project required working together in a horizontal collaboration to find new methods to overcome the technical challenges encountered along the way. The next paragraphs will describe the steps followed in both classes to create the 360° videos.

### A New Way of Approaching the Literary Text by Creating a Virtual 360° Map

By creating a 360° virtual map, this Silk Road Project aimed to realize three learning objectives. First, this project intended to show students how the study of literary texts could be approached in an unconventional way by using contemporary tools to connect students and modern society to the medieval world. As previously done, the instructors provided students with guidelines to produce their videos. Second, the project aimed to aid in language acquisition by having students continue to practice their written and oral foreign language skills through various activities through each step of the project. Finally, the project aimed to impart upon students the ever-important skill of digital literacy.

In the Italian Literature class, after students acquired knowledge on the historical background of the Republic of Venice and completed reading passages and discussed the *Travels of Marco Polo*, they were ready to start creating a 360° virtual map with their narrated 360° videos about various steps of Marco Polo's journey from Venice to China. To get things started, students created a written text related to the topic of the video assigned. Based on their created text, they then added an Italian narration and English subtitles into video. Lastly, students embedded the 360° videos in the virtual map found on Thinglink. Before diving into each step, students were divided into small groups of two for the video project. Working in pairs with a classmate provided an opportunity to build a stronger sense of community in the class

---

[10] See Thinglink, https://www.thinglink.com/welcome.

and improve confidence when by stepping out of their comfort zone with a challenging way of working on a literary text. While students could choose their working partner, the topic of the video was assigned to each group.

To create the narration, students were presented the opportunities to use the information from the reading passages on the *Travels of Marco Polo* discussed in class and add information from their additional research. Students had total agency in their choice of the narrative style as long as it was a creative presentation of the text. They could step into the shoes of Marco Polo, they could imagine being contemporary tourist guides and giving a tour of Marco Polo's journey and life in the Republic of Venice, or they could create a sort of dialogue between two college students that were studying and reading the book, and anything else they may have imagined. Creating a more personalized narration allowed the learners to better identify with their narrative text and therefore fully immerse themselves in the project and take agency.[11] Once the text was completed students turned it in to receive instructor's feedback on the content and on the grammatical structures to enhance the accuracy and appropriateness of student recordings. This was important since other students would be listening to the recordings later, so the language needed to be modeled correctly. As for length, students were not provided with a word-count for the text because they had to be able to eventually adjust the narration as described above, but they were provided with a grading rubric for this part.

Once the text was ready, students began recording their narrations by referring to the grading rubric as guidelines. Students were encouraged and advised to reserve a room at the recording facility on campus where they could find the appropriate recording equipment, or they could simply use their phone. It was crucial for students to practice multiple times before recording to make sure their narration was fluid, clear, and with an understandable pronunciation. Students were allowed to have notes, but they could not read from the written text. While this project was definitely challenging for learners at this level, it was very beneficial in building up their language speaking confidence. It made them realize they could read and elaborate on a literary text after only three semesters in the language.

In the Business Chinese class, students were first provided with an overview of the BRI from watching Episode One of the CCTV documentary series. Then

---

[11] Immersive learning enables students to be fully engaged and experience the learning process. It allows them to identify with the material they are studying.

students were divided into groups of 2-3 to dive into micro-level analysis. The instructor pre-segmented Episode Two into three 15-minute sections and listed in both English and Chinese on the handouts the places and countries that collaborated with China for infrastructure building. Each student group started by choosing one of the segmented sections to watch closely and identify the given places and countries in the video. As an example, the countries in one of the sections included Jeddah in Saudi Arabia, Khujand in Tajikistan, Danghara in Tajikistan, Tajikistan-Uzbekistan Road, Almaty in Kazakhstan, Ulaanbaatar in Mongolia, Surabaya City at Java in Indonesia, and Karakoram in Pakistan. Next, students closely watched the video segments to comprehend the ongoing cross-national business development and communication at the listed locations. Students then discussed in group to help each other comprehend and summarize how China has been collaborating with the local government and residents. Students then used their own words to introduce the business activities in forms of both written English texts and Chinese audios. Lastly, and likely the most challenging step for the Module Three test, each group developed a marketing proposal that targets the BRI economic corridor. Each group chose their targeted location and market after strategizing how the BRI might expand the market and benefit the development of their company. Such marketing proposals are presented in the form of self-filmed videos.

## Creating 360° videos

The very last part of the project before the two classes met was for students to add the recording to the 360° videos and then upload it to the virtual map through Thinglink. Students did not make the actual 360° videos since this would have required traveling abroad, but instead, they searched for freely available 360° videos on the web. One of the initial challenges they encountered at the first iteration of the project was finding a good selection of 360° videos. The second challenge was that many of the available 360° videos online did not provide students editing access. Students could not add voiceover narrations or subtitles. A solution was offered by Thinglink in a way it allows students to upload their narration and videos separately. This was still a problem for some 360° videos that already had narration in the background, so students had to mute the video and play their own recording. To address these challenges, the first author received another grant at her institution to go to Venice for a week and film her own 360° videos of some of the main parts of the city connected to the text, such as the Arsenal, Marco Polo's House, the Ducal Palace and San Marco Square. These videos were recorded very early in the morning to avoid the presence of too many tourists, and a

360° camera[12] with a selfie stick was used to record while walking to avoid having too many people in the videos. Giving students tailored videos allowed them to overlay their narration and include subtitles. To lay the audio track over the video, students used the program Adobe Premier. Then they uploaded the video to YouTube which accepts 360°videos and allows for the addition of subtitles. Once the 360° videos were completed, they uploaded them on an image of the Silk Road Journey previously uploaded on Thinglink thereby creating the virtual 360° map.

Compared with the urban locations in Venice, locations along the BRI are far less transportation accessible. In the Business Chinese class, student groups pinned down the given locations on the virtual map and added their own English text and Chinese audio introductions to each location. This step provided them with a better visual geographical understanding to navigate the ambitious BRI coverage. They also searched for 360° Aerial Panoramas or 360° images of these locations and countries to put on Thinglink VR Editor. Without editing access or software for 360° videos, students innovatively figured out to screen record the available 360° videos in order to embed their textual and audible introductions.

Once all the videos were uploaded, students of both classes met to share with each other their works as well as provide peer feedback. It is important to reiterate that for a project like this one, it is crucial for the students and instructors to seek technical support from the university's technology center.

### An Intercultural and Interdisciplinary Encounter: Italian Literature and Business Chinese

After students investigated the project from a micro-perspective in each class, it was time to bring the analysis to a macro-perspective level and to integrate the two cultures, languages, and disciplines together. By virtually travelling the Silk Road together students enhanced their intercultural skills. This was achieved by expanding their knowledge, connecting the different views of their topic of investigation, and applying this new knowledge through cultural interactions. To make the encounter between the two classes interactive and engaging, we set up a cross-class meeting to have students from both classes intermingle and then present, explain, and inquire about each other's videos

---

[12] The camera used to film the videos was a Ricoh Theta SC 360° video and still camera. After having filmed the 360° videos, it is important to take into consideration that they require some time for the editing process and a good knowledge of Adobe Premier.

and cultures. Students were given a rubric (See Appendix) in advance to guide their group presentations. During the presentations, students navigated the video using the VR headsets and virtually walked along the Silk Road from past to present. Once again, students took complete agency of the learning process by asking each other questions. They were not only in charge of explaining their own projects but also identifying with the Italian and Chinese cultures and languages respectively by representing them to their peers. Students' responses to this project were highly positive and they really valued the rich cross-cultural background that they had the opportunity to acquire throughout this collaborative work. In addition, students' feedback underlined the innovative way of approaching the material and the sense of accomplishment they experienced in being able to build a 360° map. Students showed great excitement in comments such as "loving the Google earth journey," "super fun videos," and "I'm really impressed!!!" During the cross-class meeting students were able to exchange in their group presentations the challenges they had to face while working on the project and they gave each other valuable and productive feedback. After the end of the presentations, students were asked to fill out a peer review rubric to evaluate each other's works. Many students' responses on the success of this project confirmed the effectiveness of the interdisciplinary approach since they all strongly agreed that they learned beyond their typical course boundaries. One Italian literature student commented that "I learned a lot about China that I didn't know, as well as future plans those Asian countries are making, such as a train from Hong Kong to London." Vice versa, the Business Chinese students were inspired by the historical roots of the BRI. One Business Chinese student commented "I learned a lot about the story of Samarkand, both modern and historical! I also learned about the mythical 'city of smells' and the fable behind it." In addition, many of their comments focused on the value of the opportunity they were presented with to make connections between the two disciplines. One student from the Italian literature class commented, "The Silk Road is still functioning! I had no idea that it was still a major form of transportation/trade. I am really impressed." Another Italian literature student wrote, "The Silk Road is not as historic as I originally thought. It is still functioning!" A business Chinese student commented that it was great to "earn the historical "Marco Polo's narratives with a very interesting description of the east, which seemed to have an influence on modern East-West relations". Another Italian literature student reflected, "I liked how the cities they focused on and their significance with trade and commerce was reminiscent of what we did with Marco Polo on the historic Silk Road. I learned a lot about modern day China."

The interdisciplinary approach of the project allowed the learners to overcome the boundaries of traditional classes. They surpassed the limitations presented by such a class and experienced and even promoted a more globalized and inclusive world. The cross-cultural journey ended with a banquet of Chinese and Italian foods to celebrate the students' hard work and to sustain and foster diversity and inclusion.

## Conclusions

An interdisciplinary project provides students a unique opportunity to blend learning of multiple disciplines and encourages learners to approach and analyze topics from a worldwide perspective. An interdisciplinary approach enables students to surpass the boundaries of the mono-discipline and create cooperation and connections across departments, colleagues, and students. We believe that the key to a successful cross-course interdisciplinary project is mutual commitment and effective communication between the collaborative instructors in order to guide students through the various steps in acquiring intercultural competences. In addition, interdisciplinarity cultivates a new instructor-student dynamic that stimulates cooperation by working together on projects and on developing cross-cultural critical thinking. To conclude, interdisciplinary projects are important to promote a *culturally sustaining pedagogy*. They help new generations of students to see how different cultures, languages, disciplines, and people are connected within a complex multicultural system. Importantly, a cross-course interdisciplinary approach requires instructors and students to re-evaluate their design of the course material in order to build a cross-cultural community and to bridge different disciplines.

## Appendix A: Cross-Class Silk Road Project Peer Review Rubric

Project Team members_____          Grader_____

|  | Strongly agree | Somewhat agree | Neutral | Somewhat disagree | Strongly disagree |
|---|---|---|---|---|---|
| 1. Overall, the message of this project is clear and comprehensive. | 5 | 4 | 3 | 2 | 1 |
| 2. I was engaged while interacting with the other class. | 5 | 4 | 3 | 2 | 1 |
| 3. I was able to learn something beyond my registered class through this project. | 5 | 4 | 3 | 2 | 1 |
| 4. The content is very well selected to present the learning target. | 5 | 4 | 3 | 2 | 1 |
| 5. The format is creatively designed and appealing to the audience. | 5 | 4 | 3 | 2 | 1 |
| 6. The technology chosen supports the content delivery well. | 5 | 4 | 3 | 2 | 1 |
| :) Extra points: creativity! | 5 | 4 | 3 | 2 | 1 |
|  |  |  |  | **Total:** _____ |  |

| One thing I will take away from this project: | One suggestion for future improvement: |
|---|---|
|  |  |

## Appendix B: Within-Class Silk Road Project Peer Review Rubric

Project Team members_____          Grader_____

|  | Strongly agree | Somewhat agree | Neutral | Somewhat disagree | Strongly disagree |
|---|---|---|---|---|---|
| 1. The content is very well selected to present the targeted location. | 5 | 4 | 3 | 2 | 1 |
| 2. The format is well designed and appealing to the audience. | 5 | 4 | 3 | 2 | 1 |
| 3. The technology chosen well supports the content delivery. | 5 | 4 | 3 | 2 | 1 |
| 4. The speaking in Chinese is fluent. | 5 | 4 | 3 | 2 | 1 |
| 5. The speaking in Chinese is accurate. | 5 | 4 | 3 | 2 | 1 |
| 6. The speaking in Chinese used sophisticated language. | 5 | 4 | 3 | 2 | 1 |
| 7. The material is comprehensible to non-Chinese speakers by providing English introductions/short descriptions/English subtitles. | 5 | 4 | 3 | 2 | 1 |
| 8. The project is very well presented face-to-face in an engaging and interactive way at the exhibition. | 5 | 4 | 3 | 2 | 1 |
| Extra points: Creativity | 5 | 4 | 3 | 2 | 1 |
| Total:_____ | | | | | |

## Bibliography

ACTFL. "Performance Descriptors for Language Learners." Accessed January 29, 2021. https://www.actfl.org/sites/default/files/publications/ACTFLPerformance _Descriptors.pdf

Bruner, Jerome. 1977. *The process of Education*. Cambridge, MA: Harvard University Press.

Gee, James Paul. 1990. *Social linguistics and literacies: Ideology in discourses*. London: Falmer Press.

———. 2005. "Good Video Games and Good Learning." *Phi Kappa Phi Forum* 85 (2): 34–7.

Ladson-Billings, Gloria. 1995. "Toward a Theory of Culturally Relevant Pedagogy" in *Source American Educational Research Journal*, 32 (3): 465-491.

Pace, Pino. 2010. *Il viaggio di Marco Polo da Venezia alla Cina e ritorno*. Torino: EDT.

Paris, Django. 2012. "Culturally Sustaining Pedagogy: A Needed Change in Stance, Terminology, and Practice" in *Educational Researcher* 41: 93-97, https://doi.org/10.3102/0013189X12441244.

Polo, Marco. 2003. *Il Milione Traduzione e adattamento di Elena Frontaloni*. Monte San Vito, AN: Raffaello Libri.

Stellingwerff, Irene. 2016. *Venezia nei giorni di Marco Polo*. Ficulle, TR: Comosanova.

Swora, Tamara, and James L. Morrison. 1974. "Interdisciplinarity in Higher Education." *The Journal of General Education*, 26 (1): 45-52.

Vygotsky, Lev Semenovich. 1978. *Mind in society: The development of higher psychological processes*. Cambridge, MA: Harvard University Press.

Wake Forest University Assessment of Students Learning "Core Education Competencies /Rubrics." Accessed January 29, 2021. https://assessment.college. wfu.edu/core-education-competenciesrubrics/

Chapter 4

# Bringing Culture into Language Classrooms: Creative Puppetry and the Teaching of Chinese as a Foreign Language

Jasmine Yu-Hsing Chen
*Utah State University*

**Abstract:** This chapter introduces a method for enhancing students' motivation to learn Chinese as a foreign language (CFL) by using traditional Taiwanese glove puppetry. By guiding students to create a Chinese puppet show, the instructor effectively combines language learning with drama, folklore, and culture. Previous studies argue that learning culture can help to learn a language (e.g., Nguyen 2017) or highlight the importance of introducing cultural meaning in a language class (e.g., Fatma 2014), while little empirical evidence shows how to innovatively integrate language teaching with culture. This chapter, therefore, contributes to the literature on ways to use puppetry to promote "real language" learning of CFL in higher education. Hands-on performances make the language learning process more meaningful and memorable because they not only occupy the learners cognitively but also engage them physically and emotionally. The curriculum instruction shows the effectiveness of adopting puppetry performance to enrich students' CFL learning in an interactional and communicative approach.

**Keywords:** Chinese as a foreign language (CFL), puppetry, culture-learning, performance, communicative language teaching.

\*\*\*

## Introduction: Motivate the Learning of Chinese Language and Culture through Puppetry

Educational research has long embraced the importance of integrating culture learning with students' creativity and imagination in language classrooms. Since language and culture are inextricably connected, a language teacher is also tasked with introducing students to the culture attached to the target language. Teaching culture in conjunction with language is crucial not only to develop intercultural sensitivity and awareness (Hurn and Tomalin 2013), but also because it enlivens a classroom and enhances students' learning (Bain 2004). Previous studies argue that learning a culture can help to learn its language (Nguyen 2017) or highlight the importance of introducing cultural meaning in a language class (Özüorçun 2014). Most activities emphasize improving student's reading comprehension and writing skills, while little empirical evidence shows how to innovatively motivate students' learning of language listening, speaking, and even "performing" with culture.

This chapter will begin to fill this literature gap by discussing the merits of having students "perform" with culture through the art of creative puppetry. More specifically, this chapter introduces a curriculum for instruction that utilizes performing arts, particularly Taiwanese glove puppetry, to integrate cultural education in the language classroom and enhance students' motivation to learn Chinese— particularly Mandarin in this chapter— as a foreign language (CFL). The curriculum demonstrates ways to use puppetry— including scriptwriting, play reading, communication during rehearsals, and puppet performance— in teaching CFL. Chinese/Sinophone culture is vast and varied, and it is unlikely that teachers can cover every aspect of the culture in one course. However, important elements of Chinese/Sinophone culture like drama, folklore, religious belief, and local songs can be found in its traditional puppetry. Allowing students to dive into this part of the culture can help them better connect with other parts of the culture as well. By guiding students to create a Chinese puppet show, the instructor can create a strong entry point through which students can learn the culture and authentic use of the language.

Assumingly due to how popular Muppet movies commonly target a young audience, puppets have mainly been used to attract young learners in the US. Puppets have proven to be an effective pedagogical tool in elementary education, which includes purposes such as generating communication, supporting a positive classroom climate, enhancing creativity, fostering cooperation, and providing an alternative attitude towards mistakes (Kröger and Nupponenb 2019). Scholars have noted puppets' potential for developing children's linguistic capability and encouraging them to experiment with new sounds and vocabularies; these benefits are due to how the puppet allows them to partially hide from facing their peers directly, thus settling performance anxiety (Kroflin 2012). Despite these positive findings, the existing literature has hardly examined how puppets can be a useful teaching tool in a university setting. This chapter, therefore, addresses this literature by exploring innovative approaches of using puppetry to motivate college students' learning of both language and culture.

## The Curriculum Design and Execution of the Puppet Show Project

The curriculum design was initially for a new advanced Chinese/Sinophone Theatre and Performance course taught in the target language. Course prerequisites included either having complete at least four semesters of Chinese learning or passing the equivalent placement test. The class size was relatively small with five students enrolled. All the students had served as Chinese missionaries; four of them had lived in Taiwan and one had lived in Hong Kong for two years. Their goal of registering for this course was not only to improve their language skills but also to deepen their knowledge of the culture. In response to their needs, I included a creative project of a Chinese puppet show to help them reach their goal in a lively way. The task of the project included creating the Chinese script, recording lines, choosing Chinese songs, and designing the stage and props. In addition to performing the puppetry for students in the first-semester Chinese class, students performed the puppet show in a local preschool and introduce young learners to their class learnings. The project involved students in "hands-on" experiences of connecting course materials to "real life" activities and community outreach.

I chose traditional Taiwanese glove puppetry because it is one of the most iconic practices of Taiwanese culture. Traditional puppet shows have been a common temple activity for deity birthdays and festivals in Taiwan. The origin of Taiwanese glove puppetry came from Chinese settlers who traveled from the closest mainland Chinese province of Fujian and brought their traditional forms of puppetry to Taiwan around the late nineteenth century (Chen 2007, 27-52). For over a century, repertoires based on Chinese folklore, historical legend, and martial arts novels, along with the puppets' highly choreographed movements made glove puppetry a popular form of entertainment in Taiwan. Thus, traditional puppetry is a perfect epitome of Chinese and Taiwanese culture. In Taiwan, traditional puppet shows have been typically performed in Taiwanese Holo vernacular, but I adopt Mandarin Chinese in the performance so that students can practice the language and learn the culture at the same time. The idea of using puppetry in a language class was further generated from my own performance experience. I have been a member of the Taiwan Puppet Troupe at the University of Wisconsin-Madison (UW-Madison), a student organization that has promoted Taiwanese culture in the U.S. for over twenty years. To attract the local American audience, the performance was done in English. The always-crowded audience for our puppet shows in local international festivals inspired me to integrate a performance project into my language and culture teaching. Puppetry, as a drama, is a pedagogy that reaches students of a multi-sensory mode of language learning and can be used to support the four key skills of listening, speaking, reading, and writing (Winston 2013). Thus, I decided to use a puppet show to give students a glimpse of the Taiwanese culture and help them learn the Chinese language in a performative way.

Traditional Taiwanese puppetry differs from the Muppets, and similar American puppet shows, in many ways, and can easily absorb college students' attention. In some American puppet shows, the puppeteers or other human actors interact with the puppets; however, in Taiwanese puppetry, performers usually hide behind the stage. American puppets also tend to be soft and hyper-expressive to attract children, while Taiwanese puppets are designed to be more lifelike and realistic in appearance. In the traditional form, a puppet is around an adult's palm size. A Taiwanese puppet's head is wooden, carved into the shape of a human head, and the puppet's torso consists of a glove-like, exquisite-embraided cloth costume. During performances, a puppeteer's fingers enter a puppet's hollow head and costume to make it perform. The stark contrasts between American puppets and Taiwanese puppets can quickly incite American college students' interest, which is a primary factor in motivating them to learn the performance.

What makes this teaching practice particularly malleable and universal is how the instructor can run the puppet show project with a low budget and likewise limited access to other resources. Different from the pricy handmade, wood-carved puppets, one glove puppet toy with a plastic head only costs around $12-15 and can be easily purchased on some e-shops based in Taiwan. The toy still retains the main features of the traditional glove puppet. Instructors in the U.S. can order the puppets online. Some Chinese animal puppets, such as a lion, dragon, and tiger, can be purchased on Amazon or eBay for a cost of around $20. Instructors may also consider letting students create their own glove puppets with affordable, everyday materials (Harding and et al. 2011). The stage can be made simply by connecting two tabletop display boards with hook-loop strips (**Figure 4.1**). Students can use their origami skills to make props or utilize various premade objects as props, depending on the plot (**Figure 4.2**). In sum, the instructor can easily control the cost depending on the available funding.

**Figure 4.1.** The stage can be made by lining up two tabletop display boards. The performers can easily carry, pack, and set up the stage quickly (photo taken by the author).

**Figure 4.2.** The puppet show props were made with affordable materials, which allowed students to demonstrate their creativity (photo taken by the author).

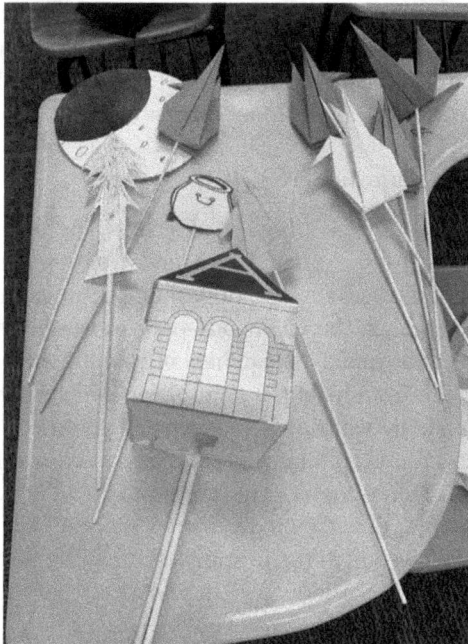

Puppetry can effectively transform a typical college language class and even be accessible to students with various social, mental, and physical differences, such as shyness or stuttering. For these students, college language classes bring a host of new obstacles. Students who took regular Chinese classes (not dual-language program or AP classes) in secondary education often equate one semester of college language class content to three years of high school language education. A college Chinese class is even more challenging because the focus is not only on listening and speaking but also on reading and writing. To balance all four language skills, college Chinese classes are often standard lectures, PowerPoints, and short group practices. A roles-play activity in a language class often takes ten to fifteen minutes, so students must quickly work out dialogues using assigned vocabulary or grammar. However, some students have social anxiety, feeling uncomfortable on the stage. Different from a role-play, puppeteers can hide behind the stage to avoid the stress of directly facing the audience while performing in the target language. A puppet show can be a long-term project that gives students time to work with each other communicatively. Some students in my class have difficulties with effective learning in a typical lecture class due to them having depression issues or attention deficit hyperactivity disorder (ADHD). Nevertheless, they were able to enjoy learning while serving as a crew member and supporting the success of the performance. The whole rehearsal process allowed the student extra time to organize their thoughts and put together a sentence naturally, as it reduced the pressure to provide an immediate response as in a typical roles-play. The following paragraphs provides instructors with the curriculum design and execution regarding the creative puppet show project.

**Read the Story and Create the Script**

The repertoire *Grant Aunt Tiger* (*hugupo*) was chosen because it represents an authentic cultural text— an often heard and well-remembered story for generations of Chinese speakers. The story shares a similar main theme with *Little Red Riding Hood,* which centers on how a clever girl tactfully killed an aggressive animal that wants to eat her, but *Grant Aunt Tiger's* cultural messages vastly differ from its popular European counterpart (Huang and et al. 1993). Students firstly watched a Chinese animation clip about the story and discussed the various cultural aspects represented within it. One of the most significant differences is the concept of a supernatural being worshipped by people. *Grant Aunt Tiger* shows that a long time ago, many people in Taiwan believed in different spirits, such as the God of the Sun, God of the Moon, God of the Earth, God of the Rock, God of the Tree, and even gods and goddesses of animals. This is different from the Christian idea that believes in only one true God. It thus created a discussion on how polytheism has been ubiquitous in traditional Chinese culture and folklore.

The introduction to different religious ideas further highlighted important cultural components of the language. Scholars have argued that it is problematic to not know the cultural components of a language. One common error of language learners is "to translate each word or expression literally. Considering how culture-bound language is, this tendency can confuse" (Neff and Rucynski 2013, 12). Regarding *Grant Aunt Tiger,* the discussion of culture bridged to the various ways to refer to a supernatural being in Chinese. Usually, for supernatural beings that would not hurt humans, they are commonly referred to as *shén* (God), but for the ones that would attack humans, the title is usually changed to *yāo* (demon). In Chinese culture, an old belief is that if an object existed or an animal lived long enough, it would possess a strange ability to transform into a human, but this human should be recognized as a *yāo*. In this case, the Chinese to refer to the grant aunt tiger, a tiger that turns to a grant aunt figure to devour children, should be *yāo* rather than *shén*.

After the discussion of the story, the translation of the script on the Google Doc expanded students' literacies with the aid of new technologies. Since the students had been already capable to conduct dialogues in plain Chinese, I requested them to translate an English script of *Grant Aunt Tiger* into Chinese so that they would learn to use some new vocabulary words. The English script was composed by a group of international graduate students from Taiwan at UW-Madison. The original script includes numerous cultural messages while the word choice is above the intermediate level, so translating the script from English to Chinese is suitable for an advanced language class. The students in my Chinese language class were divided evenly to translate a section. After they finished the first draft, each student was required to read over the translation and made comments and suggestions.

The collaborative translation on the Google Doc and the group editing practices appeared to increase comprehension and learning. One student observed the complexity and need for collaboration in the script translation because "there were multiple parts in the translation where you could translate it multiple ways" (Response form 3.1). Since he accidentally translated someone else's section, he got the chance to compare how other students' translations were to his. This helped him improve his translation skills as working on the script together allowed him to see "the diversity in translating methods" (Response form 3.1). Students could learn from each other's various word choices, grammar patterns, and impressive expressions, and then they can determine the best translation after reading the comments and discussing the subtle differences. In addition to learning from other people's different translations, the practice also created a great chance for me to introduce authentic expressions in Chinese. For example, in the story, when the mother is leaving, she hugs her children and says, "that's my sweet little girls." One student literarily translated the sentence word by word as "*wǒ tiánmì de nǚér.*" However, in Chinese daily conversations, this sentence is pretty unnatural. Because "*tiánmì de*" (sweet) is often used to describe a person only in a formal statement or in written Chinese. Considering the cultural meaning, the translation was revised to "*hǎo háizi*" (good kids), as this phrase is more colloquial in Chinese and commonly used between parents and children.

## Audio Recording and Creative Staging

When the students had the script ready, I then guided them to read the lines loudly and dramatically. Reading each word loudly can also help students improve their tones, as Chinese is a tonal language; the same syllable can be pronounced with different tones that differentiate the meaning. For English speakers, the tones are commonly challenging when they learn Chinese. The pronunciation of some phrases may need plenty of practice to get the tones correct. During the practice, the team also smoothed some sentences to fit each performer's need. This experience enabled students to learn alternative ways to represent their ideas. After each student could clearly read their lines and offer timely responses to others, we recorded the whole script. Students edited the audio file based on the recording. They then added some pieces of Taiwanese children's songs and Chinese music to enrich the soundscape of the performance.

## Rehearsal

During the rehearsal, students not only practiced how to manipulate the puppet based on the script but also learned new Chinese vocabulary words related to theatre in a communicative environment. The tools and materials they used in rehearsal, such as a stapler, super glue, tape, tabletop display board, etc. are usually not included in a regular textbook. However, through using the target language to communicate with others during the rehearsal, students learned these new words through hands-on experience. The hands-on performances make the language learning process more meaningful and memorable because it occupies students cognitively, physically, and emotionally. I also noticed that once the students learned a new word, they tended to show off and repeatedly use it in the following rehearsals. Their positive reaction is corresponding to the efficiencies of processing drama in language learning, as process drama opens the possibilities of learning "through the provision of a meaningful context for spontaneous language production" (Hulse and Owens 2019, 19). The rehearsal created a supportive cultural environment for students to spontaneously show and teach their peers the new language skills that they had learned.

### Performance

The two puppetry shows further prompted students to learn and share their language and cultural knowledge. One performance was arranged in the elementary level Chinese class, where students have learned Chinese for less than one college semester. Although the script includes numerous advanced dialogues in Chinese, the elementary-level students were still able to grasp the whole story through the performance. The second performance took place in a local preschool, accompanied by a workshop where college performers taught preschoolers the culture of Taiwanese puppetry, some simple Chinese greeting phrases, and how to play with traditional Taiwanese puppets.

### Major Reflections on Implementing Puppetry in the Learning of Chinese Language and Culture

Students showed a substantial increase in their motivation in using the language that was inspired by the puppet experience and interacting with the audience afterward. Overall, the students enjoyed putting on the puppet show, and some offered simple suggestions on how the project could be adapted to better fit their needs. The following paragraphs showcase student responses regarding this project.

### The Project Facilitated Students' Hands-on Learning of Culture

Hands-on experience can be a highly operative way to learn about different cultures because students take part in the culture, rather than observing it passively. Engaging in the art of puppetry can better help students learn about it rather than simply read a verbal introduction or watch video clips. One student share that he first learned about Taiwanese puppetry when he was studying abroad in Taiwan, but the closest he got to this subject was through YouTube videos. His hands-on performance experience made puppetry "a lot cooler than it does in YouTube videos" (Response form 1.1). Another student also commented that the performance allowed him to "understand more nuances than reading books about it." He felt the experience was priceless because it made him "fall in love with Taiwanese puppet show" (Response form 4.1*).[1] The hands-on learning more effectively deepened students' understanding of the story and the culture than simply watching videos. The experience was an unforgettable memory that could turn them into long-term learners of Chinese culture.

Although four out of five students have served missionaries in Taiwan, many of them remarked on how this hands-on experience changed their stereotype of traditional Taiwanese puppetry. Since traditional Taiwanese puppet shows were a common temple activity for deity birthdays and festivals, one student acknowledged that even though he had noticed the puppetry performance in Taiwan, he ignored it because he thought it was a solely religious activity. However, after learning and performing the puppet show in the class, he realized that "it is a lot more than what I thought it was" (Response form 3.1). Practicing puppetry enabled him to review his previous experience in Taiwan in a more intercultural approach. He believed that the puppet show is great for college students to learn and perform because "it teaches an entirely new cultural subject that is not present in western society" (Response form 3.2). He then said that "I never really ever saw puppets on my mission, but this puppet show has really opened me up to the culture diversity that is in Taiwan" (Response form 3.2). Thus, he believes that if he can go back to Taiwan, he will "find an opportunity to watch an actual [professional] performance" (Response form 3.1). Another student learned to sincerely respect professional puppeteers, as his shoulders were painful when he performed. He mentioned that "without performing the puppet by ourselves, we may never know how hard it is" (Response form 2.2*)! Involving students in "hands-on" projects is an effective way to encourage active learning and cultural awareness.

### The Project Stimulated Creativity in Language and Culture Learning

Many students have expressed that this practical learning experience sparked their creativity and helped them gain greater insight into Chinese and Taiwanese culture. One student puppeteer shared that by needing to demonstrate his puppet's personality, he "truly want[ed] to fully understand the character in the play" (Response form 5.1*). Through closely analyzing the character, it helped him and other students to grasp both the conventional

---

[1] The* indicates that the original text is written in Chinese, and the English citation is the author's translation.

and innovative aspects of the culture as depicted through the play. The script translation created a space for students "to add some part of our culture to make it more relevant and understandable to those who may not have an understanding of Chinese culture" (Response form 5.2). Thus, it is not one-way learning, but an intercultural creation. The scheduled performance for local communities strongly motivated students to put on a good show, which required them to creatively interact with the language and culture. One student was grateful that the preparation gave them the opportunity to "participate in building some creative form." Through facilitating creativity, the project made the student feel that "it was really a performance rather than merely a task. Since we hope to attract more audiences to come to see our performance, we are willing to prepare more" (Response form 4.2*). Being aware of the performance considerably enthused students to improve their language skills and performing techniques, as they wanted to offer an interesting live show that would impress the audience.

**The Project Reinforced the Language Skills**

Through this experience, the students were able to develop their vocabulary and grammar as well as valuable language skills in writing, reading, speaking, and listening in a novel and engaging way. Students thoughtfully expressed how their Chinese language has improved from this puppet show project. As the feedback suggests, the act of translating the script from Chinese to English helped students better understand the content of the text and learn about what meaning can be lost in translation. One student said that the translation is like "how to get bigger muscles, because you have to work on it to get it better" (Response form 1.1). Students also believed that the translation helped them "master what the story...and learn new vocabulary words" (Response form 4.1*); it also forced them to "be creative when using the language" (Response form 5.2*). To translate the script, students needed to have a high level of understanding of the reading and writing in the target language and culture. They had to carefully consider if the cultural elements, word choices, and lyrics convey the same meaning as they were intended in the original. By reading and comparing different people's translations on a shared Google Doc, students could recognize similarities and differences between the other translations, which also increased their vocabulary knowledge in writing.

The recording of the lines and the performance encouraged students to vigilantly practice and improve their pronunciation. By performing this puppet show, the students had to actively listen to what their classmates were saying rather than just waiting to read their next line. Students shared that the recording was particularly helpful with speaking because their desire of involving the audience motivated them to "stress more emotion in speaking and make sure [that] the tones were correct" (Response form 3.1). They also had to "carefully listen to other people's lines" during the practice and performance, so they could "accurately respond to their words" (Response form 5.1*). During the whole rehearsal process, students were required to only use Chinese to communicate with each other. These requirements turned the rehearsal into live conversations, so everyone had to actively listen and respond to each other more carefully than they would if speaking in their native tongues. The communicative environment made the Chinese learning not merely "for an exam or test" (Response form 3.1). Therefore, the rehearsal and performance helped students improve their speaking and listening ability of Chinese.

## The Project Fostered the Supportive Group Work and Community Service

The competitive character of most educational systems emphasizes self-advancement. However, a competitive attitude can also impede learning and alienate students from one another, which is why instructors must build collaboration practices into their classrooms. Collaboration also benefits students from disadvantaged backgrounds as it inspires students to learn from their peers (Dennis, Phinney, and Chuateco 2005). This style guarantees an inclusive classroom that promotes diversity acceptance. To this end, I include many collaborative dimensions in the puppet show project. Many students felt that the project made them have a strong sense of connection— in their words, "we are really friends" (Response form 4.2*). One student even mentioned that this puppet show was "a lot more group involved than most projects I have been in for my previous Chinese courses" (Response form 3.1). The community outreach performance allowed students to apply study materials in real-life situations and empowered to contribute to the cultural diversity of their communities. For this specific project, the students introduced Taiwanese folklore to local preschool children through traditional Taiwanese puppetry. A student said that he has always wanted to share the Chinese culture that he has learned with children but felt that this seemed to be a difficult task. After the performance in the preschool, he realized that a puppet show was a simple way to introduce young learners to Chinese culture. Thus, in the future, he hopes to further introduce "other traditional Chinese stories like *Monkey King* and the history of Taiwan and China by playing puppets with children" (Response form 4.2*). The performance vividly expanded young children's understanding of different cultures in a memorable and enjoyable environment. Community-service learning allowed college students to apply their scholarly knowledge of the Chinese language and culture in a context outside of academia. Further, service-learning such as this also improves the diversity acceptance of local communities and raises cultural awareness.

## Suggestions for Modifications

While this curriculum design may not be commonly used in many universities, language teachers can be some of the first to deploy puppetry as a teaching tool in their university classrooms. The cultural concepts and principles can be incorporated by language teachers into their syllabi. This curriculum approach can advance the learner's understanding of the Chinese and Sinophone culture while at the same time increasing their proficiency in the language. Based on my classroom experience, I present several possibilities for teachers to integrate these techniques into further cultural language teaching.

### Creating a transcultural script

Students can create an entire new transcultural script based on their language ability, understanding of Chinese folklore, and creativity. Since students who have grown up in the US are usually encultured differently than people in Chinese-speaking cultural environments, they may read Chinese stories through an American cultural lens. Instead of translating a long Chinese script, students in elementary or intermediate levels may use the vocabulary and grammar that they have learned to create a relatively short transcultural script.

### Memorizing the script

If the script is short enough, students may be able to memorize each line or a small part of the dialogues. Even though the dialogues were pre-recorded for our performance, students said that they had to carefully memorize the transition of each line so that they could respond with the words timely. This technique can increase students' long-term memory of the Chinese that they learned through performing the narrative.

### Using more fairy tales and folklore

Because cultures often infuse core values and ideas into children's stories, selecting stories from the target culture are an efficient way for learners to understand important cultural values. If a language class can adapt fairy tales and folklore into the curriculum and study the lessons that they teach to

Chinese people, it can help students understand the culture and learn the language in a solid pedagogic way.

## Conclusion

Cultural context is inextricably linked to language learning, either when learning in language classrooms or in more natural settings. This puppet show project is a way for students to expand their language skills building a creative performance that motivates them in the learning process. This process of rehearsing and developing a puppet show allows students to grow the intercultural communicative competence and linguistic skills that they can use in practical ways to interact in the target language. Language teachers have the responsibility of fostering students' cultural knowledge, confidence in the language, and helping them to become global citizens. These goals can be effectively accomplished through engaging, collaborative cultural activities, such as Taiwanese puppetry. Once students see the larger of the culture and culture as a concept, they are keener to accept differences with an open mind and even struggle less with difficult vocabulary words and grammar rules. Integrating culture therefore allows instructors to incorporate cognitive, affective, and behavioral patterns of language curriculum design.

## Bibliography

Bain, Ken. 2004. *What the Best College Teachers Do.* Cambridge: Harvard University Press.

Chen, Long-Ting. 2007. *Taiwan budaixi fazhanshi* (The Development and History of Taiwanese Puppetry). Taipei: Qianwei.

Dennis, Jessica M., Jean S. Phinney, and Lizette Ivy Chuateco. 2005. "The Role of Motivation, Parental Support, and Peer Support in the Academic Success of Ethnic Minority First-Generation College Students." *Journal of College Student Development* 46 (3): 223–36.

Harding, D.P., W. Alexandra Marsh, and Donald Seager. 2011. *Glove Puppetry: How to Make Glove Puppets and Ideas for Plays-Three Volumes in One.* Redditch: Read Books.

Huang, Chih-chun, and Huang Chengzeng, Annette Specht, Gu¨nter Lontzen and Jacques Barchilon. 1993. "The Earliest Version of the Chinese 'Little Red Riding Hood': The Tale of the Tiger-Woman." *Merveilles & Contes* 7 (2): 513-527.

Hulse, Bethan, and Allan Owens. 2017. "Process drama as a tool for teaching modern languages: supporting the development of creativity and innovation in early professional practice." *Innovation in Language Learning and Teaching* (13): 1-14

Hurn, Brian, and Barry Tomalin. 2013. *Cross-Cultural Communication.* London: Palgrave McMillan.

Kroflin, Livija, ed. 2012. *The Power of the Puppet.* Zagreb: The UNIMA Puppets in Education, Development and Therapy Commission.

Kröger, Tarja and Anne-Maria Nupponen. 2019. "Puppet as a Pedagogical Tool: A Literature Review." *International Electronic Journal of Elementary Education*: 393-401.

Neff, Peter and John Rucynski Jr. 2013. "Tasks for Integrating Language and Culture Teaching." *English Teaching Forum*, 51 (2): 12-24.

Nguyen, Trang Thi Thuy. 2017. "Integrating Culture into Language Teaching and Learning: Learner Outcomes." *The Reading Matrix: An International Online Journal* 17 (1): 145-155.

Özüorçun, Fatma. 2014. "Teaching Culture as A Fifth Language Skill" *The Journal of International Social Research* 7 (29): 680-685.

Winston, Joe, ed. 2013. *Second Language Learning through Drama: Practical Techniques and Applications.* London: Routledge.

Chapter 5

# Documentary Filmmaking: A Digital and Innovative Language Teaching Method

Eda Başak Hancı-Azizoglu

*Mediterranean University*

Maha Alawdat

*Academic College of Education and Ort Abu Rabe'a*

*Multidisciplinary School*

I think documentaries are the greatest way to educate an entire generation that doesn't often look back to learn anything about the history that provided a safe haven for so many of us today.

**Steven Spielberg**

**Abstract**: The ever-changing societies and the influence of technology push people to the boundaries of feeling empathy towards other cultures. It is no longer possible to intentionally overlook the disasters that are being experienced across borders in far lands anymore because the borders on the world's map are just an illusion now in this information age. With the web of information technologies, it takes seconds for an unfortunate event in one remote place to affect another place and context despite cultural and geographical distances. In the first place, it seems clear that cultural values, beliefs and traditions are being altered by the young generation since they create their own shared culture through digital and innovative platforms. The culture they share through technology and media transforms and unites the youth under one roof of empathy when they watch the same movies and listen to the same songs with similar heartbeats. By this definition, this study proposes a cross-cultural language teaching method that is designed specifically for multilingual students: Documentary Filmmaking.

In a multilingual classroom or setting, documentary filmmaking can be an effective ice-breaker in that the participants not only could feel a sense of belonging but they would also develop both self-discovery and empathy for other communities and cultures. Since empathy deficit is absolutely one of the major flaws of the current educational systems', teaching the concept of empathy would transform the learning environment into a more peaceful and globally sensitive environment (Obama, n.d). Moreover, welcoming other cultures and showing tolerance to cultural differences require empathy. Empathy has a broader term beyond the classroom: "Empathy is a quality of wisdom. Empathy is what human beings require to become kinder to Earth and to every living being on Earth. Empathy is far beyond living for your selfish self. Empathy is the will to be part of a harmonious planet by accepting the fact that your endless freedom should be restricted once it interferes the freedom of another living being. Empathy equals to respect." (Kavaklı and Hancı-Azizoglu 2021, 67). With documentary filmmaking, students will be culturally sensitive, respecting and valuing other cultures, which is a demanded skill for today's peacemaker global citizens. In one sense, documentary filmmaking helps language learners to discover other cultures, and in another sense, they can gain metacognitive awareness on their own culture and language by being exposed to other cultures. Second language learners, in this sense, acquire new cultural and linguistic-based experiences, which affects learners positively or negatively based on the focus of the learners and what they watch. In educational settings, however, documentary films are under the control of the teachers who expose their students to structured meaningful linguistic contents.

In this regard, learners have the opportunity to develop meaningful and in-context culturally oriented films. In addition, documentary filmmaking can reduce the affective filter in a language classroom, and students would feel appreciated when their cultural values are celebrated rather than perceived as interference (Canagarajah 2018). For this purpose, this proposed chapter theorizes several perspectives as a response to create a digital language pedagogy including (a) focusing on a rationale to implement higher-order skill development for digital natives in language classrooms; (b) liberating language learners by creating both a culturally responsive and innovative language teaching pedagogy through documentary filmmaking; (c) implementing documentary filmmaking as culturally responsive short film making approach to teach an additional language effectively.

**Keywords:** Documentary filmmaking, communicative language learning, communicative language teaching, multilingual classroom, technology integration.

***

## The Context of DOCUMENTARY FILMMAKING in a Language Classroom

"Documentaries have the power to immerse us through images and stories in the reality experienced by others. They bring together complex representations of social issues with the personal experiences of protagonists, expressing the diversity of our shared humanity and expanding our empathy" (Briciu 2020, 1). Documentaries reflect the actual world through real series of events that are formerly experienced. Documentaries record the feelings of real people by preserving the authenticity of the original without altering the irresistible world of fiction that is often shaped by endless options of human imagination.

Through documentaries, human imagination is activated by feelings of affection, compassion, sympathy and empathy. Documentaries often motivate people to be put in someone else's shoes with a virtual but realistic experience. In one sense, documentaries provide virtual insights and experiences for people to avoid similar mistakes in their course of life, and they indeed function as essential life lessons. In another sense, documentaries show people the essence of what it means to be a human who can feel other people's worries, pain and happiness without having the need to experience the same series of events. This combination changes the way people behave in certain circumstances and has the power to alter a community's perception of the concept of civilization.

Documentaries affect humans' feelings, attitudes and even behavioral patterns of empathy considerably (Eğeci and Gençöz 2017; Khusumadewi and Juliantika 2018; Powell et al. 2006; Rimonda et al. 2018). It is quite fascinating how movies, which are the product of human imagination, have remarkable power over human attitudes and behaviors when considering the fact that movies are often the product of random human imagination within a plot and series of events. In parallel with this thinking system, it is highly likely for documentaries to alter, modify or shape human emotions and behavior when the same plot and series of events belong to real people and real life without any filter. Therefore, documentaries that focus on culturally derived tolerance for diverse cultural attitudes and differences promote peace and cultural sensitivity in a learning setting.

The cultural documentaries that are proposed within the context of this chapter objectify strategies to promote cross-cultural perspectives along with multiple effective objectives. The theme of these documentaries is designing mini-cultural documentary filmmaking that will report and reflect on cultures to represent different cultures with respect and care. The audience and the participants of the project proposed in this chapter can be given brief training on how they should follow the code of ethics at all times during the preparation and application of this project. The designing part of the documentary filmmaking project consists of phases of designing stages where the participants take the variables of the cultural theme, audience and objectives into consideration. The first and foremost prerequisite of documentary filmmaking is to research facts whether it is for a short documentary for a classroom project or a larger project for professional documentary filmmaking. Within this part, the students should be taught how to conduct research depending on their maturity level, and they should be aware of ethical and proper citation to acquire habits that prevent intellectual theft. The other most critical part is the script writing. There is a crucial relationship between documentary filmmaking and writing skills. Principally, second language learners tend to report what they understood from the film, how they relate to the content by eventually connecting it to their culture when they are asked to reflect on a documentary film in their language classrooms.

Research shows that this critical relationship helps to improve learners' writing skills (Nunun 2010; Haris 2013; Anggraini et al. 2014; Abdul Rahman 2017). Planning, outlining and crafting a storyline is the next significant step for focusing on a wholesome and detailed theme. One crucial element that stands out a particular documentary is to avoid superficial approaches that lack a unified theme or a course of plan. A story outline gives the documentary a hierarchical flow of logically sequenced events that could make the short documentary filmmaking project a more appealing and interesting one in ideal circumstances. The unsettling fact that is worth noting that in a classroom with limited resources out of financial burdens, making a documentary filmmaking can be an unrealistic choice.

In a study conducted by Hasan Haris (2013), it is stated that:

> Most students agreed that the use of video in learning process is an interesting medium which can help the students to get their attention. Moreover, the students also could release their boredom toward English lesson because of the limited technique or media used by the teacher. Only few students thought that video was not interesting. Some of the students said that video can be used not only for writing but also for other skills (6).

From this perspective, using documentaries as a medium of the language learning process surround students with an innovative intellectual setting, where language learning involves more convenient resources that help students acquire language along with cultural values. The interactive devices of media in terms of pictures, videos and music not only can aid language learners to grasp the target language faster, but it also removes negative feelings of boredom and disorientation of rote learning styles (Haris 2013). In this vein, image file types and resolutions for video quality should be provided so that no student will be out of reach from the required digital resources to be able to present their project with the latest technology. Color and motion effects can be taught through recent and updated programs that are user-friendly.

Finally, professional documentary filmmakers' advice the fact that less is more. It is advisable to students to focus on a few more themes of their choice of significance rather than trying to cover all cultural elements that are specific to a particular culture. Upon completion of these documentaries that would reflect each student's cultural heritage and assets, students are expected to learn how to plan, process and take roles in a documentary filmmaking project. If some students share the same culture, they can do a group project by managing the tasks that are specifically related to their roles. In case the number of students is inconsistently distributed, some students can represent other cultures to create a balance for the cultures to be represented through the documentary filmmaking (Shinnick 2019; "The University of British Colombia" 2021). Finally, students should be encouraged to avoid discourse that can sound rude or racist. For this purpose, it is highly advised for language teachers to check the initial draft to detect inconvenient and culturally hostile styles to overcome linguistic and cultural inequalities.

## The Contextualization of Culture in Documentary Filmmaking

Language is power, and power is often in hands of the privileged. The access to resources of health, wealth and education provides what is known to be a privilege (Simpson 2019). Language variations, and how one dialect or a variant belongs to an upper or lower class is not a coincidence but all because of power (Cameron et al. 2018). The reality is quite more complicated than that though. Basically, the language of the powerful creates a linguistic illusion and then a perception that the language variation of the people of health and wealth becomes the standard over time through codification (Holmes and Wilson 2017).

Within the same parallel, the language of the weak is often disrespected and disregarded regardless of the fact that all languages are equally and linguistically competent and wholesome. Over time, the perception of one variant's classy status gets highly accepted that the language of education is indeed codified by the people of health and wealth as the classy and desirable accent of that certain language variation. That's how you are watching a sharp-looking news reporter who specifically talks the variant that is considered highly sophisticated.

But there is a hidden sociolinguistic reality in the process of how one language variant is perceived as superior as opposed to other variants. All could have been just the opposite if the power exchange changed the course of this perception within an insignificant historical game-changing event. In that case, that sharp-looking news reporter would talk exactly sound like a cowboy in some remote village, and all would perceive that language variant as the desirable and high-status one. In an ideal world, the purpose of intellectuals and decision-makers must be spreading peace regardless of language and cultural differences through equal distribution of education. Even though there are rare cases of success stories for reaching out to ultimate success without the privilege of accessing equal education, it often remains as a fact that people's success rates are shaped by the privileges they are born into. Therefore, it is the power relations that certainly determine which particular language variant will be high-status as opposed to others, and that's how perceptions on cultures in terms of high class versus low class shape. Unfortunately, societies often give unwritten cultural messages as to no languages and cultures are indeed equal and people of health and wealth rule the game of superiority and dominance despite the lawful institutions that claim to protect the rights of all the children regardless of their sociocultural and economic status (Waldron 2017).

The interesting reality reflects that classrooms have more culturally diverse students than before through global interactions among cultures (Forghani-Arani et al. 2019), and the invisible borders that divide countries seem less visible through the impact of new technologies (Western 2019).

An overwhelmingly increasing number of multicultural students are now enrolling at schools today that represent a wide spectrum of cultural diversity. In an ideal world, these students are expected to be educated in harmony and peace with the same educational standards. Despite curriculums and planning that target equality and standard education for all, the reality of educational barriers reflects another side of the story. Multicultural students often fall behind in standard curriculums due to English language deficit, and mainstream teachers experience hardship in educating multicultural students since they wrongfully assume that it is not their job to educate these children because they are not language teachers (Hancı-Azizoglu 2021; Gallagher and Haan 2018; Lee and Oxelson 2006).

Unfortunately, it is the multicultural students who suffer the most in such circumstances. This is because the power relations among the privileged prevent substantial consequences when these students do not have equal access to one of the fundamental rights for children: education ("Say No to Discrimination in Education" 2020).

The mainstream educational settings that are designed for Anglo-Saxon cultures propose a monolingual English-only policy as the medium of education, often unwelcome to hear other languages in educational settings. This strictly monolingual attitude often results in teachers often making a remark in public schools such as: "English Only!" so that these multicultural students could quickly immerse in the target culture as a result of assimilation (Sigsbee 2002). A high number of multilingual students experience heartbreak since their cultural heritage is often overlooked and ignored by similar educational approaches and policies (Kaveh 2020; Wiley and Garcia 2016; Flores 2014; Pennycook 2002).

Within this context, schools are the sole remedy to welcome and unite all cultures of languages under one safe roof to create welcoming, equal and nurturing surroundings for students.

> What the best and wisest parent wants for his own child, that must the community want for all of its children. Any other ideal for our schools is narrow and unlovely; acted upon it destroys our democracy. -John Dewey

For this purpose, this study proposes a cross-cultural linguistic, digital and innovative method that would create a serenity between diverse cultures of multilingual students. In a multicultural classroom, where some of the students belong to minority languages and cultures within the group, it is essential to activate the affective filter of the students to promote a nurturing and culturally sensitive learning environment (Man et al. 2021; Chen 2020; Wang 2020; Lin and Lin 2020). Documentary filmmaking as a language teaching method may offer endless digital opportunities for students to document their cultural richness and values from their elevating and vivid perspectives.

All cultures, regardless of their strengths and weaknesses, are valuable. Valuing only a few cultures among many is overlooking the knowledge and teachings of other cultures, which describes and defines the world with a limited worldview. Ignoring other cultures and languages that are different than one's own is indeed not only missing their literature and wisdom but is also missing the possibilities of a wide spectrum of cultural access to endless possibilities of experience and knowledge.

## Documentary Filmmaking: A Digital and Innovative Language Teaching Method

The U.S. Department of Education declare actual and research-based statistics that American Schools involve 800 different languages, but neither schools' and colleges' infrastructures nor teacher training programs prepare institutions to welcome this broad cultural diversity (Hancı-Azizoglu 2021; Takanishi and Le Menestrel 2017). Not a single day passes that a language teacher is in demand of a better and more interactively designed language method that is both appealing and functional (Scala 2021; Kirsch and Duarte 2020).

This chapter theorizes a digital and innovative documentary filmmaking pedagogy as a language teaching method that multilingual and multicultural students would find the opportunity to feel liberated through sharing their cultural values. With the help of interactive short documentary filmmaking methods, language teachers could benefit from domain and grade level specific lesson plans and rubrics that can particularly target an additional language teaching subject of preference. Documentary filmmaking on multicultural students' unique cultural qualities can function as an ice-breaker in a large learning setting, where participants need to develop cultural sensitivity for each other's diverse heritage. Through an effective culturally derived documentary filmmaking language technique, students will be able to acquire the following life lessons that last a lifetime in their personal and professional careers.

**Figure 5.1.** Culture Sensitive Documentary Filmmaking

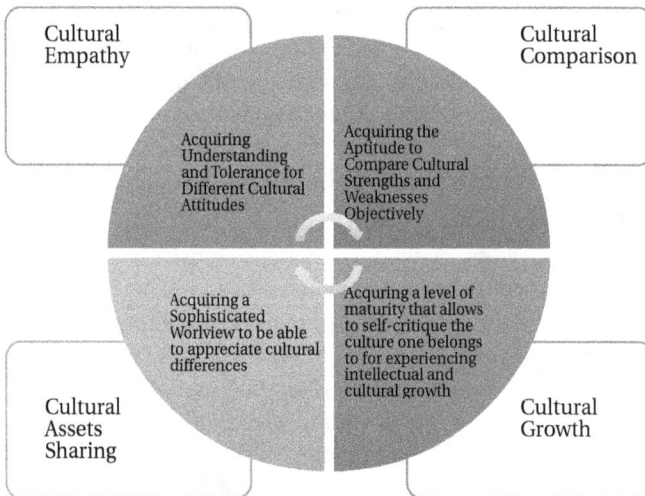

Cultural Empathy

Acquiring Understanding and Tolerance for Different Cultural Attitudes

Cultural Comparison

Acquiring the Aptitude to Compare Cultural Strengths and Weaknesses Objectively

Acquiring a Sophisticated Worlview to be able to appreciate cultural differences

Acquring a level of maturity that allows to self-critique the culture one belongs to for experiencing intellectual and cultural growth

Cultural Assets Sharing

Cultural Growth

***Cultural Empathy:*** After being exposed to new cultures through documentary filmmaking in a classroom environment, students will have the chance to develop an awareness and tolerance for cultural attitudes and approaches that they might have been previously unfamiliar with. It is clearly beneficial that students are exposed to other cultures through watching documentary films in addition to be motivated and encouraged to understand the cultural contents of the films. Abdul Rahman et al. (2017) claimed that "The most intense emotional change was when learners realized that they not only understand the document's main content, but could also produce their own meanings due to the convergence of their learning experience" (104). Documentary filmmaking and film watching produce open-minded learners who build an understanding of others, their cultures, and their lifestyle. They also lead to a new trend of language learners who could use the language of the Other and might also adapt beneficial culturally rich life norms and standards. By being in touch with intellectual understandings of cultural empathy and experiences, learners can further improve their learning experiences by gaining emotional maturity.

***Cultural Comparison:*** After being exposed to documentary filmmaking in a classroom environment, students will have the chance to be aware of the unwritten rules that indeed make up the distinctive features of diverse cultures. To illustrate, documentary filmmakers often wish and anticipate that the migrant and refugees have better life conditions without traumatic events in their new lands after they record their sufferings. They hope that people relate to and feel the pain of the migrants and refugees when they are desperate for new land for survival or decent living standards, which should be the right of every human being on Earth. From the filmmakers' perspective, the audience is expected to become aware of how humanity can be in need of seeking help from others to continue to make a living again with great tolerance and patience. Documentaries that tell the vivid stories of immigrants and refugees clearly represent the necessity of acquiring social and cultural consciousness to make a difference in people's future when their life is in turmoil (Briciu 2020).

Within the same line of thinking, this study offers a learning setting through documentaries for students to internalize the fact that people are born within a system of culturally derived rules that transfer from one generation to the next through an invisible memory transfer among generations (Ramstead et al. 2016; Hancı-Azizoglu and Kavaklı 2021). With this language technique, students will have the chance to compare cultures, and this analytical approach and thinking can create a sophisticated worldview of apprehending the fact that each culture has its strengths and weaknesses depending on the time, context and variables triangle. Acquiring such consciousness is quite an essential skill in a multilingual learning environment that will not only promote effective learning but also critical thinking skills for real-life applications to live in a better world.

*Cultural Assets Sharing:* After being exposed to documentary filmmaking in a classroom environment, students will have the chance to recognize the significance of how sharing cross-cultural assets is essential for the world's well-being. Not attempting to understand other cultures through isolation is no longer a realistic or logical goal or policy at the political level. Within a world that gets closer through a shared media culture, people perceive the recent changes and updates around the world with similar technological channels and devices.

In this way, the world alters and gets much narrower than people anticipate with digital communication styles through the same news platforms.

Nowadays, the necessity to learn about other cultures is apparent, and ignoring another culture prevents surviving and succeeding in both physical and digital environments that are constantly subject to change with rapidly growing technologies. The most vivid example of this fact in our desperate present time is that all humanity is still fighting a pandemic no matter which culture they belong to:

> "People everywhere," it states, "want to get back to their lives as soon as possible—to see family and friends, celebrate, learn and work alongside one another." But if different countries move at different speeds then there is no guarantee that life will ever be the same. (Damadoran 2021)

No matter who you are, and whichever high-scale society you consider yourself to belong to, it is not possible to recover from the pandemic or the restrictions soon without unification and integration through the same line of planning and rationale despite different culturally derived thinking systems. This living example alone symbolizes the essence of adapting multiculturally originated interactive language teaching techniques that focus on respecting cultural differences.

Obviously, multicultural students need opportunities to express their cultural assets through creative language teaching approaches to acquire a more sophisticated worldview to be able to appreciate cultural differences with wisdom. One way to achieve this goal is cross-cultural documentary filmmaking, which is a digital and innovative language teaching method.

*Cultural Growth:* Human history consists of a wide variety of crises, turmoil and conflicts that occur due to cultural misunderstandings. What is more unfortunate is that distant representatives of opposing thinking styles often insist that each one of them is the absolute symbol of morality and righteousness. What is often overlooked is the way that they perceive the very same situation quite differently due to their perceptions that are shaped by unwritten cultural and social rules (Hofstede n.d.). One of the very unfortunate examples of such a misperception due to cultural barriers is undoubtedly experienced when a single Japanese word "mokusatsu," is misunderstood and mistranslated in the course of history and results in the other party dropping the world's first atomic bomb killing tens of thousands of innocent people. During World War II in 1945, Japanese president Suzuki is believed to reject an ultimatum for peace offered by the United States; however, the word he used "mokusatsu" reflects the Japanese culture regarding a concept of remaining in wise and masterly inactivity.

The other linguistic meanings for this single word are to treat with silent contempt, take no notice of or ignore by keeping silent (National Security Agency Central Security Service n.d.).

This tragedy shows how just one word of a language cannot be translated in a sense-for-sense translation (Munday 2016), and this miscommunication between cultures has been the sole cause for people, including innocent children, to lose their lives over cultural misconceptions. It does not really matter which party is indeed right after children tragically died just because two diverse cultures could not find a way to overcome their cross-cultural differences to communicate effectively. But the lesson of this horrific incident and many others are vivid examples to prove that people need to experience cultural growth.

Within the context of this study, cultural growth is acquiring a level of maturity that allows to self-critique the culture one belongs to for experiencing intellectual growth. The purpose of this digital and innovative teaching method offers a vivid technique for multilingual and multicultural students to learn about other cultures. After being exposed to documentary filmmaking in a classroom environment, students will have the chance to evaluate their own cultures with a new set of eyes of an outsider.

What's more crucial is that students will be surrounded by a unique opportunity to gain self-consciousness for their own cultures after internalizing other cultures from a variety of perspectives with real data and documentation. With the above-mentioned consciousness, students can develop an aptitude to compare familiar cultures with unfamiliar ones to recognize the fact that all cultures indeed have strengths and weaknesses, and there is not a culture-perfect country in the world.

# Bibliography

Abdul Rahman, Tg Ainul Farha Tg, Chik Abdul Rahman Muhammad Sabri Sahrir and Mohd Shukri Nordin. 2017. "A Review of Documentary Film as Authentic Input in Enhancing Writing Skills in ASL Setting." *Journal of Nusantara Studies* 2 (1): 99-110.

Anggraini, Yessi, and A. Yasin and Radjab Desmawati. 2014. "Improving students's writing skill of narrative text through video at Grade XII IPA 2 of SMAN 2 Bukittinggi." *Journal English Language Teaching* 2 (2): 78-92.

Briciu, Bianca. 2020. "Anyone Can Become a Refugee: Strategies for Empathic Concern in Activist Documentaries on Migration." *Emotion, Space and Society*, (37): 100737: 1-19.

Cameron, Deborah, Elizabeth Frazer, Penelope Harvey, M.B.H. Rampton and Kay Richardson. 2018. *Researching Language: Issues of Power and Method.* New York: Routledge.

Canagarajah, Suresh. 2018. "Transnationalism and translingualism: How they are connected." In Transnational Writing Education: Theory, History, and Practice, edited by Xiaoye You, 41–60. New York, NY: Routledge.

Chen, Cuicui. 2020. "The Application of Affective Filter Hypothesis Theory in English Grammar Teaching." *Journal of Contemporary Educational Research* 4 (6): 71-74.

Damadoran, Ramu. 2021. "Why We Care." March 12. United Nations. https://www.un.org/pt/academic-impact/why-we-care-12-march-2021

Eğeci, İ. Sine, and Faruk Gençöz. 2017. "Use of Cinematherapy in Dealing with Relationship Problems." *The Arts in Psychotherapy* (53): 64-71.

Flores, Nelson. 2014. "Creating Republican Machines: Language Governmentality in the United States." *Linguistics and Education* (25): 1-11.

Forghani-Arani, Neda, Lucie Cerna and Meredith Bannon. 2019. "The Lives of Teachers in Diverse Classrooms." *OECD Education Working Papers* (198): 1-49.

Gallagher, Colleen E., and Jennifer E. Haan. 2018. "University Faculty Beliefs about Emergent Multilinguals and Linguistically Responsive Instruction." *TESOL Quarterly* 52 (2): 304-330.

Geert Hofstede. Last modified 2022, https://geerthofstede.com/culture-geert-hofstede-gert-jan-hofstede/6d-model-of-national-culture/

Hancı-Azizoglu, Eda Başak. 2021. "Culturally and Linguistically Diverse Students: (Re) imagining Multilingual Education." In *Interdisciplinary Approaches Toward Enhancing Teacher Education*, edited by M. Dolores Ramirez-Verdugo and Bahar Otcu-Grillman, 202-220. New Jersey: IGI Global.

Hancı-Azizoglu, Eda Başak, and Nurdan Kavaklı. 2021. "Creative Digital Writing: A Multilingual Perspective." In *Digital Pedagogies and the Transformation of Language Education*, edited by Matthew Montebello, 250-266. New Jersey: IGI Global.

Haris, Hasan. 2013. "The Use of Documentary Video to Teach Writing News Item Text to the Tenth Grade Students in SMAN 4 Bangkalan." *Journal RETAIN Universitas Negeri Surabaya* 1 (3):1-9.

Holmes, Janet and Nick Wilson. 2017. *An Introduction to Sociolinguistics*. New York: Routledge.

Kavaklı, Nurdan, and Eda Başak Hancı-Azizoglu. 2021. "Digital storytelling: A futuristic second language writing method." In *Futuristic and linguistic perspective on teaching writing to second language students*, edited by Nurdan Kavaklı and Eda Başak Hancı-Azizoglu, 66-83. Hershey, PA: IGI Global.

Kaveh, Yalda. M. 2020. "Unspoken Dialogues between Educational and Family Language Policies: Language Policy Beyond Legislations." *Linguistics and Education* 60: 100876.

Khusumadewi, Ari and Yeni Tri Juliantika. 2018. "The Effectiveness of Cinema Therapy to Improve Student Empathy" Conference, Indonesia, July 28. ICEI, Atlantis Press.

Kirsch, Claudine and Joana Duarte, eds. 2020. *Multilingual Approaches for Teaching and Learning: From Acknowledging to Capitalising on Multilingualism in European Mainstream Education*. New York: Routledge.

Lee, Jin Sook, and Eva Oxelson. 2006. "It's Not My Job": K–12 Teacher Attitudes toward Students' Heritage Language Maintenance." *Bilingual Research Journal* 30 (2): 453-477.

Lin, Yulan, and Yuewu Lin. 2020. "The Enlightenment of Affective Filter Hypothesis and Risk-Taking on English Learning." *Studies in Literature and Language* 20 (2): 51-57.

Man, Chang Fui, Sabariah Sharif, Andrea Lee Jen May, Rosy Talin and Soon Singh Bikar Singh. 2021. "The Effects of Drama-Based Activities as a Language Learning Tool on Learners' Motivation in Non-Malay-Medium National Schools in Malaysia." *Indonesian Journal of Applied Linguistics* 10 (3): 603-614.

Munday, Jeremy. 2016. *Introducing Translation Studies: Theories and Applications*. New York: Routledge.

National Security Agency Central Security Service. Last modified 2022. https://www.nsa.gov/Portals/70/documents/news-features/declassified-documents/tech-journals/mokusatsu.pdf

Nunun, Indrasari. 2010. "Improving students' writing skill of narrative texts by using short videos." Master's thesis, Sebelas Maret University.

Obama, Barack, "Goodreads." January 29, 2022. https://www.goodreads.com/quotes/9609019-the- biggest-deficit-that-we-have-in-our-society-and

Pennycook, Alastair. 2002. "Mother Tongues, Governmentality, and Protectionism." *International Journal of the Sociology of Language* 154: 11-28.

Powell, Micheal Lee, and Rebecca A. Newgent and Sang Min Lee. 2006. "Group Cinematherapy: Using Metaphor to Enhance Adolescent Self-esteem." *The Arts in Psychotherapy* 33 (3): 247-253.

Ramstead, Maxwell J. D., Samuel P. L. Veissière and Laurence J. Kirmayer. 2016. "Cultural Affordances: Scaffolding Local Worlds through Shared Intentionality and Regimes of Attention." *Frontiers in Psychology* (7): 1090.

Rimonda, Rubi, and Mungin Eddy Wibowo and Muhammad Jafar. 2018. "The Effectiveness of Group Counseling by Using Cognitive Behavioral Therapy Approach with Cinematherapy and Self-talk Techniques to Reduce Social Anxiety at SMK N 2 Semarang." *Jurnal Bimbingan Konseling,* 7 (2): 145-152.

Scala, Carmela. 2021. "How to Foster Equality in the Language Classroom." In *Rhetoric and Sociolinguistics in Times of Crisis,* edited by Eda Başak Hancı-Azizoglu and Maha Alawdat, 115-130. New Jersey: IGI Global.

Shinnick, Tanner. 2019. "The Beat: 5 Tips on How to Create a Great Short Documentary Film." July 18. The Beat. https://www.premiumbeat.com/blog/5-tips-for-great-short-documentary/

Sigsbee, David L. 2002. "Why Americans Don't Study Foreign Languages and What We Can Do About That." *New Directions for Higher Education* (117): 45-52.

Simpson, Paul, Andrea Mayr and Simon Statham. 2019. *Language and Power. A Resource Book for Students.* New York: Routledge.

Takanishi, Ruby, and Suzanne Le Menestrel. 2017. "National Academies of Sciences, Engineering, and Medicine: Promoting the Educational Success of Children and Youth Learning English: Promising Futures." *National Academies Press.* https://eric.ed.gov/?id=ED582056

"The University of British Colombia." 2021. Project 7: Mini Documentaries. Accessed January 30. https://people.ok.ubc.ca/creative/AdobeTeachingResources/DigitalVideo/dvcg_cs4_project7.pdf

UNESCO. "Say No to Discrimination in Education". Accessed November 26, 2020. https://en.unesco.org/news/what-you-need-know-about-right-education

Waldron, Jeremy. 2017. *One Another's Equals: The Basis of Human Equality.* London: The Belknap Press of Harvard University Press.

Wang, Ling. 2020. "Application of Affective Filter Hypothesis in Junior English Vocabulary Teaching." *Journal of Language Teaching and Research* 11 (6): 983-987.

Western, Simon. 2019. "The Making and Unmaking of Borders." Room, February 2. https://www.academia.edu/37704823/The_Making_and_Unmaking_of_Borders

Wiley, Terrence G., and Ofelia Garcia. 2016. "Language Policy and Planning in Language Education: Legacies, Consequences, and Possibilities." *The Modern Language Journal 100*: 48-63.

Chapter 6

# Animated Cartoons to Promote 'Real Language' Learning: Attitudes of Undergraduate Students of Italian

Stefano Maranzana

*Southern Methodist University in Dallas*

**Abstract:** This study explores the use of the cartoon series *Peppa Pig* as a resource to enhance listening comprehension skills, vocabulary and grammar acquisition while engaging college learners of Italian. It enquires on how undergraduate third-semester students perceive the effectiveness of the use of Italian (dubbed) children's cartoons in their second language (L2) course. Qualitative data collected throughout a 16-week semester suggest that including this kind of media may help familiarize learners with authentic L2 speech. The cartoon offered learners an opportunity to experience the dynamics of daily-life conversation and acquire new vocabulary and idiomatic expressions within a highly contextual environment. Students acknowledged that behind a children's cartoon lay rich and authentic everyday L2 speech that is rarely represented in traditional textbooks. Though featuring authentic speech, students found the cartoon appropriate to their proficiency level, particularly with captions. Indeed, students could follow along with each episode thanks to the straightforwardness of the plots, the short episode length, the rather slow speech rate and the strong connection between language and images. Finally, most students welcomed the activity as entertaining and valuable. Humor was reported to have made the learning process less stressful and engaging while providing them with a respite from traditional textbook-oriented tasks.

**Keywords**: animated cartoons to promote 'real language' learning, Italian language, humor in the language classroom, language in context through animated cartoons.

***

## Introduction

Listening comprehension, i.e., the individual's ability to decode and interpreting spoken language in real-time, is a difficult skill to acquire owing to its high cognitive demand, especially for novice language learners (Bae and Bachman 1998; Vandergrift and Goh 2012; Vandergrift and Baker 2015). Compared to writing, reading and speaking, listening comprehension is generally seldom a focus in second language (L2) classrooms and learners' ability to understand spoken language in real-life settings is often underdeveloped (Becker and Sturm 2017, 147; Verspoor and Hong 2013, 3). Consequently, conversations occurring in the traditional L2 classroom between the instructor and the students or among students often tend to stagnate around a typical classroom discourse encompassing academic/formal registers. This restricts students' exposure to the variety of vernacular registers, which are typically available only outside of the classroom (i.e., through exposure to media and in study abroad contexts) (Bahrani 2014; Lafford 2006). Vernacular social registers or languages are socially-situated language styles with distinctive collocations or patterns of lexical and grammatical resources in relation to specific identities and activities. They are utilized by individuals in various forms in "everyday" communication and their acquisition are part and parcel of one's language development, be it of one's first language (L1) or L2 (Gee 2015, 37). Because of their lack of experience with authentic and diverse speech, students, even when exhibiting a high level of competence in the classroom, often realize that their competency is limited or inappropriate when engaging in out-of-class situations (Wilkinson 2002; Sánchez-Hernández and Alcón-Soler 2019; Isabelli-García and Isabelli 2020).

However, the use of technology in the classroom can widen the spectrum of registers allowing the learner greater exposure to authentic and diversified speech. This study focuses its inquiry on children's animated cartoons as a resource to create a constructive environment for second language acquisition (SLA). Specifically, I will discuss the use of the British educational cartoon series *Peppa Pig* (Davies 2004; henceforth only *Peppa Pig*) in its Italian-dubbed version to be used as authentic video material, with and without same-language captioning for "real language" learning."

The traditional language course is conventionally built around a textbook that guides the curriculum. Such textbooks act as "building blocks," introducing the L2 to the students, generally, topic by topic, with the supporting or guiding grammar structures and vocabulary lists recapitulated in end-of-chapter "boxes" (Payne 2011). This systematic and structured presentation of language has its undeniable benefits, as it serves as a functional reference and as a support for the learner (Foncesa 2016), yet, language in textbooks is often presented in a decontextualized fashion, where vocabulary is submitted through a list of terms pertaining to a given topic or issue (i.e., the school, the house, the stores, etc.). Furthermore, grammatical structures are detailed as discrete points of information that are subsequently exemplified with phrases aimed at illustrating how the structure is should be - employed. Little context is thus provided for making sense of how "real language" works.

Students' own lay beliefs about SLA are often left aside, or even dismissed as mere "misconceptions" (Barcelos 2003, 11). However, understanding students' beliefs about their L2 education is vital as they have strong consequences on the outcomes of their overall L2 development (Barcelos and Kalaja 2011; Mercer 2011; Dörnyei 2014). To investigate undergraduate learners' attitudes towards the use of this cartoon for L2 acquisition, I conducted the present study in one section of a third-semester Italian language course in a large American university of the South West. Qualitative data was collected throughout one 16-week semester.

## Background
## Rationale for the Study

SLA researchers have been urging educators to recognize the emerging needs of the younger generations of learners, illustrate encouraging programs, theorize promising practices, and identify the usefulness of current technology for second language (L2) instruction, be it generally (Heift and Vyatkina 2017) or in more specific domains, e.g., telecollaboration (Antoniadou 2011; Grazzi and Maranzana 2016), mobile-assisted language learning (Loewen et al. 2019), social media (Shafie and Singh 2016; Alam 2019), video conferencing (Lenkaitis 2019) and virtual reality (Berti, Maranzana and Monzingo 2020). To identify ways of introducing authentic L2 Italian speech that would familiarize students to vernacular social registers, I conducted this research, reasoning that educational children's video cartoons would allow for a streamlined, yet authentic, "real language" exposure. The logic for choosing children's animated cartoons is comparable to that of Ecke's (2019): the intention to have L2 learners engage with authentic material, produced for native speakers of Italian, that is not linguistically complex, familiar, not too complex, and rich with reiterations of structures, vocabulary, and images (7-8).

## Significance of the Study and Research Question

The findings in this study will contribute to the practice of language teachers who are concerned with their students' struggle to comprehend authentic, everyday L2 speech, and are seeking effective and engaging approaches to engage with "real language." Language teachers need to be aware of all potential forms of audiovisuals that are available, recognize their benefits as well as their limits, and know how to include them in the academic curriculum (Oddone 2011; Robin 2011).

SLA researchers seem to agree that compared to traditional textbook-bound L2 instruction, the use of video for pedagogical purposes provides significant enhancements in terms of context, discourse, paralinguistic features, cultural aspects and students' motivation (Bahrani 2014; Oddone 2011; Swaffar and Vlatten 1997; Verspoor and Hong 2013; White, Easton and Anderson 2000). In spite of the growing body of research on the use of video, with and without captioning, for SLA (Chai and Erlam 2008; Danan 2004; Montero Perez et al. 2014; Vanderplank 2010; Winke, Gass, and Sydorenko 2010), with the exception of Saeedi and Biri (2016), who investigated the attitudes of Turkish and Persian students toward using animated cartoons in an English as a Foreign Language (EFL) grammar class, there have been no published investigations of undergraduates' perceptions and attitudes towards using children's cartoons in the language classroom. The current study aims to help fill this gap by investigating the attitudes of university-level students toward the use of children's cartoons.

## Literature Review
### Animated Cartoons in L2 Instruction: Peppa Pig

There is a relatively small body of literature that is concerned with the use of animated cartoons for the development of adult learners' L2 acquisition (Bahrani 2014; Bahrani, Tam and Zuraidah 2014; Bahrani and Sim 2012; Bahrani and Soltani 2011; Clark 2000; Saeedi and Biri 2016; Vulchanova et al. 2015; Maranzana 2022). According to Bahrani (2014, 555), the advantages of using cartoons in an L2 pedagogical setting are the following: (1) cartoons often capture the viewer-learner's attention, (2) they display a strong picture-to-word correlation, (3) dialogues are simple and complete, (4) with numerous repetitions, and (5) the rate of speech might be relatively low, depending on the cartoon. Cartoons, especially those that are created for young children, often involve more distinctly articulated speech in standard L2 accents (Vulchanova et al. 2015).

Inquiring into the effectiveness of exposure to three different types of authentic audiovisuals (news, cartoons, and films), Bahrani and Sim (2012) implemented a 10-week study involving 60 low-level learners of English. Participants were divided in 3 groups: the first was exposed to news, the second to cartoons and the third to film. The results of the post-test indicate that the first group (news) did not improve language proficiency overall, while the other two groups (cartoons and film) gained significant competence, especially the group that watched cartoons. Low gains were found in the group who watched newscasts arguably because of the degree of specialized terminology present in this type of media.

Saeedi & Biri (2016), aimed at assessing the benefits of twelve episodes of the cartoon *The Looney Tunes Show*. Episodes were shown to EFL Turkish and Persian students for six sessions. The authors compared the performances of two groups of learners exposed to two different teaching approaches for the conditional form: explicit instruction without video (control), instruction through the use of the cartoon (experimental). When a conditional sentence was used by a cartoon character, the teacher paused and replayed the clip, drawing the participants' attention to form. While revealing positive attitudes towards the use of cartoons to learn the language, participants of the experimental group exhibited greater proficiency on the conditional in the post test than the control group.

Vulchanova et al. (2015) looked at the effects of captions and subtitles using video cartoons on English comprehension and acquisition in a group of 114 Norwegian High School students. The authors selected the American animated cartoon series *Family Guy* because they deemed it was more likely understood by participants, both in terms of language and plot.

## The Role of Humor to Stimulate L2 Learning

Gardner and colleagues have played a significant role in drawing attention to socio-affective factors and the importance of positive attitudes in language learning (Gardner and Lambert 1972; Gardner 2010). As Deneire (1995) argues, the L2 language classroom presents high levels of tension/anxiety for the learner. Not only do students strive to communicate in a new and unfamiliar tongue, but they also have to do so in front of peers. This triggers a distinctively tense/anxious learning atmosphere because the student is divested of his or her L1 language expertise, and consequently also of part of his or her personal and cultural identity (Deneire 1995; Askildson 2005). Language teachers are conscious of the importance of diffusing that tension in the classroom and of how the L2 learning process is supported, not only through a variety of effective pedagogies, but also by nurturing the positive emotions which are essential for the long-term success of language learning (MacIntyre and Mercer 2014). However, "[w]e still live," argues Watson (2013), "with the outdated idea that learning must be hard work, and must NOT[1] be fun" (2). Humor provides teachers and students with an occasion for a respite from the formal and "serious" assigned material, affording a change of pace that may contribute to lowering the tension that many learners experience during the learning process. Humor is in fact regarded as a valuable medium for students to learn the vocabulary, syntax, semantics, and conventions of the language they are studying, as well as to achieve a better understanding of its culture (Bell, 2009; Askildson, 2005).

## Captioned Videos for L2 Development

In one of the earliest studies on captioned video's effect on comprehension, Price (1983) found that the 450 participants improved comprehension when the video was accompanied with captions. Most of the subsequent studies have supported the opinion that the use of captioned videos in L2 instruction enhances learner's comprehension (Chai and Erlam 2008; Danan 2004; Montero Perez et al. 2014; Vanderplank 2010; Winke, Gass, and Sydorenko 2010; 2013). Danan's (2004) meta-analysis provides a wide-ranging summary of the benefits and limitations of captioned video that have been documented by researchers. As for the limitations, captioning may prove to be unsuitable for lower-level learners or learners with limited reading proficiency (Danan 2004, 70). Taylor (2005) found that captions benefited third-year college students better than first-year students, who found the simultaneous presentation of sound, image, and captions to be distracting.

Benefits associated with captions seem to include improvements in language production, increased word identification and vocabulary building skills, greater ability to detect nuances of speech, and reduced learner's anxiety (Danan 2004, 75). Winke, Gass, and Sydorenko (2010, 255) suggested that captions can improve learners' attention and advance their learning by connecting with their previous knowledge. A key factor in learners benefiting from captioned video is the increased degree of heightened conscious attention paid to language use (Vanderplank 1990, 225). In other words, conscious language learning, i.e., the effort the learner exerts to read the captioned video, as opposed to just passively watching the video, results in substantial language acquisition (Vanderplank 1990, 2016). Captions can help

---

[1] Emphasis in the original.

learners to isolate and notice lexical elements, hence clarifying potentially ambiguous input and enabling word/phrase recall more accurately (Chai and Erlam 2008; Montero Perez et al. 2014). Consequently, by promoting form-meaning mapping, an important process for L2 acquisition, captioning helps learners to process and decode what they hear through visualization and the identification of word boundaries (Winke, Gass and Sydorenko 2013, 255).

In sum, captioning may act as a useful scaffolding device, furthering learners' comprehension and reinforcing acquisition, especially when the audio stream is particularly challenging, as when using authentic materials (Vanderplank 2016, 80).

## Research Methods and Data
## Peppa Pig Videos

The video cartoon selected for this study is *Peppa Pig*, a British children's educational animation series launched in 2004 in the United Kingdom. The series has acquired vast popularity worldwide and it is translated and broadcasted in 180 countries (Nightingale 2014). The plot of *Peppa Pig* involves the title character, Peppa, and her family of anthropomorphized pigs. The stories show interactions within the family and with other anthropomorphized animal characters in typical everyday activities of family life (e.g., going on trips, grocery shopping, visiting family and friends, etc.). Because the series is designed to be both educational and recreational for children, the use of the language is age-appropriate. In other words, the individual characters speak in turn, have a clear pronunciation, and the dialogues use basic vocabulary with frequent repetitions. Furthermore, the episodes are lighthearted and humorous, and entirely devoid of violent or sexual content.

Each episode of *Peppa Pig* is approximately five minutes in length, making them an ideal audiovisual for language courses. Indeed, research shows that short narratives with simple plots and familiar themes are less demanding in terms of attention span and background knowledge than longer videos, such as movies (Oddone 2011; Moser 2008; Robin 2011). While the original version is in English, the version used for this study is dubbed in Italian.

All data collected for this research stems from the viewing of 7 episodes of Peppa *Pig* (see Table 6.1), first without then with captioning. The episodes' themes did not relate to the themes covered in the syllabus.

Table 6.1. Titles of Peppa Pig episodes

| Title of episode in Italian | Original English title | Episode |
|---|---|---|
| 1. Vacanze al Sole | Flying on Holiday | Series 1 - Episode 36 |
| 2. La festa di beneficenza | The Children's Fete | Series 6 - Episode 4 |
| 3. Il riciclaggio dei rifiuti | Recycling | Series 2 - Episode 11 |
| 4. La macchina nuova | The New Car | Series 1 - Episode 11 |
| 5. Papà appende una foto | Daddy Puts up a Picture | Series 1 - Episode 45 |
| 6. Papà fa ginnastica | Daddy Gets Fit | Series 1 - Episode 40 |
| 7. Una giornata molto calda | Very Hot Day | Series 1 - Episode 35 |

## Setting

Participants to this study were 21 intermediate students enrolled in a third-semester four-credit Italian language course at a large American university. A qualitative approach was employed, as through narration and reflection students become aware of their beliefs, their feelings and their difficulties and have the possibility to express their opinions in their own words (Aragão 2011; Benson 2014; Ritzau 2013).

## In-class Activity and Pedagogy

In this study, I incorporated the *Peppa Pig* cartoon series in an intermediate classroom within a pedagogy informed by the Multiliteracies Approach. I aimed at interpreting the videotext while nurturing critical awareness of the relationship between spoken, written, visual and audio-visual texts, discourse practices, and social and cultural contexts (Dupuy 2011). The episodes of the cartoon were used as a springboard for instructor-facilitated whole classroom discussions on language use, but also on cultural and social contexts.

Traditional language lesson plans are often based on oral instruction or visual demonstrations of the learning content, which is generally followed by learners' practice sessions. Instead, during these sessions, I acted as facilitator, trying to stimulate students' thought, reflection, ideas and acquisition of knowledge on language and through language. The activity (about 40 minutes long) incorporated the screening of *Peppa Pig*, two matching vocabulary tasks, a comprehension task, followed by a discussion. Each of the episodes were screened once a week, first without captioning and then with captioning. Portions of each episode were presented a third time during the class discussion. The results of the matching vocabulary tasks and comprehension tasks are not reported in this study as they are beyond the scope of this research.

The discussions involved discussing any relevant lexical or grammatical features appearing in the episode and responding to questions posed by the students. Additionally, the discussions aimed at eliciting students' L2 production while promoting active engagement of critical thinking from the entire class, drawing attention to the link between the language used in the specific episode and attitudes, values, conventions, ideals and beliefs (Kern 2000, 17).

### Online Survey

The purpose of this survey was to inquire about their perceptions on the role of video cartoons used in class to foster their proficiency in Italian as an L2. The total number of respondents was N = 15. The survey included questions about participants' backgrounds as well as Likert-type and open-ended questions asking participants to evaluate the usefulness of the cartoons. The quantitative data acquired through the survey will not be discussed here. The open-ended questions inquired into participants' perceptions of children's animated cartoons in Italian (with and without captions) to enhance their L2. Data was also collected via other methodologies which aimed at eliciting participants' thoughts and beliefs through narration and reflection, such as writing a brief reflective statement and a final reflective essay in Italian. 3 students were also invited to take part in an individual face-to-face interview.

### Reflective Statement and Final Reflective Essay

Participants were asked to compose a brief written statement in English (approximately 200 words) in which they were to reflect upon the perceived benefits and limitations of watching cartoons with and without captions for their Italian L2 development. In order to collect data specifically to learn about participants' attitudes towards the in-class pedagogy, students were asked to write a 300-word final essay in Italian that was graded as a homework assignment. The title of the essay translated from Italian was "Describe in Italian your experience with the use of *Peppa Pig* in the classroom. Try to honestly express a positive or negative opinion". All the essays have been coded from the original Italian version and the portions that are quoted in this chapter are my translation from Italian into English.[2] 21 students submitted their final reflective essay.

## Interviews

Individual face-to-face interviews with 3 participants were conducted at the end of the project, soliciting a cumulative evaluation of their experience of watching cartoons. Participants were given the opportunity to compare their comprehension and vocabulary matching tasks in order to elicit their reflections and comment out loud on their own learning experience.

All qualitative data, including the transcribed interview responses, was sorted and itemized in MS Word documents and added to the Atlas.ti software's pool of data to be analyzed qualitatively.

## Results

**Table 6.2.** Abbreviations

| Source | Abbreviation | Explanation |
|---|---|---|
| Survey Question #8 | S8 | "Did you find it beneficial to have the captions on? Why?" |
| Survey Question #9 | S9 | "Any comments or suggestions regarding the project?" |
| Reflective Statement | RS | "What are the benefits and limitations of watching cartoons with and without captions?" |
| Final Reflective | FE | n/a |

We now turn to an in-depth analysis of the participants' attitudes towards the use of animated cartoons to promote L2 learning. Direct quotes from students and their interpretations are provided throughout the following sections. Several abbreviations will be used when presenting participants' direct quotes (see Table 6.2). This information is given in parenthesis, followed by

---

[2] Because this assignment was completed by intermediate students during the final weeks of their third semester of Italian instruction, all were able to produce a text that, despite the occasional error, was entirely comprehensible and straightforward.

the source of the quotation. A separate section will be devoted to the interviews. All student names quoted here are pseudonyms.

### The Role of Humor

Generally, participants' attitudes towards watching cartoons to enhance their Italian L2 appear to be very positive. Participants of both classes agreed that watching the episodes of *Peppa Pig* as a tool to enhance their Italian L2 was an enjoyable experience and acknowledged its potential as a learning tool.

> Peppa Pig was a very helpful tool and made words more familiar in our vocabulary and the videos were also very enjoyable. (Miriam, RS)

The humorous and lighthearted nature of the cartoon series was recognized by most participants as a positive characteristic that nurtured a relaxed and informal learning environment, one that gave them a respite from the habitual tasks and exercises found in the classroom. This view is expressed by Wendy and Cody:

> These assignments were refreshing and different from the usual things that are expected in a language class. (Wendy, FE)

> I enjoyed watching Peppa Pig. It really made stressful weeks somewhat better because it allowed me to escape for a while. (Cody, RS)

This last sentiment should be emphasized in the broader context of the student's attitude towards learning Italian as a life skill or valuable pursuit. If the learning of a second language is understood as stressful, most students are likely to abandon that language as soon as the academic requirement is achieved. Yet, if humor and spontaneity can be incorporated within the curriculum, the possibility that the student will make a positive emotional connection with the target language is much stronger, with important implications for later learning. Participants consistently regarded watching the episodes as a fun activity, crediting the humor present in the show as an attention-grabbing device that supported memorization, united the class and motivated the students to learn the language:

> Humor is very important in the class and in learning in general as it helps to remember important information. (Charlie, FE)

I like how the authors use humor. I think that humor is very important in class. Humor connects the class to their teacher and helps to learn. (George, FE)

Nevertheless, some participants expressed a negative attitude towards watching the cartoon. A few explicitly stated that they found the cartoon either too childish, unrelated to the formal class curriculum or simply annoying. Predictably, the most common criticisms alluded to the content of the cartoon as being unsuitable for a college-age student:

[T]he cartoon lacks an important aspect. Because it's an animated cartoon for children, the themes in the episodes are very simple and positive, so some issues that arise in adults' everyday life are not discussed. (Dana, FE)

Indeed, the stories are very simple because they are targeted toward young children. This proved to be a double-edged sword as, while it provided accessible content even to novice-level students, it also induced some participants to find it too childish and disengaging. Although a few participants admitted that they felt slightly embarrassed or dispassionate, the majority did not find it demeaning.

I don't think it's degrading to watch cartoons because they can help to learn a new language. (Andrew, FE)

I can't think of anything negative about watching a cartoon that is intended for children. (Wendy, FE)

George observed the simplicity of the cartoon was perceived as a facilitating learning:

Watching basic cartoons may seem silly but the simplistic grammar and concepts help people that are in the early learning stages of learning a language. It aids in grasping proper grammar as well as pronunciation (S9)

In sum, though a few expressed a negative view about watching the episodes as they regarded the cartoon as childish, inappropriate for their age and unrelated to the material covered in class, most students welcomed it as engaging and beneficial material for language acquisition. The general theme that emerges is that the humor of the interactions made the activity of viewing an episode in an L2 context less stressful and therefore aided, not only in the retention of vocabulary and grammatical contexts but also in engaging the students.

## The Role of Captions

Generally, participants stated that understanding the cartoon was too difficult without the aid of captions. Although they failed to understand accurately all the dialogues, participants frequently asserted that they could follow along with the story as they relied extensively on the visuals to gather the main gist. With captions on, however, they asserted that they reached greater comprehension of the dialogues, as exemplified by these statements:

> For me, personally, when I watched an episode the first time, it was difficult to understand what the characters said (Dillon, FE).

> When we first started watching the Peppa Pig videos, I found the exercise to be difficult. The first video without subtitles was difficult for me to understand and I found myself only able to understand about half of the content without subtitles. In the second video with subtitles, I still had some difficulty at first, but as we continued these exercises each week I noticed that my comprehension skills greatly improved. (Andrew, S8)

With captions, the viewers could parse the sentence, i.e., to identify the constituents of the phrase, such as verbs, nouns, etc., while the visual prompts displayed, not only the spelling of the words but also the boundaries between each word, as exemplified by the following quotes:

> When viewing [the episode] without captions it was harder to understand what they are saying because I would think some words were combined when they weren't. (Miriam, RS)

Hence, captions were considered a practical scaffolding device that allowed the learner to visualize what was being said and, importantly, to cue them on where each word ends:

> Particularly at the beginning, I observed that watching the episodes with captions was easier. When the characters spoke, all the words sounded like a jumble. The captions help me understand the

separation of words. But after a while there was a slowing down of the words in my brain and I could understand everything without captions. (James, RS)

Captioned viewing was reported to serve other purposes. Many participants noticed that hearing and seeing simultaneously a new word would help them to associate spelling and pronunciation while increasing the chance of recall. Some reported that captions helped strengthen the acquisition of familiar vocabulary and structures. The standard written representation of a language does not show which syllable is accented, how words in certain linguistic environments glide together or subtly change the pronunciation of the beginning of an adjacent word:

> W/o captions, I missed a lot of the storyline. Also, being able to read along as the characters were speaking helped me understand the pronunciation of the Italian words. (Arthur, S8)

> I think [captioning] is good because it connects what they are saying with what the words look like and looking at how to pronounce words. (James, S8)

When viewing an episode of *Peppa Pig*, students began to pick up on these captions, hearing the pronunciation of words strung together creating units of meaning. In addition, they began to develop strategies to listen for short words, such as pronouns, which can be almost imperceptible to new Italian language learners.

In summary, captions are perceived as a useful scaffolding device that increases the learners' comprehension in both levels. Adding same-language word-by-word captions provides a decisive visual cue to the viewer/listener that supports the interpretation of the content of the audio, acting as a "safety net," as Irene, a participant, put it (S8). With captions turned on, the students felt they could understand almost all of them. Other than aiding with comprehension, the perceived benefits of captions include the acquisition of new L2 vocabulary, the reinforcement of prior knowledge of both vocabulary and grammar, and a source of examples of how words are spelled and pronounced.

### The Interviews

The main interview questions for each participant concerned their attitude towards watching the cartoon, their perceived benefits for language acquisition and their thoughts about the use of captions. The quotes were selected according to their pertinence to the study's research question and based on whether they supported or not the findings outlined in the previous sections or offered further insights into students' attitudes.

The participants interviewed were Irene, Charlie, and Miriam. Asked if he enjoyed watching the episodes of the cartoon, Charlie acquiesced enthusiastically:

> I like the whimsical aspect of the episodes because they are whimsical. They are kinda fun, and targeted to the kids, they are easier to understand as opposed to, you know, a movie. An Italian movie where you gotta pick up a plot, you know some elaborate schemes. But when it comes to Peppa Pig, it's a simple story, and it throws in some idioms from Italy, like "boh" or "mamma mia," things that maybe you don't hear in class, but it's just how Italians talk in Italy and you get that kind of flavor in those episodes.

Charlie welcomed the humorous aspect of the series and appreciated that, because of its simplicity, the medium was more accessible than other authentic alternatives, such as movies. Again, we see the emergence of a theme that has been cropping up all over the data: the chance to be exposed to idioms that are usually not covered in class. Despite being a cartoon for young children, Charlie perceived it as a sample of "how Italians talk in Italy," therefore authentic. A similar opinion was held by Irene, when asked if she enjoyed the episodes:

I did, because it gave me kind of an insight into how real Italians are speaking, even if it was kind of a lower level for children. That's basically the level where I am at in speaking, so I thought it was great because you get to hear words in context, new vocabulary, and kind of real reactions that Italians would say or have to certain situations, which normally you don't get in classroom settings. You don't get to hear colloquial speech ...you get to learn educational speech and structures of language.

I asked Irene if she meant that she perceived the language in the cartoon as authentic, to which she replied without hesitation: "Oh yeah! Because it was real Italians speaking and real Italian dialogue" (Irene). Irene, despite her being among the highest achieving students of her Italian class, felt as if she were, linguistically speaking, at a child's level, hence she found the cartoons suitable for her developmental stage. Just as Charlie, she recognized the value of being exposed to a type of language that is not typically incorporated in the traditional L2 classroom, where, she felt, the emphasis is laid on the study of speech created for language-learning purposes ("educational speech") and grammar. Miriam affirmed that she enjoyed watching the episodes, explaining that she appreciated the entertaining and humorous aspects of them as well as the perceived simplicity of the language:

> I enjoyed watching the cartoons. I thought they were entertaining and they, like, broke things up easier, so I thought it was better to understand. I did like when there were the subtitles instead of just hearing it because it was easier to understand. And I feel it was, like, lower-grade Italian, so I feel that helped. And then that they made jokes and made it kind of more entertaining.

Arguably, Miriam's definition of the style of language featured in the cartoon as "lower-grade Italian" should be interpreted rather as being simple or straightforward than of an inferior nature.

When participants were asked if they thought to have improved in their overall Italian proficiency, all three responded positively, especially for what concerned listening comprehension:

> Sure, I mean, in my reading comprehension of the language and the listening part. I notice it now, like going through your class and going through it now, I have a much better understanding, maybe I'm not able to speak it as well, but when [his current teacher] speaks in class, I know what she's saying. Yeah, I feel that I have improved. (Charlie)

Charlie attributes the cartoon as impacting positively his listening skills and overall understating of Italian; however, he did not feel as having improved his speaking skills. Irene expanded on the topic, recognizing that typically she is only exposed to her Italian instructor's speech, while the cartoon has given her an opportunity to experience and "train her ear" to how other Italians speak, while Miriam underscored how the episodes offered her examples of language interactions and conversations:

> Most of the time I only ever hear my professor speaking in Italian, so it's...it's hard when you're listening to other Italians speak because they have different ways of speaking. So, when I got to watch [Peppa Pig] I got to see or hear how other people speak, and kind of train my ear to recognize how to understand how other people are speaking too. (Irene)

Yes, it helped me kind of learn the flow of the talking with someone in Italian and responding and watching it. The interactions between people and conversations. (Miriam)

Talking about the benefits of captions, all three interviewees stated that they enhanced their comprehension skills. Charlie considered captions as useful because during the first viewing he felt that the speech was too fast. Miriam stressed that the captions provided her with a visual reinforcement of what was being said, and thus helped her understand more:

Yes, because I kind of, like, would see how the word was said and then spelled at the same time, so subtitles helped me understand a lot better what they said [...] I did understand some parts, but I didn't understand the full extent without subtitles. It wasn't something that was above me, but now we're still learning the basics, you know?

Irene admitted that the speech rate was challenging but that the captions helped to parse the words, thus improving her comprehension:

When they're speaking really quickly, because most Italians, I have noticed, speak very quickly, you kind of hear the words running together, so the captions helped with that.

Reflections were solicited also upon the usefulness of the in-class activity. Miriam found the activity beneficial as watching the video a third time because pausing the video and discussing about it gave her time to understand it better:

When we reviewed the video, or like when we paused each time and kind of go over what they were talking about, or what the scene was, I feel that that helped a lot. Because it kind of broke it down and helped you understand what was happening instead of watching it all at once.

Reiterating what was maintained in his final reflective essay, Charlie replied that the in-class discussions reinforced his prior knowledge of vocabulary and his understanding of grammar in use:

In class you look at vocab, and you make that connection of a word that you knew. Definitely, going over it as a class, like the grammar points we would go over and you'd be like "This is something we'll be covering later, so it's important" or the pronouns that were the hardest thing we did in that class, and you'd be "This is why and it's here, and it's really basic for us who spoke the language for years and it's easy."

The in-class discussion served also to draw the students' attention to the contextual use of grammatical constructions that had either previously been taught in class or that were expected to be covered in subsequent sessions. Irene focused on the opportunity to pose questions to the instructor, achieve greater understanding of the plots and learn new vocabulary or idiomatic expressions:

> When we did the activities in class, I really had to focus and I picked up on small details, and things like that, which I thought was really helpful, uhm, cuz I got a deeper understanding of the plot and the words, vocabulary...I really enjoyed going through it together in the class with you because you were able to kind of answer the questions that I had, and that maybe I couldn't figure out on my own.

### Discussion

This study sought to enquire on how undergraduate students of Italian perceive the effectiveness of the use of animated cartoons to promote real language. Most students welcomed it as an engaging and valuable activity for language acquisition. Humor was reported to have made the activity less stressful and engaged the students giving them a respite from the traditional textbook-oriented occupations. Participants found that humor helped them to be more receptive to the material that they were exposed to, as found in the literature on the use of humor in the classroom (Askildson 2005; Bell 2009; Garner 2006; MacIntyre and Mercer 2014). The cartoon brought to the classroom an authentic material that presented "real language", an aspect that was regarded favorably by participants. They acknowledged that behind a "silly" children cartoon lay rich and authentic every-day L2 speech that is seldom represented in the traditional textbook. The sociocultural understanding of second language acquisition which has supported my study favors the contextual and social character of language characterized by a deviation from the traditional teacher-oriented grammar-based L2 instruction (Pavlenko and Lantolf (2000).

The cartoon offered the learners an opportunity to experience the dynamics of daily-life conversation and acquire new vocabulary and idiomatic expressions within a highly contextual environment. As maintained by the literature, exposing learners to materials that are not intended for language learning provides them with richer samples of the target language that allow them to discern the dynamics of authentic communication where the emphasis is on the message and not on language per se (Gilmore 2007; Torregrosa Benavent and Sánchez-Reyes Peñamaría 2011).

In general, despite the relatively slow pace of the speech, even the most proficient participants failed to understand the dialogues without captions. In accordance with the findings in studies on captioned videos in L2 instruction (Chai and Erlam 2008; Danan 2004; Montero Perez et al. 2014; Vanderplank 2010; Winke, Gass and Sydorenko 2010; 2013), greater accessibility to the videos was attained by participants when the captions were turned on. Participants were able to see what was said in real-time and identify what, during the first viewing, seemed as an indistinct string of sounds. They could not only parse the sentence, but they could also distinguish the boundaries between each word (Vandergrift and Baker 2015; Winke, Gass and Sydorenko 2013: 255). Captions helped learners to isolate and notice lexical elements thus clarifying indistinct input and enabling word/phrase recall with more accuracy (Chai and Erlam 2008; Montero Perez et al. 2014; Winke, Gass and Sydorenko 2010). Furthermore, hearing and reading the words also helped students to learn how words in Italian are pronounced.

Some students appreciated the different strategies that are applied and skills that are necessary when listening to speech a) with captions, i.e., reading skills and activation of prior knowledge, and b) without captions, i.e., exploiting the available context and paralinguistic clues. This finding corresponds to the conclusions reported by Chai and Erlan (2008) and Sydorenko (2010). Being able to read the dialogue catered to their prior knowledge, boosting their comprehension. Participants frequently asserted that their comprehension increased as they watched more episodes and familiarized themselves with the language. This tends to suggest that students at least perceived an improvement in their listening comprehension skills, which may in turn impact positively their motivation to study their L2 (Dörnyei 1990; Kilickaya 2004; Dewi 2018). Analogous conclusions as to the importance of exposing learners to videos with and without captions are put forth by Syderenko's (2010). Alternating captioned and non-captioned audiovisuals, as done in the present study, would allow students to focus on vocabulary acquisition (captioned) as well as on listening strategies (non-captioned).

The study also aimed at identifying participants' attitudes towards the in-class discussion, which also incorporated a supplementary viewing of some excerpts of the episode. The intermediate students regarded the activity as worthwhile because they were able to watch the episode a third time and thus notice new details and confirm or refute what was previously understood. Noticing unfamiliar terms in the input is the first step in the language acquisition process (Huckin and Coady 1999; Hulstijn 2001). Digital video allows to "move back and forth, to repeat, to pay close attention to language and other features of the communicative situation, and to stop and reflect on the components that contribute to a deeper understanding of linguistic and semiotic data and to the language learning process" (Tschirner 2001, 307). Particularly, students appreciated the opportunity of posing relevant questions to their instructor aimed at clarifying meaning or reinforcing previous knowledge of grammar[3], vocabulary and idiomatic expressions. Furthermore, being exposed to Italian idioms in context alongside the elucidations of the instructor was very often referred to in the data as a positive characteristic of the in-class discussions because they recognized that this type of language is not usually taught in the formal L2 classroom.

This article offers insights for language teachers as to how students assessed the usefulness of children's animated cartoons to promote "real language" learning. Results of this study can inform L2 pedagogy and help language instructors be aware of the potential of using children animated cartoons in the classroom, not only for Italian but for other languages as well. However, there are two main limitations in this study. First, the sample being limited in number could not warrant for complex statistical analysis that might quantify the participants' language gains. Future research should survey a larger sample of intermediate L2 learners. This would offer a more in-depth understanding of the impact that children's cartoons may have on the learners of that level. Secondly, the cartoon episodes used in this study did not have direct bearing with the material that was covered in the class. Incorporating the episodes according to their relevance to the syllabus would increase the pedagogical importance of the episodes, by providing reinforcement to what is formally learned, while exposing the students to new vocabulary and idioms that otherwise would not be taught.

---

[3] Though *Peppa Pig* is intended for an audience of preschoolers and the plots are exceedingly simple, a close look at the grammar employed by the characters and the narrator reveals considerable complexity. For instance, in just 5 minutes, the episode 'La macchina nuova' (*The New Car*) features dialogues containing the use of: 1) the present tense; 2) the simple past and the imperfect past tenses; 3) the subjunctive; 4) the future tense, and 5) both the direct and indirect object pronouns.

# Bibliography

Alam, Zahangir. 2019. "Facebook as a Formal Instructional Environment in Facilitating L2 Writing: Impacts and Challenges." *International Journal of Language Education* 3 (2): 41-48.

Antoniadou, Victoria. 2011. "Telecollaboration 2.0: Language, literacies and intercultural learning in the 21st Century." *Language and Intercultural Communication* 11 (3): 285-288.

Aragão, Rodrigo. 2011. "Beliefs and emotions in foreign language learning." *System* 39 (3): 302-313.

Askildson, Lance. 2005. "Effects of humor in the language classroom: Humor as a pedagogical tool in theory and practice." *Journal of Second Language Acquisition and Teaching* (12): 45-61.

Bae, Jungok, and Lyle F. Bachman. 1998. "A latent variable approach to listening and reading: Testing factorial invariance across two groups of children in the Korean/English two-way immersion program." *Language Testing* 15 (3): 380-414.

Bahrani, Taher. 2014. "An overview on the effectiveness of watching cartoons as authentic language input for language learning development." *International Journal of Language Learning and Applied Linguistics World* 5 (2): 550-556.

Bahrani, Taher, and Tam Shu Sim. 2012. "Audiovisual News, Cartoons, and Films as Sources of Authentic Language Input and Language Proficiency Enhancement." *Turkish Online Journal of Educational Technology-TOJET* 11 (4): 56-64.

Bahrani, Taher, Sim Shu Tam, and Mohm Don Zuraidah. 2014. "Authentic language input through audiovisual technology and second language acquisition." *SAGE Open* 4 (3): 1-8.

Barcelos, Ana Maria Ferreira. 2003. "Researching beliefs about SLA: A critical review." *Beliefs about SLA*. Springer, Dordrecht 2: 7-33.

Barcelos, Ana Maria Ferreira, and Paula Kalaja. 2011. "Introduction to beliefs about SLA revisited." *System* 39 (3): 281-289.

Becker, Shannon R., and Jessica L. Sturm. 2017. "Effects of audiovisual media on L2 listening comprehension: A preliminary study in French." *Calico journal* 34 (2): 147-177.

Bell, Nancy D. 2009. "Learning about and through humor in the second language classroom." *Language Teaching Research* 13 (3): 241-258.

Benavent, Gabriela Torregrosa, and Sonsoles Sánchez-Reyes Peñamaría. 2011. "Use of Authentic Materials in the ESP Classroom." *Online Submission* (20): 89-94.

Benson, Phil. 2014. "Narrative inquiry in applied linguistics research." *Annual Review of Applied Linguistics* (34): 154-170.

Berti, Margherita, Stefano Maranzana, and Jacob Monzingo. 2020. "Fostering Cultural Understanding with Virtual Reality: A Look at Students' Stereotypes and Beliefs." *International Journal of Computer-Assisted Language Learning and Teaching (IJCALLT)* 10 (1): 47-59.

Chai, Judy, and Rosemary Erlam. 2008. "The effect and the influence of the use of video and captions on second language learning." *New Zealand Studies in Applied Linguistics* 14 (2): 25-44.

Clark, Cary. 2000. "Innovative strategy: Concept cartoons." *Instructional and learning strategies* (12): 34-45.

Danan, Martine. 2004. "Captioning and subtitling: Undervalued language learning strategies." *Meta: Journal des traducteurs/Meta: Translators' Journal* 49 (1): 67-77.

Davies, P. (Producer), Astley, N., Baker, M., Hall, P., & Van Hulzen, J. (Directors). 2004. *Peppa Pig.* England: Astley Baker Davies Ltd.

Deneire, Marc. 1995. "Humor and foreign language teaching." *Humor* 8 (3): 285-298.

Dewi, Resti Citra. 2018. "Utilizing Authentic Materials on Students' Listening Comprehension: Does it have Any Influence?" *Advances in Language and Literary Studies* 9 (1): 70-74.

Dörnyei, Zoltán. 1990. "Conceptualizing motivation in foreign-language learning." *Language learning* 40 (1): 45-78.

———. 2014. "Researching complex dynamic systems: 'Retrodictive qualitative modelling'in the language classroom." *Language Teaching* 47 (1): 80-91.

Dupuy, Beatrice. "CLIL: Achieving its goals through a multiliteracies framework." *Latin American Journal of Content & Language Integrated Learning* 4.2 (2011): 21-32.

Ecke, Peter. 2019. "Planning and Assessing Group (Video) Projects in Foreign Language Classes." *Handbook of Research on Assessment Literacy and Teacher-Made Testing in the Language Classroom.* IGI Global: 126-139.

Foncesa, Mónica Patarroyo. 2016. "Textbooks Decontextualization within Bilingual Education in Colombia." *Enletawa journal* 9 (1): 87-104.

Gardner, Robert C., and Wallace E. Lambert. 1972. *Attitudes and motivation in second language learning.* Vol. 786. Newbury: Rowley.

Gardner, Robert C. 2010. *Motivation and second language acquisition: The socio-educational model.* Vol. 10. Peter Lang.

Gee, James Paul. 2015. "Three paradigms in reading (really literacy) research and digital media." *Reading at a Crossroads?* Routledge: 49-58.

Gilmore, Alex. 2007. "Authentic materials and authenticity in foreign language learning." *Language teaching* 40 (2): 97-118.

Grazzi, Enrico, and Stefano Maranzana. 2016. "ELF and Intercultural Telecollaboration: a Case Study." *Intercultural Communication. New Perspectives from ELF.* 109-133.

Heift, Trude, and Nina Vyatkina. 2017. "Technologies for teaching and learning L2 grammar." *The handbook of technology and second language teaching and learning.* 26-44.

Huckin, Thomas, and James Coady. 1999. "Incidental vocabulary acquisition in a second language: A review." *Studies in second language acquisition.* 181-193.

Hulstijn, Jan H. 2001. "Intentional and incidental second language vocabulary learning: A reappraisal of elaboration, rehearsal and automaticity." *Cognition and second language instruction* 3: 258-286.

Isabelli-García, Christina L., and Casilde A. Isabelli. 2020. "What Is the Impact of Study Abroad on Interlanguage?" *Researching Second Language Acquisition in the Study Abroad Learning Environment.* Palgrave Pivot, Cham, 65-96.

Kern, Richard. 2000. *Literacy and language teaching.* Oxford University Press.

Kilickaya, Ferit. 2004. "Authentic materials and cultural content in EFL classrooms." *Internet TESL Journal* 10 (7): 1-5.

Lafford, Barbara A. 2006. "The effects of study abroad vs. classroom contexts on Spanish SLA: Old assumptions, new insights and future research directions." *Selected proceedings of the 7th conference on the acquisition of Spanish and Portuguese as first and second languages.* Somerville, MA: Cascadilla Proceedings Project. 1-25.

Lenkaitis, Chesla Ann. 2019. "Technology as a mediating tool: videoconferencing, L2 learning, and learner autonomy." *Computer Assisted Language Learning.* 1-27.

Loewen, Shawn, Dustin Crowther, Daniel R. Isbell, Kathy Minhye Kim, Jeffrey Maloney, Zachary F. Miller, and Hima Rawal. 2019. "Mobile-assisted language learning: A Duolingo case study." *ReCALL* 31 (3): 293-311.

MacIntyre, Peter D., and Sarah Mercer. 2014. "Introducing positive psychology to SLA." *Studies in Second Language Learning and Teaching* 4 (2): 153-172.

Maranzana, Stefano. 2022. "Intermediate Learner Opinions on Captioned Video Cartoons for Language Acquisition." In *Emerging Concepts in Technology-Enhanced Language Teaching and Learning.* IGI Global: 232-252

Mercer, Sarah. 2011. "Language learner self-concept: Complexity, continuity and change." *System* 39 (3): 335-346.

Montero Perez, Maribel, Elke Peters, and Piet Desmet. 2014. "Is less more? Effectiveness and perceived usefulness of keyword and full captioned video for L2 listening comprehension." *ReCALL* 26 (1): 21-43.

Moser, Amelia. 2008. "Chapter Seven Azione! Teaching Listening Skills Through Video: A Web-based Program of Film and Television Segments Designed for Italian Language Courses." *New Approaches to Teaching Italian Language and Culture: Case Studies from an International Perspective,* 158-172.

Nightingale, Richard. 2014. "Well I never!: formulaic language as a pragmatic resource in child entertainment media." *Studying Second Language Acquisition from a Qualitative Perspective.* Springer, Cham, 203-218.

Oddone, Cristina. 2011. "Using videos from YouTube and websites in the CLIL classroom." *Kalbų Studijos* (18): 105-110.

Pavlenko, Aneta, and James P. Lantolf. 2000. "Second language learning as participation and the (re) construction of selves." *Sociocultural theory and second language learning* (3): 155-178.

Payne, Mark. 2011. "Exploring Stephen Krashen's 'i+ 1'acquisition model in the classroom." *Linguistics and Education* 22 (4): 419-429.

Ritzau, Ursula. 2013. "A qualitative investigation of the dynamics and complexity of language learner beliefs through written protocols." *Linguistik Online* (2): 97-111.

Robin, R. 2011. "Listening comprehension in the age of Web 2.0." *N. Arnold, & L. Ducate, Present and future promises of CALL: From theory and research to new directions in language teaching.* 93-130.

Saeedi, Zari, and Aso Biri. 2016. "The application of technology in teaching grammar to EFL learners: The role of animated sitcoms." *Teaching English with Technology* 16 (2): 18-39.

Sánchez-Hernández, Ariadna, and Eva Alcón-Soler. 2019. "Pragmatic gains in the study abroad context: Learners' experiences and recognition of pragmatic routines." *Journal of Pragmatics* (146): 54-71.

Shafie, Latisha Asmaak, Shafie, Latisha Asmaak, Aizan Yaacob, and Paramjit Kaur Karpal Singh. 2016. "Negotiating multiple audiences of L2 learners on Facebook: navigating parallel realities." *International Education Studies* 9 (10): 95-104.

Swaffar, Janet, and Andrea Vlatten. 1997. "A sequential model for video viewing in the foreign language curriculum." *The Modern Language Journal* 81 (2): 175-188.

Syodorenko, Tetyana. 2010. "Modality of input and vocabulary acquisition." *Language learning & technology* 14 (2): 50-73.

Taylor, Gregory. 2005. "Perceived processing strategies of students watching captioned video." *Foreign Language Annals* 38 (3): 422-427.

Tschirner, Erwin. 2001. "Language acquisition in the classroom: The role of digital video." *Computer assisted language learning* 14 (3-4): 305-319.

Vandergrift, Larry, and Susan Baker. 2015. "Learner variables in second language listening comprehension: An exploratory path analysis." *Language Learning* 65 (2): 390-416.

Vandergrift, Larry, and Christine Goh. 2012. *Teaching and learning second language listening: Metacognition in action.* Routledge.

Vanderplank, Robert. 1990. "Paying attention to the words: Practical and theoretical problems in watching television programmes with uni-lingual (CEEFAX) sub-titles." *System* 18 (2): 221-234.

———. 2010. "Déjà vu? A decade of research on language laboratories, television and video in language learning." *Language teaching* 43 (1): 1-37.

———. 2016. *Captioned media in foreign language learning and teaching: Subtitles for the deaf and hard-of-hearing as tools for language learning.* Springer.

Verspoor, Marjolijn H., and Nguyen Thi Phuong Hong. 2013. "A dynamic usage-based approach to Communicative Language Teaching." *European Journal of Applied Linguistics* 1 (1): 22-54.

Vulchanova, Mila, Vulchanova, Mila, Lisa Aurstad, Ingrid vygKvitnes, and Hendrik Eshuis. 2015. "As naturalistic as it gets: subtitles in the English classroom in Norway." *Frontiers in psychology* (5): 1510.

Watson, Etain Caitlin. 2013. "Teaching Italian with the Virtual Reality of Video." *AISHE-J: The All Ireland Journal of Teaching and Learning in Higher Education* 5 (2): 1-11.

White, Cynthia, Pamela Easton, and Colin Anderson. 2000. "Students' perceived value of video in a multimedia language course." *Educational Media International* 37 (3): 167-175.

Wilkinson, Sharon. "The omnipresent classroom during summer study abroad: American students in conversation with their French hosts." *The Modern Language Journal* 86 (2): 157-173.

Winke, Paula, Susan Gass, and Tetyana Syodorenko. 2010. "The effects of captioning videos used for foreign language listening activities." *Language Learning & Technology* 14 (1): 65-86.

———. 2013. "Factors influencing the use of captions by foreign language learners: An eye-tracking study." *The Modern language journal* 97 (1): 254-275.

Chapter 7

# A Pedagogical Model for Integrating Interdisciplinary Approaches in Second Language Acquisition

Elena De Costa
*Carroll University*

**Abstract:** The challenges of translating research into classroom practice have been widely acknowledged (e.g., Spada and Lightbown 2019). This chapter aims to present recognized theory and research in Second Language Acquisition (SLA) and bilingualism and to discuss its implications for language pedagogy. The importance of differentiating between two broad domains of language, mental representation and skills is well-known (Krashen 1988; VanPatten 2006) Within this context, grammar, as part of mental representation, cannot develop through explicit instruction and practice, but only through input processing. Skill, on the other hand, is acquired by engaging in the very behaviors that learners wish to develop. While a great deal has been written on the theory and practice of communicative language teaching, there have been relatively few studies of actual communicative language practices both inside and outside the classroom. Active learning devices using a variety of interdisciplinary approaches are particularly powerful pedagogical tools that can help improve the linguistic skills of second language learners since they focus on the communicative act in interpersonal settings. This chapter will present a language teaching approach that advocates the addition of the following pedagogies: (1) the effective use of *cortometrajes* or short films to foster communication and critical thinking in the target language; (2) experiential learning in service learning community contexts; (3) composition and conversation instruction using a journalistic approach to inform a more sociocultural nuance in learning; (4) the creation of short digital narrations to share cultural and intercultural competencies, while encouraging aesthetic appreciation of knowledge from personal and group experiences; and (5) the production of bilingual theater adaptations in one-act plays to foster cultural and linguistic proficiencies in public performance spaces. Such pedagogies support a pedagogical model designed to help students develop linguistic, cultural, and intercultural competencies while encouraging the aesthetic appreciation of interdisciplinary forms.

**Keywords:** active learning, natural language learning, communicative language learning, spontaneous linguistic production

***

### A pedagogical model for integrating interdisciplinary approaches in SLA

How do we engage second language learners in authentic learning experiences that model the real world they will enter after graduation? How do we collaborate with students using a learner-centered model to facilitate learning despite limited linguistic proficiency, grammar, vocabulary, and sentence structure? Which pedagogical approaches and strategies improve language learners' comprehension and recall while allowing them to apply their knowledge and skills in meaningful ways related to the real world? Effective teaching is all about authentic learning. How is the learner going to use this information and skills learned in the foreign language classroom in the real world?

Authentic experiential learning is not a new concept. Indeed, the developmental psychologist Jean Piaget as early as the 1950s had become a staunch advocate of getting learners actively engaged in real-world learning by connecting new knowledge with prior knowledge within a meaningful context. Within this constructivist pedagogy, learners are perceived as active participants in the learning process as opposed to passive recipients. When there is an absence of meaning and engagement in the learning process, a disconnect occurs between knowledge and its application, motivation is lowered, and learning transfer becomes inhibited (Brown et al. 1989). Following this constructivist premise that learners learn best when they are actively involved in the process of their own learning, we would expect that there is no skill more authentic, more active, more meaningful than language acquisition. Why is it, then, that learners in SLA (Second Language Acquisition) classes often experience such a high degree of anxiety in the learning process and such a low yield in communicative skills even after several years of language study? Why do some second language learners express that they have invested their time in a low-yielding endeavor, unable to communicate effectively, especially in the oral skills of language proficiency? And, finally why do second language learners often feel that their coursework bears little or no resemblance to real-world transfer in any meaningful, authentic way, when language is a critical skill that is put to use daily in professional and personal settings? The purpose of this essay is to illustrate the complex role of active learning as a central approach to second language teaching and learning where interdisciplinary activities, experiential learning, and community engagement are core goals. Creative approaches to foreign language teaching in authentic, real-world contexts provide learners with the opportunity to effectively build language skills while increasing motivation for learning. In well-constructed, learner-centered, non-threatening activities, the learner is focused on interactive communication, dialogic encounters with a purpose. In such contexts, anxiety is diminished since assessment becomes more holistic rather than centered on a single task in an isolated moment of time. Authentic learning in this sense includes real-world tasks with value beyond the classroom. It is interdisciplinary, uses a variety of learning styles, and provides learners with agency as they take ownership of their learning. Authentic learning is student centered with the instructor as facilitator encouraging collaborative engagement in meaningful scenarios.

Intercultural communication, community, and global engagement can empower language programs with relevance and prepare students to transfer and apply their language skills beyond the walls of the classroom. In a related way, community and global engagement prepare students for civic engagement, the workplace, and our interconnected globalized society. Language educators must design and facilitate learning experiences that are grounded in authentic communication and issues with community and global significance. They must introduce students to career opportunities for language, intercultural and global competence. These factors underscore the importance of relevancy and its relationship to increased motivation and thus language proficiency. Classroom language learning is directed at learning the rules of language or "formal knowledge" of a language, for the most part. The classroom is not structured for language acquisition in a limited time segment with multiple learners, each different in their abilities and interests (Krashen's acquisition learning distinction). Yet, research has shown (Krashen, Krashen and Terrell 1983) that affective-humanistic and problem-solving activities can yield linguistic development particularly in the active skills by lowering the affective filter and increasing engagement in relevant speech patterns. The subject divided curriculum is a fragmentation of the coherent interrelationship of knowledge. It focuses on an area of learning that might be a weaker discipline rather than integrating more than one subject area to call upon the potential strengths inherent in an interdisciplinary approach that deflects from the limitations of a single subject approach. In the 1950s Jean Piaget was already advocating active learner engagement in real world learning. But what exactly is authentic or real-world learning and how can it be accomplished in the process of second language acquisition? Constructivist theory underscores that learners can become active when they connect new knowledge with prior knowledge within a meaningful context (Brown et al. 1989). This hypothesis relies on the premise that bringing the real world into the classroom by connecting disciplines in practical, meaningful ways for learners (a departure from traditional learning situations) leads to greater student motivation and engagement. The pedagogical applications that follow are designed to test the efficacy of this premise in the college undergraduate classroom.

Treating culture and language as *performance* of the target culture permits us to systematically accommodate culture while the language is being learned and taught, practiced, and creatively adapted to meaningful situations that *the learner* wishes to communicate. Active learning in which the learner becomes meaningfully and significantly engaged in the learning process may be defined as involving "students in doing things and thinking about the things they are doing" (Bonwell and Eison 1991, 2). In more specific pedagogical terms, active learning encompasses a broad array of learning strategies including experiential learning; learning by doing (hands-on learning); applied learning; service learning; peer teaching (in various contexts); lab work; role plays; case-based learning; group work of various kinds; technology-based strategies such as simulations, games, clickers, and various smartphone applications; and classroom interaction, with participation and discussion probably being the most widely used of all active learning approaches (Carr, et al. 2015, 173). Building on these strategies are theories such as constructivism that have focused on student centered approaches that promote student autonomy, self-direction, and self-regulation of learning. It is unclear how and where such strategies and approaches belong in the active learning domain, not to mention which ones are best suited to learners. Certain strategies will fit well with specific kinds of content and learning outcomes. Specific strategies promote learning more effectively for the unique learning style of individual students. But even a cursory review of what is active learning makes one feature clear: active learning engages students individually and collectively to different degrees. It is completely plausible that individual students and whole classes of students can be actively engaged at different levels during a single activity or across several of them. That raises the question of the level of active learning needed to influence learning outcomes. Can active learning strategies even be measured? What level of involvement or how many active learning events does it take before the effects start showing up in assessment measures such as test scores or in other measurable ways? I surmise that active learning is occurring when I see certain behavioral manifestations, such as critical thinking in projects and reflective journaling, creative application of skills from other disciplines, engaging performative tasks inside and outside the classroom and in the wider community. Performing a culture means interpreting *language as culture*, not divorced as a separate entity from culture. Of course, active learning strategies are much more difficult to assess than vocabulary and verb conjugation memorization. I could argue that memorizing facts is an active process even though it might not involve much thinking. However, memorization does not invite critical thinking, nor does it engage the learner in meaningful, motivational tasks that lead to a personally designed and fulfilling result.

### Task-Based language teaching from passive to active learning: journalism as messaging

In my intermediate to advanced language classes, I design classroom resources and educational experiences with the focus on sharing global news in the Hispanic world. I am passionate about social justice issues and a firm believer in the power of storytelling to cultivate empathy.

Empathic response tends to enhance motivation to learn and to communicate reactions to situations, thus increasing the desire to communicate in the target language. Culture, literature, theater, and community engagement are all logical manifestations of responding to societal problems. The idea behind combining journalism with Spanish language, literature, and culture in a single course (*Hispanic Studies through Journalism and Literature*) is for students to develop areas of academic or personal interest into journalistic pieces and communicate their knowledge and perspectives to a broader audience. They compose articles for their fellow citizens in a Spanish language magazine (*El Coloso*), 28-pages of text that is published in print and online for university and community distribution. Each student undertakes one or two reporting projects on his or her own topic about Hispanic culture, history, politics, literature, in-country experiences, as well as other relevant issues and works to craft the final written product under the supervision of the course instructor. This journalism class equips students to embark on their own journalistic projects. Students connect with one another and with resources in the community as they brainstorm challenges and opportunities for integrating resources shared during interactive sessions. They research stories, many of which are under-reported news items, related to local, national, and international Hispanic issues. They tell these stories through photojournalism, descriptive and editorial writing, investigative journalism, reviews, and interviews, among other strategies. In this way, journalism skills are used as a tool to increase student engagement, critical thinking, and empathy (empathic response or active listening). They include a photographic component to their reporting, bringing to life those affected by changes in society, policy, or environment. Depending on the topic, some students investigate academic and government reports in the target language, searching for the root causes to the issues on which they report. Some students focus on storytelling to overcome reporting roadblocks in the project's development. In classroom sessions, we delve into basic reporting techniques, interview techniques, journalism's code of ethics, and issues in today's media landscape. This is a unique initiative in language practice in an interdisciplinary setting designed to provide deeper global learning and storytelling experiences for students.

Founded on the premise that second language acquisition must parallel first language acquisition, Krashen's theory of comprehensible input insists that language must be taught through meaning and context. Language proficiency is a skill that develops over time and never reaches perfect communicative abilities. Language instructors must accept that mistakes indicate progress, transfers will eventually be made from the native language and that the emphasis of instruction should remain on clear communication. Paying attention to what is being communicated orally and in writing, as opposed to *how* it is being said, only enhances the affective domain, which, in turn, impacts successful language acquisition. Self-esteem, self-confidence, risk-taking, empathy, extroversion, lowered anxiety, and heightened motivation to engage in meaningful communication are all critical to SLA. The classroom must provide students with opportunities to develop as independent thinkers and self-reliant problem solvers. Indeed, the affective filter hypothesis embodies Krashen's view that the affective variables *facilitate* SLA. None of the methodologies used in the classroom over the years (audio-lingual and grammar-translation, in particular) has proven successful in achieving SLA since they are cognitively based with emphasis on rule-bound communication. Authentic or communicative learning, what Krashen refers to as acquisition learning or the *natural approach*, allows students to explore, discuss, and meaningfully construct concepts and relationships in contexts that involve real world problems and projects that are relevant to the learner. An intense desire to open new channels of communication to overcome language barriers in the communication-oriented classroom must pervade every element of instruction. The primacy of learning a language as a means of communicating with others is underscored when students are given tasks that are meaningful, relative to real world issues of *their* choosing, requiring *their* creative input, *their* engagement in what *they* want to say, whether it be in an oral or written context. The efficacy of the journalism course, for example, is that students conduct research for their articles in both written and oral formats using native informants. They problem solve in how and where they will identify their sources. They must be proficient in interview techniques to engage the native informant in conversational dialogue while they are asking questions about the content of their topic. In short, the interview is a conversation *not* an interrogation. It must be conducted with professionalism yet be informal and conversational in nature to maximize the information sought. A follow-up written correspondence of gratitude for time invested in the interview process is expected. The process involves multi-tasking, so anxiety is not focused on simple language production. Initial anxiousness is necessarily dispersed over a multiplicity of tasks, thus lessening focus on any single portion of the interview information gathering process. After completing the interview, the student experiences a heightened sense of accomplishment and self-confidence. Conducting a formal interview with a stranger is, of course, a very challenging assignment for anyone even in one's native language.

### Interdisciplinary strategies: performing culture in the public performance space

Languages are thought to be acquired by understanding messages and providing comprehensible listening and reading opportunities. According to VanPatten (2006), in order to approach acquisition, learners need to understand a great deal of input through the passive skills of reading and listening so they can begin to mimic and absorb the natural usage of a language and produce ideas that the speaker wants to convey in meaningful contexts. In their 2010 publication of *Key Terms in Second Language Acquisition*, Bill VanPatten and Alessandro Benanti define the distinction between incidental and intentional learning by underscoring that "research on native vocabulary acquisition suggests that most speakers' vocabularies are a result of incidental learning." (93). This assumption would suggest that learning in context and reinforcement by multiple sensory input is a more "natural approach" to learning both in isolated and whole speech second language acquisition. By placing language in the broader context of a theatrical performance with dialogic exchanges, soliloquies, audience asides, and other interactive language formats, the focus shifts from learning for assessment to learning for communication in a public performance space. Communication to elicit audience reaction becomes the motivating factor—

laughter, gasps, outcries of outrage, applause—all such audience responses signal to the speaker that communication has been effective. Audience responses of this nature provide unintentional feedback to the student performer in the form of self-confidence by collective acknowledgement of comprehension of the spoken word. The relationship between motivation and success correlated with individual differences in SLA has been well documented by VanPatten (2003) and more extensively by Zoltán Dornyei and Peter Skehan (2010). While integrative motivation or the internal impetus to learn is ideal from a teaching perspective, most students operate on instrumental motivation, the purposeful or beneficial use of language. I always tell students during theater rehearsals to focus on meaning even when they miss or forget memorized lines. In this way, they are consciously aware of what they are saying and what is being said to them. Since our performance texts are adaptations of plays, they often add text or revise lines or even add new roles to the performance during rehearsals. They are given the permission to control their situation, to repair miscommunication, to be fully heard, to make choices. Communicating the message for audience comprehension is the key even when they invent lines to make up for a missed cue. Effective language usage relies on interacting with the environment, a specific situation or individual in particular ways. It has long been my philosophy that SLA learners can become *native-like* if given the proper instruction, input, and real world contexts in which to practice speech. Parsing or the moment-by-moment (real time) process of tagging words with syntactic rules, projecting syntactic structure, is a way to make sense of keywords used in context to interpret or intelligently guess what is being said in context. The speech patterns or grammatical structures that are created on the spot outside of the memorized lines might not be perfect grammatically, but they do communicate the message and inspire the student with positive feedback from audience response. In their distinction between performance and competence, VanPatten and Benati (2010) affirm that "Performance is limited by such things as working memory... fatigue... style of language... there are performance factors that limit what people do with language even though they know more than what they can do" (124). This is particularly the case with speech in a public performance space even for native speakers!

What makes interdisciplinary applications of language learning such an effective mechanism for second language acquisition? How does the interdisciplinary nature of this strategy lower the affective filter and increase motivation to use language? Why does teaching in silos prove to be ineffective? Can the Humanities and the Sciences cross-pollinate to yield advantages in both areas, or does the interdisciplinary nature of teaching and learning need to be restricted to subjects only in one area and not in the other? Blending second language instruction with another discipline or activity shifts the focus away from the language alone. Learner engagement in different environments with different activities results in ancillary talents and skills combining with and strengthening SLA perceptions and thus the outcomes from the blending of disciplines. Additionally, interdisciplinary environments that combine language instruction with another area of study add novelty and increase motivation and engagement of students in these settings. The pedagogical implementation of active learning such as collaboration, feedback, and activities that have a communicative purpose, yield the best results. To be certain, this pedagogical strategy is challenging and requires creative approaches and an energized, motivated, self-confident instructor who is constantly re-assessing activities and building collaborations both on campus and in the larger off-campus community. When successful, however, designated learning outcomes exceed those produced in a traditional language instructional setting, even one that focuses on the communicative approach. Settings in which students are assessed on free and effective communication, as opposed to linguistic exactness, provide language learners with *agency*, communicative meaning, and relevancy driven by their need to communicate in their own way. Often such communications are self-initiated, wherein the instructor becomes the facilitator with the learner intentionally and proactively personalizing communication. Research on affect in language proficiency motivation places learner agency in a central position. Learner agency demonstrates a shift from the cognitive to the sociocultural perspective in language learning. In many SLA motivation theories, the student's sense of agency is central to increasing language learning, as asserted by the extensive research of Chie Muramatsu and Tomoko Yashima (2015).

Of course, linking language and meaning in the context of SLA interdisciplinary teaching and learning is not a new pedagogical strategy. An interdisciplinary approach to language teaching in a dual-focused classroom was originally identified in 1994 as *Content and Language Integrated Learning* (CLIL) and was launched by the University of Jyväskylä and the European Platform for Dutch Education (UNICOM) with subjects taught in a foreign language. The learning outcomes centered on the mastery of content in the subject area (journalism, theater, civic engagement, history, etc.) and the simultaneous learning of a foreign language. CLIL advocates Krashen's theory of the *natural approach* in an immersion situation. Of course, when the language learner resides in an environment different from one in which the target language is spoken almost exclusively outside the classroom, conscious or cognitive learning of the target language takes precedence. Interdisciplinary or cross-curricular language teaching derivatives of CLIL include the following: situational learning or language presented in real world contexts; focus on language acquisition over conscious learning with the functional-notional syllabus; the communicative approach to language learning focusing on fluency as opposed to grammatical accuracy ("interlanguage"); language learning linked to enhanced motivation relative to a topic of interest (subject content) together with the simultaneous need for communication in the target language; and, finally, a whole language approach of speech taught in chunks, as in the lexical approach with grammar as secondary to lexis. In the interdisciplinary language classroom, learners are required to communicate content to each other, and skills are integrated with each other using language input. Learner needs are of primary concern, and learning styles are addressed in the variety of tasks available to the learner depending on the subject matter. Focus is on content and knowledge progression in the subject area. Indeed, *content, language* (including the specialized language of the discipline), *cognition* (the development of critical thinking skills), and *culture* (alternative perspectives) are the hallmarks of the interdisciplinary approach to language teaching, especially at the more advanced levels of instruction. Interdisciplinary courses such as *Latin American Civilization* with binary world views of the indigenous populations in contrast to the Spanish Conquistadors and later the Neo-Colonial United States policy-makers, *Hispanic Cultural Studies through Journalism and Literature, Spanish for the Professions, Spanish Translation in Professional Settings, Medical Interpretation, Bilingual Theater Production, Civic Engagement in Latino Communities, Experiential Learning in Community Contexts* (internships)—all these courses provide the second language learner with exposure to alternative perspectives and shared understandings which deepen awareness of otherness and self in addition to polishing language proficiency. Interdisciplinary teaching helps learners to apply, integrate and transfer knowledge, and fosters critical thinking. Interdisciplinary or cross-curricular teaching has the capacity to increase students' motivation for learning a second language due to the additional subject matter with which it is paired. In contrast to learning skills in isolation, when students participate in interdisciplinary experiences, they see the value of what they are learning and become more actively engaged. Interdisciplinary teaching provides the conditions under which effective learning occurs on two or more subject levels. Students learn more when they use language skills to explore, write, and speak about what they are learning.

### Digital narration: storytelling as messaging of shared experiences

Today's learners are very adept at electronic communication used for a variety of communicative purposes in diverse formats. It can be used to convey stories very aptly. Storytelling is a uniquely powerful linguistic technique to process learning. We celebrate the power of true and personal stories to connect individuals through universal experiences. Stories build a neighborhood, stable neighborhoods connect communities, diverse communities strengthen a city. In short, community bonds are strengthened through the art of storytelling. Just as shared stories create the linchpin of communities, stories also bring students together in shared experiences and endeavors in the classroom. This is particularly true in the case of the digital narrative. A digital storytelling project allows language learners to express themselves creatively and to convey meaning using a medium with which they are eminently familiar. Once again, language learners are combining their focus of the spoken word in the target language with another discipline. But this time the companion discipline is a mode of production and not another academic subject. Story circles, visuals, voice overs, music, video, and text intersect in the digital narration. With the advent and availability of new technology, various forms of digital media production have become quite common, so that the language learner is able to produce a *cortometraje* or short video with relative ease, especially if it is assigned as a small-group project. The potential for learning and showcasing second language acquisition is broad. Depending on the assignment, the medium can be used to develop oral, written, or digital skills. Digital storytelling can focus on a goal, such as to develop content understanding by providing a *moraleja* or moral to a literary or historical reading. In a group setting, learning is perceived as being active and ongoing in the learning process of teaching others, documenting, and sharing knowledge. Students not only learn from their own digital storytelling contributions but also from those of their classmates.

One example of an assignment that I give to students in an intermediate language class requires students to focus on their own culture and the target culture with their similarities and differences through the digital narrative. Everyday people share aspects of their story centered on an enduring question, experience, or memory about culture to keep the viewer's attention, using powerful emotional content to connect the audience with the storyline, personalization to help the audience understand the story context, meaningful images, and an appropriate soundtrack. Digital narration is a cooperative learning process which involves team discussion and reflection that engages students as they work together to storyboard, shoot, and edit their digital stories using the target language and even learning new technical vocabulary in the process. This use of technology within the framework of social construction motivates language learners to focus on the contextual use of language rather than basic vocabulary development in isolation, such as in topical vocabulary lists. The affective filter of anxiety is lowered while the levels of student motivation and self-esteem are heightened, since the L2 learner brings together oral storytelling with images, music and audio, enhancing the storyteller's personal view. As a teaching and learning strategy, digital storytelling promotes critical thinking, connects new content with prior knowledge, enhances memory, and fosters an understanding of language structures to communicate effectively. If students interview and/or involve native informants from the campus or community in the project, they also learn about identity negotiation and the ways culturally and linguistically native informants make meaning out of their lives.

One of the assumptions of intercultural communication is that all of us have been shaped on a fundamental level by one or more cultures. Our family upbringing, our education or religious affiliation, our gender and the roles our culture assigns to it—these and many other factors have done their work, often invisibly, to make us who we are. The more we know about ourselves, the more we know about how our cultures have affected us, the easier time we will have as we try to communicate across cultures. The purpose of this storytelling project (an auto-ethnography or cross-cultural ethnographic study of Hispanic/American cultures) is to make the students aware of the hidden values of their own culture and the culture of the "other" and the hidden ways in which culture has shaped identity. In a normal ethnography, an outside observer participates in a foreign culture in order to learn from the inside what that culture is about and how it functions. In an *auto-ethnography,* the observer studies his or her own culture and the influence that it has had on his or her own self. As students work through course materials, they reflect on who they are and how their culture has shaped their identity. Class discussions address these questions of identity as they develop underlying concepts in greater depth, providing students with insights and approaches. We explore the concept of culture through the lens of Hispanic cultures, particularly immigrant cultures in the United States.

Why assign a storytelling project? Each of us has a powerful story to tell about our culture. All human beings have an innate need to hear and tell stories, and so storytelling is the ultimate cross-cultural bridge, a timeless way to make strangers into friends, to communicate to others a message, a lesson, information. Stories are how we learn since they can illustrate ideas clearly and concisely. We have difficulty remembering abstractions and lectures, but we always remember a good story told in a creative, interesting way. If you tell me, it's an essay. If you show me, it's a story. Stories are powerful because they delight, enchant, amuse, touch, teach, inspire, motivate, and challenge. When we share life-changing moments and surface our deepest motivations, we touch other people more profoundly than if we repeat a list of talking points, even well-researched ones. A good story trumps a mountain of facts. If you want to understand people, ask for their personal stories. Listen long enough, and you learn not only the events of their lives, but their sources of meaning, what they value. We define our culture through the stories we tell—our family histories, our traditions, our shared experiences.

Why assign the digital storytelling format? The digital format of this assignment provides a familiar medium in a non-threatening environment, allowing for student collaboration, revisions, creative development, and above all, reflective critical thinking. It is also a change from the usual assignments and therefore refreshing, motivating. The assignment allows students to demonstrate their strengths and learn from the strengths of others at the same time. What follows are some of the instructor's open-ended instructions given to the class for this project:

- Your group might tell a short narrative story collectively.

- You might include performance, dramatization, music, song, dance, poetry, collage, photography.

- You might use art, projections, a mural or cultural "mapping," or infographics of your ideas.

- You might begin with your own story and end with the story of the "other" culture.

- You might explore a single idea or link together a series of related ideas with a moral to the story, a lesson learned.

- You might focus on a sociocultural problem and offer clarity about its roots and visions about ways to solve it.

- You might tell a story of someone who finds courage and discovers what it means to be human in today's world within a cross-cultural context.

- You might incorporate film, theater, and music to explore cultural identity after speaking with local Hispanic immigrants.

And finally, why focus on the topic of culture? Culture is more than what meets the eye (traditions, practices), more than what touches the soul of a people (beliefs, values). Culture is lived experiences, what has been passed on from one generation to the next (one's heritage). It is what has been lived in the present moment and how the experience of this present moment impacts the evolution of culture in a future moment. Culture is informed by the individual interacting with his surroundings with all the teachings of his ancestors which have made him who he is. Culture is defined by the experiences of both the individual and his patrimony. And these cultural experiences are more than the surface components that communicate with our five senses. They are physical, emotional, intellectual, and spiritual. They are both logical and inexplicable to those who are not members of the cultural group. They are spoken and heartfelt. Culture defies simple definitions. Culture defies full comprehension by both those inside the cultural group and outsiders. Culture begs maintenance and continuity, while it is always in a constant state of flux, change, development, re-defining itself, re-inventing itself over time. Culture is sameness. Culture is change. Culture can be seen and experienced (as is the case of the ethnographer), yet the true meaning of any culture is always invisible, evasive, profound in its simplicity. While each of us is a unique representation of our culture, each of us represents cultural components that are uniquely identified with our cultural associations. My culture is shared with my compatriots. Yet my culture is as unique to me as my experiences are unique. Culture must be experienced. Culture must be lived. Language *is* culture, and language cannot be taught. Language must be *experienced*. Culture cannot be cataloged in a book. It cannot be found on a tourist trip. Culture cannot be discovered in a classroom. Culture is a lifetime of interactions, experiences, dialogues with self and others—others like me and different from me. And for all these reasons, culture is an enchanting mystery that begs a constant struggle to grasp and understand, communicate, and embrace. Culture cannot be learned in any single course nor in many courses. Cultural knowledge, cultural awareness, and cultural sensitivity are all on-going processes for all of us, regardless of our educational preparation and life circumstances.

Integrated learning and student engagement are a challenge to twenty-first century faculty in the foreign language classroom. Effective teaching depends on the link between what you teach and how you teach it, between content and pedagogy. But there are other connections besides those between academics and methodologies. The obstacles to good teaching and learning have not really changed that much—student passivity, lack of motivation, low self-esteem, less than adequate study skills, and excessive grade orientation. What has changed are some interference mechanisms that did not exist in earlier generations, i.e., electronic devices used in inappropriate ways during class sessions to text, email, instagram, google, etc. While good scholarly work on teaching and learning is being done in every discipline, much of that work addresses issues about shared aspects of teaching and learning. There are peer-reviewed articles on cellphone use, clickers, group work, evidence-based teaching, classroom management, and engagement in pedagogical periodicals. One way to ensure that language learning occurs in a meaningful context and that language processing goes beyond the level of isolated sentences is to develop pedagogies where language and content are closely intertwined. Numerous scholars have shared their research on the value of immersion and content-based instruction or CLIL (*Content and Language Integrated Learning*) for the teaching of foreign languages. Some prominent examples of CLIL research include Krashen (1988) and Shrum and Glisan (2000). Simply teaching content through language or language through content will not lead to linguistic proficiency nor engage the modern-day student more completely. As with any pedagogical approach, the instructor must integrate form-focused activities and content-based assignments creatively in response to individual and group needs in order to achieve the best results. Such content-driven second-language instruction is much more apt to allow for the weaving of soft social skills, the interpersonal level of communication in small groups, with the focus on identifying, discussing, and offering resolution to some social issue in blogs, electronic and face-to-face interactions. In other words, emphasis must be placed on the topic under consideration in the target language rather than the grammatical accuracy of isolated sentence patterns that are devoid of a larger significance. The application of content-based methodology implies a multiple focus on language, learning, and cognition; the creation of safe and enriching learning environments; the use of authentic materials and interactions; the promotion of active learning or learner centered teaching; the combined use of macro- and micro-scaffolding in student learning aimed at learner agency or autonomy; and the promotion of cooperative learning among peers and between students and teachers/facilitators of learning. Additionally, content-based instruction shifts the focus of traditional language instruction by providing learners with every opportunity to engage in meaningful exposure and use of the target language through the delivery of engaging and purposeful content of a topic or academic subject in the target language (García and Navés 2009). In this way, the target language not only becomes the medium of instruction but also the focus of communication.

To me, motivation to communicate is a vital concept in second language acquisition. The challenging question arises on *how* learners develop second language proficiency in such a way that it becomes a tool used to share information as well as their intentions and to share their views and values and those of others, thereby turning the target language into something that represents part of their self-concept and their desire to engage with others in a meaningful way. The motivation to communicate emerges from engagement with others of diverse perspectives (instructors, co-learners, authors, native informants) in an interactive dialogic space. Ideas are exchanged with the focus on the efficacy of message delivery more so than on how accurately (from a linguistic perspective) that message is delivered. The success of content-based instruction on language acquisition ironically comes from its focus on non-linguistic outcomes. Motivation, self-confidence, and the willingness to communicate are equally valued goals of foreign language instruction and might even have a longer impact on students' learning behavior. Focus on the learner and the learner's ability to communicate content-specific information are a major shift in a field of study dominated by descriptions of language and teaching techniques. It is a shift to a greater consideration of the contributions that learners make to their own language learning if given the opportunity.

Today's language learners require a positive learning environment that leads them to construct meaning and apply new learning using a variety of differentiated and stimulating learning strategies. In the classroom, the instructor needs to promote language learner engagement by creating an atmosphere that is conducive to the learning experience, that is, by setting the stage for learning. The content-based strategies suggested in this chapter promote student engagement, independence, and interdependence in learning. Such strategies facilitate a positive learning community that is responsive to and respectful of the learning needs of today's active learner. Today's SLA instructor must plan instructional approaches and activities that engage students in rigorous and relevant learning in context to promote their curiosity, both cognitively and affectively, and engage them while activating background knowledge. Participatory learning, emphasizing authentic learning in meaningful, energizing contexts, embodies not only the use of problems and issues in the real world, but also the methods that are used to approach them—teamwork, collaboration, technology, critical thinking, and creativity. Such learning experiences from interdisciplinary contexts to performance texts, from community-based projects to film shorts, increase student motivation. They do so because they involve active engagement and meaningful outcomes used in real world settings on the job, in interpersonal relations, in everyday life circumstances. In their study *How People Learn: Bridging Research and Practice,* (Donovan et al. 1999), the authors underscore the concepts of meaningfulness, the real world, and relevancy as being important to authentic learning. They also stress the importance of the more affective attributes of negotiating meaning, gaining trust, building understanding. Today's instruction should be learner centered with the instructor orchestrating or facilitating how knowledge is shared with authentic experiences and assessment strategies, and target language immersion as much as possible. By engaging students in learning experiences that model the real world, the work that the learner will ultimately be asked to undertake, the instructor/facilitator collaborates with the learner in the process of his/her own learning process. At the same time, the learner is invited to share his/her knowledge and expertise with others *actively* as a "teacher" in his/her own right. The active learner is the engaged and motivated learner promoting cultural dialogue in varied authentic settings from print media to stage, from classroom discussions to professional settings. Language is much more than isolated words, grammar rules, and syntax. Language is cultural communication in meaningful contexts; it is learning the behaviors of a society and its cultural customs. Indeed, self-determination theory (Ryan and Deci 2017) suggests that learners engage in a holistic model of language learning opportunities with a sense of competence, autonomy, and relatedness. Learners need to believe that they can successfully manage learning that is of value to them, that they have some choice in what they do and how they do it, and that this can all be done within a supportive, low-anxiety community of peers bolstered by the instructor as facilitator. All this returns us to where we started earlier in this chapter with Krashen's "Natural Approach" to language acquisition and his "affective-humanistic activities" that engage students' "feelings, opinions, desires, reactions, ideas, and experiences" (Krashen 1988, 100) with the focus on content. Developing creative delivery of interdisciplinary content in foreign language teaching provides students with the opportunity to effectively build language skills and increase their motivation for learning by active engagement, while acquiring content information in another discipline. Interdisciplinary content learning in the foreign language classroom develops skills for local and global community engagement through course content that is relevant, authentic, engaging, developmentally appropriate, and linguistically and culturally responsive. Interdisciplinary language learning environments facilitate meaningful communication and purposeful second language acquisition that can be used within and beyond the classroom. The additional advantage to such a pedagogical approach is the focused purpose and context of second language acquisition with the content of another discipline. Psycho-social and informational-cognitive uses of language thus merge to fully engage today's learners with this pedagogical model of language learning.

# References

Bonwell, Charles C. and James A. Eison.1991. "Active Learning: Creating Excitement in the Classroom." ASHE-ERIC Higher Education Report, No. 1. Washington, D. C. The George Washington University, School of Education and Human Development.

Brown, John Seely, Allan Collins, and Paul Duguid. 1989. "Situated cognition and the culture of Learning." *Educational Researcher* 18 (1): 32-42.

Carr, Rodney, Stuart Palmer and Pauline Hagel. 2015. "Active learning: The Importance of Developing a Comprehensive Measure." *Active Learning in Higher* Education 16 (3): 173-186.

Donovan, M. Suzanne, John D. Bransford, and J.W. Pellegrino. 1999. *How People Learn: Bridging Research and Practice.* The National Academies Press.

Dornyei, Zoltán. 2014. "Researching complex dynamic systems 'Retrodictive qualitative modeling' in the language classroom." *Language Teaching* 47 (1): 80-91.

Dornyei, Zoltán, and Peter Skehan. 2003. "Individual Differences in Second Language-Learning." In *The Handbook of Second Language Acquisition,* edited by Catherine Doughty, and Michael H. Long, 589-630. Wiley-Blackwell.

García, Ofelia. 2008. *Bilingual Education in the 21st Century: A Global Perspective.* Wiley-Blackwell.

Hammond, Jennifer, ed. 2001. *Scaffolding. Teaching and Learning in Language Literacy Education.* Australia: PETA.

Krashen, Stephen D. 1985. *The input hypothesis: Issues and implications.* Longman.

———. 1987. *Principles and Practice in Second Language Acquisition.* Prentice-Hall International, 1987.

———. 1988. *Second Language Acquisition and Second Language Learning.* Prentice-Hall International.

Krashen, Stephen D., and Tracy D. Terrell. 1983. *The Natural Approach: Language Acquisition in the Classroom.* Prentice Hall Europe.

Lee, James F., and Bill VanPatten. 2003. *Making Communicative Language Teaching Happen.* McGraw-Hill.

Muramatsu, Chie. 2013. "Portraits of Second Language Learners: Agency, Identities, and Second Language Learning." PhD diss. University of Iowa.

Navés, Teresa. 2009. "Effective Content and Language Integrated Learning (CLIL) programmes." In *Content and Language Integrated Learning Evidence from Research in Europe,* edited by Rosa Yolanda Ruiz de Zarobe, and Jiménez Catalán, 22-40. Bristol: Multilingual Matters.

Piaget, Jean. 1954. *The Construction of Reality in the Child.* Basic Books.

Ryan, Richard M., and Edward L. Deci. 2017. *Self-Determination Theory. Basic Psychological Needs in Motivation, Development, and Wellness.* The Guilford Press.

Shrum, Judith L., and Eileen Glisan. 2000. *Teacher's Handbook: Contextualized Language Instruction.* Cengage Learning, 2000.

Spada, Nina, and P. M. Lightbown. 2006. *How Languages are Learned.* Oxford University Press.

Spada, Nina and Patricia M. Lightbown. 2019. "Second Language Acquisition." In *An Introduction to Applied Linguistics*, edited by Norbert Schmitt and Michael P.H. Rodgers, 111-127. Routledge.

VanPatten, Bill. 2003. *From Input to Output: A Teacher's Guide to Second Language Acquisition.* McGraw-Hill.

———. 1996. *Input Processing and Grammar Instruction: Theory and Research.* Ablex.

VanPatten, Bill, and Alessandro G. Benati. 2010. *Key terms in Second Language Acquisition.* Continuum.

VanPatten, Bill, Megan Smith, and Alessandro G. Benati. 2019. *Input Processing and Grammar Instruction: Theory and Research.* Cambridge University Press.

Yashima, Tomoko. 2015. JALT2015 Conference Plenary Speaker Interview with Yashima Tomoko. Interview by Stephen Ryan. *The Language Teacher,* May/June. Retrieved from https://www.academia.edu/14848236/An_interview_with_Tomoko_Yashima

Chapter 8

# Domesticating the Virtual Wild: Implementing Online Informal Language Learning in the Formal Language Classroom

Iwona B. Lech

*University of Illionois*

**Abstract:** Learning another language (L2) through exposure to authentic unaltered L2 resources in online spaces (i.e., movies, television shows, news, articles, discussion forums, music, blogs, vlogs, or social media) has increasingly been receiving attention. A growing body of research suggests not only positive outcomes in the L2 itself, but also significantly greater learner engagement and perseverance in learning compared to traditional classroom instruction.

This chapter describes the existing research and discusses the next step: Implementing OILL in the *formal* language pedagogy. Following the idea of Wagner's (2015) merger of classroom learning with experiences in the "Wild" (i.e., interactions in an L2 community), I suggest embedding the *virtual* Wild resources and designing a pedagogical approach for their effective use in the classroom without stripping them of their informal character.

**Keywords:** Language Learning in the Virtual Wild, Online Informal Learning of Language, OILL, incidental learning, usage-based model of language, informal learning, constructivism, learner autonomy, CALL

\*\*\*

"Given the growing abundance of authentic L2 content found online, a teacher's primary role will no longer be to provide linguistics input and corrective feedback but rather to help learners curate their personalized learning experiences" (Blyth 2018, 230)

## Introduction

Since the beginning of the twentieth century, modern language teaching methodology has centered on language use (e.g., communicative tasks, model dialogs, role plays and needs analysis), but the truly authentic, colloquial language, unplannable contexts, and situations common in everyday life have rarely been employed as a systemic resource in the language classroom (Clark et al. 2011). In many colleges and schools, the common method of teaching a foreign language still constitutes a model Taylor (2008, 863) calls the "vocabulary + grammar" approach. It involves a textbook-based program organized according to the complexity of grammatical structures—from the easiest (but not necessarily the most frequently used) to the most complex—and lists of disconnected lexical items (Gettys and Lech 2013).

Even though most programs are prescribed to use a communicative approach that emphasizes "meaningful and authentic language use rather than merely mechanical practice of language patterns" (Richards and Rodgers 2014, 90), the typical syllabus is still organized according to grammar topics. Consequently, "meaningful and authentic language use" is often reduced to practicing grammar patterns in prescribed, and generally not very natural, speech instances. With these common program standards and the time constraints instructors face, they do not have many opportunities to create a truly meaningful and authentic language-use environment.

At the same time, there is growing interest in naturalistic, largely incidental, usage-oriented ways of learning other languages in online environments (Cole and Vanderplank 2016; Godwin-Jones 2019; Jijang 2019; Lech and Harris 2019; Sockett 2014). Referred to in literature as Online Informal Learning of English (OILE) or of Language (OILL), Web-Based Informal Language Learning (WILL), Informal Online Language Learning (IOLL), or language learning in the Virtual Wild (among others), the idea centers on the notion of learning another language through exposure to authentic resources in L2 available online. These resources include watching television series, movies, short videos, vlogs, reading articles, blogs, interacting on social media, listening to music, playing synchronous video games, etc.

Researchers in this area consistently agree that exposure to such sources, guided largely by the individual interest in the source rather than by the desire to learn the language, creates higher learning gains when compared to traditional language instruction (Cole and Vanderplank 2016; Lech 2018). It also significantly lowers affective filter and foreign language anxiety, fosters higher engagement, and develops autonomous learning skills (Cole and Vanderplank 2016; Lech 2018; Sockett 2014). Additionally, given the current affordances of technology, OILL serves as an extremely rich and valuable source of immersion-like experiences in L2 communities and cultures in environments in which direct contact with L2 communities is not available. Thus, it should not only be much more widely advocated for use among learners of other languages, but it should also become an inextricable part of any language instruction.

With the growing body of research on OILL and its positive results (Godwin 2019; Lech 2018), with the development of technology and increased access to it, and with the common knowledge that immersive-like environments are the best way to learn another language, there is still a lot of resistance to Wild resources (Sockett 2014). Some researchers (e.g., Reinders and White 2011) argue that uncontrolled and unguided access to authentic materials can be more harmful than helpful to the learning process. Many teachers shy away from the messy unstructured input that stands in opposition to the well-established and followed idea of the comprehensible input (Krashen 1985). It is a fact that OILL can be quite messy and is impossible to (and should not be) control, i.e., to build assignments on or merge it into the textbook-guided course program. However, these very qualities are also the qualities of every language and, thus, are the most realistic and authentic version of the language that exists. Embracing OILL in all its messiness and unpredictability and not trying to modify it in any way to create an impossible fit may just be the missing element that language instruction, often ineffective (Gettys and Lech 2013), needs.

However, a question arises about how to embed such resources into the actual instruction, how to make them work with the traditional instruction or a textbook in symbiosis. The main aspect that makes OILL what it is is its incidentality and that the learner 1) has a choice of what to engage in and 2) does not engage for the learning purposes. We cannot just assign students to watch a video or listen to a song (and this is why doing so has more characteristics of regular instructional activities rather than qualities or results aligned with OILL). Thus, an approach is needed in which OILL resources are not modified to fit the instruction but left in their original format, are introduced only as options and ideas, and students are taught how to use them, so they develop an individual comfort to go 'into the wild' on their own.

Following these tenets, the chapter proposes connecting OILL and traditional instruction with these principles in mind. I describe the key aspects of OILL and its theoretical framework grounded in the constructivist theory of usage-based model of language and language acquisition. I indicate how OILL fosters development of learner autonomy for future language learning beyond the classroom and how it develops the overall learning skills of language students. Next, I suggest how OILL can be merged with any formal instruction and pedagogical program without changing the two and without stripping OILL of its main characteristics. Finally, I propose activities and an organizational structure for such a merger as well as pedagogical strategies to teach students how to navigate in the OILL world to eventually become fully autonomous OILL users as well as autonomous language learners.

## Part I: Theoretical Framework
## What is OILL

The online informal learning of language (Lech 2018) or learning language in the Virtual Wild (Lech and Harris 2019) refers to organic unplanned and unstructured exposure to L2 online through activities like watching original television shows, movies, videos, or vlogs; listening to music, audiobooks, podcasts, reading blogs, news, magazine articles; interacting on social media; playing synchronous video games; and similar. These resources are not created for or altered in any way for educational purposes; instead, they are simply cultural products of the L2 community created by default for the L2 community and L2, usually native, speakers. The defining characteristic of OILL is that it is unintentional, unconscious, and incidental and the learner is largely unaware that learning is taking place (Lech and Harris 2019; Sockett 2014). It occurs "naturalistically, using resources not specifically tailored for educational purposes and which are situated outside of any institutional context" (Sockett 2014, 11).

An OILL learner engages in activities to e.g., exchange opinions about their favorite TV show or musician. Thus, learning of language is "merely a by-product of this decision" (Sockett 2014, 130). An OILL activity may not necessarily be defined as informal, but the decision to engage in it may be, and OILL happens without following any order or progression known to the learner without following any timetable.

It is important to note that many other technology-oriented language learning solutions are different than OILL. Programs like *Rosetta Stone* or *Duolingo,* chat and language exchange apps like *Hello Talk* or *Tandem,* and numerous websites with conversation exchange options like *LiveMocha* are created specifically for educational purposes, even if outside of the formal instructional context. Similarly, any solutions connecting technology with language learning and teaching that fall under Computer Assisted Language Learning (CALL) are pedagogically adapted, involve conscious and deliberate learning, and are fundamentally different than OILL.

This distinction between OILL and tailored CALL is especially important because the greatest benefit of OILL is its incidentality (Lech and Harris 2019; Sockett 2014). The learner engages in OILL activities due to the learner's interest in the specific item, e.g., the newest episode of a favorite show, a song, a social media post on a specific topic, etc. The learner focuses on enjoying the specific item, often being unaware that learning is taking place. The driving force of this engagement is the learner's decision to choose and engage in the activity (Sockett 2014). Because the choice is guided by the specific interests and situational context of each learner, it is driven by a unique type of intrinsic motivation (Sockett 2014) and carries meaning for the learner that is irreplicable by any pedagogically designed tools or materials. Thus, limiting any of these characteristics can potentially harm the benefits of OILL.

In the following part of this contribution, I describe the most important aspects of OILL and how they align with current research in second language acquisition (SLA).

## OILL is usage-based

Over the last decades, the field of SLA has turn to a view, based on extensive empirical evidence, that language learning is essentially formed by experience and social practice (Clark et al. 2011). In the usage-based (UB) model of language and language acquisition (Bybee 2010; Ellis 2003, 2006; Tyler et al. 2018; Tomasello 2009), language learning is gradual, contextualized, social, and based on the general cognitive principles of learning and development (Tyler, Ortega, Uno, Park 2018). All language knowledge "is 'constructed' on the basis of the input" (Goldberg 2009, 93), meaning that true participation in *usage events* (i.e., situated instances of the language user producing or understanding language to convey particular meaning in a specific social situation) can happen only through active participation of the learner who extracts information and *constructs* a new set of skills based on it (Kemmer and Barlow 2000; Tyler et al. 2018). Language *emerges* from use and *shapes* the use of it further.

In the UB view, language learning is governed by the same cognitive and emotional processes that govern acquisition of any skill; thus, the usual learning conditions, including exposure to the subject and repetition, are required (Bybee 2008). The main difference from the traditional theories of and approaches to language learning is that "the grammar and syntax is not the foundation upon which the remainder of the language is built and it does not drive the language" meaning that "language is not an analytical system in which small parts make a whole, but a holistic system that is more than the sum of its parts" (Verspoor 2017, 145).

Consistent with this premise, the OILL environment gives learners the opportunity to truly engage in the real-life events and construct their own learning through online informal experiences (Lech and Harris 2019). In OILL, learners engage in the real raw language, and this engagement exposes learners to a wide selection of phrases used in various situations as well as idiomatic expressions, slang, and abbreviations, which are a mirror of the usage events present in real life. This language is hard to implement in an actual classroom following a textbook-based program with prescribed events and language samples. Learners who engage in OILL activities have an opportunity to interact with usage events and, in this way, to really experience the language. Additionally, in activities like blogging, chatting, or social media interaction (e.g., exchanging comments via Facebook), learners *use* language instances and co-create linguistic structures through language use.

### OILL aligns with constructivists framework of learning

The UB model of language is, essentially, a constructivist theory of learning. Constructivism asserts that "knowledge cannot be taught but must be constructed by the learner" (Candy 1991, 252). In the UB view, all language knowledge "is 'constructed' on the basis of the input" (Goldberg 2009, 93), so true participation in usage events can happen only through active participation of a learner who extracts information and *constructs* a new set of skills based on it. Learners create their own learning, i.e., they transform and organize reality extracted from interactions with the environment using common intellectual principles (Candy 1991; Schunk 1996). Thus, knowledge is produced through interpretation of socially conditioned messages, i.e., language that is used in social situations (Benson 2001).

Effective learning involves learners' active participation, through social interaction, in determining their process of learning and deciding what meaning it has for them. Therefore, learning will be most effective when learners are fully involved in decisions about the content and process of learning (Benson 2001). This idea supports the main tenant of OILL in which learners *choose* to engage in the online activities and choose how active they wish to be and how they use the knowledge extracted from these activities. OILL environments give learners an opportunity to truly engage and actively participate in the real-life events and to construct their own learning. They interpret the situations and messages encountered in the Virtual Wild and learn from those instances.

## OILL develops learner autonomy

Constructivist philosophy implies that learners must take ownership of their learning process and meaning making, consistent with Little's (1994) claim that all successful learning is autonomous, i.e., in that learners develop their own ways of extracting knowledge. Autonomous learning involves learners having responsibility for all aspects of their learning, including determining the objectives, defining the content and progression, selecting methods and techniques to be used, monitoring their progress, and evaluating what they have experienced (Holec 1981). This control over learning may take a variety of forms in the learning process for different individuals (Benson 2001).

Learning autonomy stands at the core of OILL, as learners take responsibility for their learning while they determine the objectives, content, and their own progress. However, it is also a skill conditioning any OILL involvement, and it is a skill that significantly lacks support in many language classrooms (Lech 2018). Thus, creating an environment in which autonomous skills are taught and gradually developed following zone of proximal development (ZPD) has the potential to create independent autonomous learners truly successful in learning another language.

## OILL fills the void of not enough input

A traditional undergraduate language course in the U.S. is either 45 (3 credit course) or 60 (4 credit course) instruction hours (50-minute periods) per semester. Given different program-related requirements and even taking into consideration the time students spend on homework, this is a very limited time to create an opportunity for abundant and meaningful input. Class instruction is largely dedicated to grammar explanations and limited practice of prescribed patterns (Lech and Harris 2019). Additionally, students mostly practice with each other, and thus, the source of their input, beyond the teacher, falls on fellow classmates. Common textbook-based exercises involve mostly talking about textbook fictional characters, which is not very meaningful for students (Gettys and Lech 2013), and chances to talk about themselves are highly limited, being typically the last activity on the list. This summary is, certainly, a large simplification and may not apply in many instances; nevertheless, the 150-200 minutes of instruction per week give very little opportunity for L2 input. To be effective, language instruction should involve "large amount of input – preferably as authentic as possible" (Verspoor 2017, 151).

Embedding OILL into the L2 classroom presents an opportunity to address this situation with relatively little effort or time investment. The idea behind using OILL is such that it becomes more of a hobby than obligation. Learners engage in the activities like interacting on social media, watching movies, shows, programs, listening to podcasts or music, or gaming online and develop an interest in particular topics and products. For example, a learner who enjoys German music may end up listening to Rammstein for many hours a day. Another one interested in a story presented in a television show may engage in binge-watching for several hours a week. At a minimum, any niche a learner finds particularly interesting has the potential of becoming from a few to several hours of input on a regular basis.

## OILL creates immersive environments

Another advantage of OILL is its immersion-like character. It is a well-known fact that immersion is the best possible way to learn another language and OILL constitutes an alternative to the in-person interactions with L2 communities. Especially in communities where the real-time L2 is not easily accessible, but there is available internet, OILL can be a great source of real-life and meaningful interactions with native L2 speakers and often may present possibilities even greater than living in an L2 country. With increasing access to all parts of the world and its resources with a click of the mouse, it seems prudent to find strategies to use these opportunities as much as possible, especially in learning about other cultures and languages.

## OILL fosters engagement and resilience

Research in OILL suggests that the success of OILL environments is associated with the positive emotions present during engagements that fosters students' intrinsic motivation, resilience, and autonomy (Lech 2018; Sockett 2014). In particular, these emotions come from the freedom of choice in OILL (Cole and Vanderplank 2016; Roed 2003; Sockett 2014). Sockett (2014) suggests that learners engaged in OILL activities are not exposed to affective pressure and are highly motivated. This is because they chose their own content, are not being evaluated, and the OILL context is synonymous with leisure and, "as such, is low on anxiety and high on motivation" (Sockett 2014, 25). Online environments may also constitute a safe zone of learning, eliminating many of the negative aspects present in a classroom setting and reducing foreign language anxiety (Horwitz 1986; Roed 2003).

Positive emotions are believed to broaden perception, attention, motivation, reasoning, and social cognition, and therefore foster more effective and pleasurable learning experiences (Cohn and Fredrickson 2009; Fredrickson 2001). But even more importantly, while being just fleeing moments, positive emotions build long lasting resources that can later be accessed in challenging situations. Associating exposure to L2 resources in the Wild with positive emotions can make learners more resilient in more difficult aspects of learning a language (i.e., parts of the formal instruction; Lech 2018). This adds to lifelong perseverance in learning another language.

Lech's (2018) study indicated that the emotions for learners engaged in learning German stayed consistently positive in both OILL and traditional learning groups, however, only for the participants who persevered in the entire intervention of 10 hours of learning. Given that three times more participants completed the full study, Lech suggested that learners exposed to OILL and experiencing positive emotions during this engagement are three times more likely to persevere in learning. Additionally, since all participants were highly motivated German learners who engaged in the study for the mere reason of enhancing their German skills, it is highly likely that less motivated learners would not even constitute the one third of participants in the traditional learning group (Lech 2018).

## OILL fosters a true cultural immersion

Language learning is essentially formed by social practice, experience, and socialization (Clark et al. 2011), and it is often argued that authentic experiences with the language (Kemmer and Barlow 2000) cannot happen behind the classroom door (Clark et al. 2011). Learning happens "through practice…in the everyday activities of communities of language users" (Duff and Talmy 2011, 96), and L2 learners often not only have the goal of speaking another language but also of becoming a part of its community and engaging in the social and cultural environment of that language (Wagner 2015). Thus, language learning through real usage events can only happen *in the wild* – that is, through unplanned and unanticipated interactions with native speakers handling a situation in the L2 (Wagner 2015).

According to Verspoor (2017, 144), "language is not a system on its own, but is part of, interrelated with, and embedded in our cultural, sociological, and psychological lives, each of these levels interacting over time with the other." The central function of language is to interact socially, and language learning is "part and parcel of social and cultural learning, a holistic process within a social and cultural context, in which cognitive development also plays a role" (144). It is essentially formed by social practice, experience, and socialization, and while adults build their L2 skills on already acquired languages, they still learn language in their social practice (Clark et al. 2011, 1). Thus, it is necessary to rethink the ideology and practice of second language teaching and learning and to "understand the challenge as a social and not solely a linguistics one" (Clark et al. 2011, 2).

OILL represents language with all its socio-cultural characteristics and linguistic variations and perhaps does so better than any other instructional and theoretical approach. It constitutes an organic version of the linguistic and cultural worlds that are the mirror of the reality present in an L2 community. Having no local or other limitations, it may be even a more accessible source of socio-cultural reality. L2 learners, using OILL resources, are able to participate in the online version of the context, practice, and "everyday activities of communities of language users" (Wagner 2015, 75). OILL users can become "part of social and cultural environment in which this language is used" (75). Watching movies, series, shows, or programs, interacting on social media, reading forums or articles, or listening to music all ensure a direct or indirect contact with the L2 culture.

**OILL is informal and why that matters**

As Cross (2007, 17) notes: "Most learning experiences blend both formal and informal aspects. Sometimes public transport is the best way to get somewhere; other times it's better to take one's own path." Yet, in many classrooms the necessity for mutual support of formal and informal learning is ignored. In a typical foreign language (FL) classroom, while there is a lot of pressure on teachers to use authentic materials and communication, teachers are often confused as to how to navigate between the textbook (e.g., teaching students rules of conjugations) and authentic materials (often filled with grammar that has not been discussed in class). Allowing students to be more autonomous and engage on their own in wild experiences with the L2 is an example of *taking one's own path*, as contrasted with the *public transport* of carefully designed instruction. Supplementing classroom instruction with OILL exemplifies the blending of formal and informal learning.

Informal learning is important in L2 learning for several reasons. First, learning another language is a life-long process. Whoever wants to achieve a working level of an L2 must engage in language-related activities far beyond the end of classroom instruction. Another reason informal learning is important for success in learning an L2 is that any learning of an L2 in a classroom is merely an introduction to basic rules, words, and structures. Learning strategies and ways of extracting knowledge of constructions and language elements (e.g., words, structures, grammatical rules) from formal and informal materials and events contribute to the development of successful language learners. Unfortunately, these skills are rarely taught in FL classes; instead, determined or gritty students figure them out on their own, leaving the majority of the less gritty ones at loss. The source of these skills and methods for teaching them lie in the realm of informal learning.

**Why we need to domesticate OILL**

With the current affordances of technology and common engagement in the virtual worlds, especially in case of younger learners, it may be hard to believe that students are not already engaging in OILL. And yet, Lech's (2018) study indicated that out of 57 highly motivated intermediate to advanced German learners, only 16.1% of participants admitted to engaging in any OILL-like activities often or sometimes. The vast majority of 21.6% and 57.5% reported engaging in OILL-like activities rarely or never, respectively (58). These results suggest that even highly motivated and apparently autonomous learners shy away from the Virtual Wild.

While the reasons for these numbers may lie in reliance on an educational environment (i.e., a class) as the exclusive medium of knowledge as well as the common lack of trust in the informal uncontrolled environments (Lech 2018; Sockett 2014), it is important to acknowledge that it is also difficult to immerse oneself into a completely unfamiliar Wild environment, especially for beginning or intermediate language learners (Lech 2018). Moreover, English is the dominant language of the Web worldwide, and for native English speakers who are learners of other languages, it is particularly difficult to fight through the automatic translations and array of tools and extensions that make browsing in a community in which English is a dominant language a rather monolingual experience and may almost give an impression there is no other language in the world.

Thus, building a merger of OILL and traditional instruction has the potential for being an ultimate language learning experience with meaningful and positive environments and well-designed scaffolded support.

## Part II: How to build a merger

In this section, I propose a pedagogical approach, based on existing research and theoretical underpinnings, to implement OILL into the language classroom instruction. The design of this merger is based on two studies: The Icelandic Village study, a project of implementing the experience of L2 learners in the specially designed Wild environments in an L2 community, and Language Learning in the Virtual Wild study, which compared learners exposed to L2 in traditional instructional setting and in the Virtual Wild (=OILL) setting.

As next, I suggest how the domesticating of OILL can be organized in four main steps: 1) Building the OILL library; 2) Creating OILL activities; 3) Guidance through the Wild; and 4) Making space for OILL in the instructional program. I describe each step with attention to not stripping the wild activities from their Wild character and preserving all linguistically and psychologically positive elements of OILL.

### The Icelandic Village Project

The Icelandic Village Project was hosted by the University of Iceland and described by Wagner as "a project that builds bridges between the classroom of early newcomers and the everyday life in Iceland" (2015, 93). It is an example of designing language learning in the Wild (Clark et al. 2011; Eskildsen 2009; Wagner 2015). Wagner borrowed the term "in the wild" from Hutchins (1995) who described the learning conditions in everyday environments as unstructured and depending on real life events and reactions. He argued that bringing the lab tools into the wild creates an opportunity to truly understand the actual occurrence. Following this concept, Clark, Wagner, Lindemalm, Bendt (2011) and Wagner (2015) argue that L2 learning in the wild should be *connected* to traditional classroom instruction rather than kept separate at the discretion of the already more autonomous learners. Activities in the classroom can initiate, form and support language practice and learning outside of it, and, in turn, activities in the wild can be harvested and reflected on to strengthen language learning and develop resources for language learners (Clark et al. 2011).

The Icelandic Village Project came from the need to expand the repertoire of situations familiar and mostly predictable for the newcomers to develop their flexibility in a variety of new situations and to expand their growing localized second language competence (Wagner, 2015). It was dictated by the challenge of limited possibilities to use the local language "since the friendly locals happily switch to English when they are approached in an obviously non-fluent version of the local language" (Wagner 2015, 93).

The organizers of the project established a network of service places (e.g., cafes, bakeries, bookstores, libraries) where newcomers were welcome to exercise their Icelandic. The *friendly locals* in those places would not switch to English whenever a challenge appeared, but rather allowed the newcomers develop their skills in Icelandic. The Village, thus, constituted "a protected language arena for newly arrived foreign language students" (Wagner 2015, 94). The newcomers were able to spend time in the Village to observe and learn how locals organize their activities and learn about their culture. Moreover, they were able to video-record their activities and encounters to discuss them later in detail in the class.

While all visits to the Village were carefully planned through various role-plays and activities similar to those used in a typical language classroom, the stories and recordings that students brought back from their excursions revealed interesting and often surprising insights. For example, such simple everyday tasks like ordering a coffee would often bring in multiple challenges and rarely ever go "by the book" (Wagner 2015, 94). Wagner (2015) summarizes that "going out into the wild is not helpful *per se* but that newcomers need support, coaching, and debriefing to normalize the sense they give to unexpected experiences" (94). This idea also stands at the core of the hereby proposed approach and is a response to the common reluctance of advocating for OILL.

### The Language Learning in the Virtual Wild

The Icelandic Village Project, as well as previous studies on online informal learning of English (OILE) became the groundwork for a study called Language Learning in the Virtual Wild. The study proposed designing a "Virtual Wild" (Lech 2018, 5) learning environment and compared such learning with a more traditional textbook-based setting. Both settings were designed as online learning environments, gathering either a) OILL resources in the experimental setting or b) traditional textbook activities in the control setting. The target language of the study was German as an example of a commonly taught foreign language in the U.S. and a language different than English (the only language used in research on OILL at the time of the study was English).

The study created a digital library of resources in either condition, organized in comparable seven thematic modules on topics: family life and me, love and relationships, community and environment, leisure time, work and learning, everyday life, and media and science. The content of the modules, however, included different materials and activities centered around the thematic lexical items for the two groups. The control group involved more specific thematic subcategories like "family life" and "me" (in the first module) and so on. Each module also included the subcategory of "Grammar." The organization of the control condition of traditional textbook-based learning mirrored a typical instructional program.

The experimental condition exposing the participants to OILL, on the other hand, employed subcategories of the types of resources: readings, music, films, funny programs, media, social media, television, and games. They were still in the area of each Module's topic but did not focus on any specific language items other than a general connection to the theme. To mirror the idea of supporting learning in the wild, both groups of participants were told that the teacher is always at their disposal and they could contact her with any questions. Interestingly, only the experimental group participants reached out with questions and ideas, some quite often, usually inquiring about the meaning of words and phrases in the specific contexts (e.g., songs). The control group participants almost never asked questions, despite the control condition being a very teacher-dependent method of learning. This may suggest that learners engaged in cultural products they liked for their own sake, rather than for the purpose of studying the language, were more interested in the object of their attention (the questions were as much about the meanings of the words as of the cultural background or circumstances) and wanted to dig deeper, planting the first seed to develop autonomous learning skills in L2.

The Language Learning in the Virtual Wild study showed that designing a Virtual Wild environment, mirroring the Icelandic Village project, is not only possible but also brings in positive results; fosters students' engagement, intrinsic motivation, and resilience;[1] and can be created for any language other than English (Lech 2018). Thus, it seems prudent that the next step is creating strategies for 1) preparing learners for the visits to the 'Virtual Wild Village' and 2) creating time and space in the classroom for learners bringing their experiences in. I argue that such a merger based on similar successful attempts and positive research results may be an ultimate way to enhance language instruction and give language learners not only unique language

---

[1] The referenced study resulted in three times more learners completing the project (10 hours of the intervention) in the OILL setting than in the traditional one. Read more about the study and results in Lech, 2018.

skills and culture knowledge but also teach them to be independent self-learners necessary when anybody wants to become a proficient speaker of any language.

**Step 1: Building the OILL library**

Based on these two ideas of a) designing for the Wild, and b) gathering a digital collection of OILL resources, I propose to build an OILL library for use in every language classroom. To create a library of OILL resources, it is critical to understand what constitutes OILL and what does not. In the richness of resources available online, it is easy to fall into the trap of using resources that qualify as CALL or to strip OILL of its incidental or choice-conditioned character. Thus, it is important to remember that true OILL means the learner has an absolute choice to engage in an activity and select its type. The learner's engagement in a more instructional type of a resource can still qualify as OILL as long as the learner chooses it on their own. Thus, I propose not including such resources in the library but instructing students that they can explore any types of activities they wish. The OILL library should only be the starting point, everything in it is merely a gate to the actual Wild that needs to be explored on their own by every student based on their likings, interests, and passions but with the teacher's scaffolded guidance.

Below, I list examples of OILL resources that could be compiled in the library.

1. To watch: movies (original or translation, but if the latter, then with dubbing), television series, telenovelas, television programs, shows, reality TV, videos of different nature, vlogs, short movies, filmed interviews and talks, talk-shows, comedy shows, concerts, documentaries, reportages, news and all elements of the news (e.g., weather forecast or sport reportage), cartoons, children television (e.g., Sesame Street), commercials, and similar.

2. To read: books, original or translated (novels, short stories, dramas), poetry, newspaper and magazine articles, street and place signs, children stories, fairy tales, and other literary works, any descriptions, blogs, forums, social media posts, written or illustrated jokes, and similar.

3. To listen: music, radio programs, interviews and conversations, radio news and commercials, audiobooks, podcasts, stories, and similar.

4. To interact: social media (e.g., Facebook/Instagram interest pages and groups, Twitter interest accounts or accounts of famous people), chat

(e.g., chat with other L2 speakers), interest forum websites (e.g., Reddit), interest forums and groups (e.g., Slack, Discord), music communities or groups (e.g., YouTube channels or Spotify), synchronous video games (e.g., Day of Defeat), online virtual reality games like Second Life, etc.

5.  To play: a virtual version of Hangman game, crossword puzzles, psychological tests (e.g., the types from magazines), various word building games (usually phone apps), and similar.

It is important to note that building the library does not belong to the teacher only, but rather it should be a collective work of the teacher and all students. This is how OILL remains in its organic format and also saves the teacher's time. However, because many students need help being introduced to the Wild and guiding them, especially in the beginning, the teacher must be the organizer of the library and of the guidance practices. One way to employ an OILL library is to begin with a few categories like music, movies/videos, readings/websites, or similar. Each category, besides the OILL resources, should include possible places where other OILL resources can be found. However, it is also important to make the search as easy and guided as possible, including a rich list of examples, items to be searched, names of people, musicians, movies, programs, etc. since, especially the beginners, will not know what to search for even if they know where.

### Step 2: Creating OILL Activities

To embed OILL in the class program, the teacher needs to create a meaningful set of activities. These activities cannot be activities like a cloze test on a song or a mandatory watching of one movie with a follow-up quiz or exercise. The guiding idea for creating OILL activities is not to instructionalize OILL but rather to invite students into the Wild and engage them in the joy of discovering and sharing. Some possibilities for activities fostering such an engagement could be 1) Building chunks of the OILL library; 2) Choosing the best song/video/show/movie/commercial/audiobook/podcast, etc.; 3) Creating a playlist of songs, movies, shows, vlogs, etc.; 4) Sharing findings in class presentations; 5) Sharing findings in Discussion Forums; 6) Setting up a social media account or computer in L2 and sharing experiences; 7) Keeping a journal (individual or group) on experiences in the Wild, etc.

### Step 3: Guidance through the Wild

A crucial part of embedding OILL into the regular instruction is the scaffolded support of the teacher and other students. One of the most problematic aspects of the Wild is how difficult it is to explore in the English-dominated world (particularly the virtual part of it). It can also become very easily overwhelming, especially for the lower-level learners (Lech and Harris 2018; Lech 2018). This guidance should be based on Vygotsky's (1978) concept of the zone of proximal development (ZPD), which stipulates that through interacting with more knowledgeable peers (here: the teacher and other students), one gradually develops an independent problem-solving mechanism.

With this scaffolded guidance, learners, even those who engage in wild experiences on their own, have a valuable resource in the person of their teacher to help them understand many aspects of the wild language that they encounter (Clark et al. 2011; Eskildsen 2009; Lech 2018; Wagner 2015). The teacher is the first to open the gate to the Wild and to lead the learner through this domesticated version of it, supporting the learner with not only examples of the resources themselves but also with strategies and ways of handling them and being around when needed for immediate help. They can not only explain the language, structures, or cultural circumstances for the learner's Wild experience but also lead them through more focused steps to find out more about the topic or to practice observed language through structured activities and build on them. This support can not only enhance learners' skills but also encourage them to undertake an autonomous exploration of similar activities.

### Step 4: Embedding OILL in the course program

For many instructors, embedding OILL may seem difficult in the limited class time and with a prescribed textbook or program of learning. However, it is worth rethinking the typical structure of the course and finding elements for which OILL may be a good substitute. For example, many textbooks have a cultural component that involves reading a short text about a cultural aspect of the L2 with a short quiz or exercise as a follow-up. OILL content, however, may be a source of much richer cultural information than many specifically crafted cultural notes in the textbook. One does not necessarily have to cut all cultural textbook components, but some of them could be easily substituted by engagement in the authentic L2 culture. The advantage of OILL is the fact that if a learner finds their niche of interest, they will probably spend more time with the L2 input than could ever be fostered in traditional class time or homework. Thus, whichever part needs to be given up making place for OILL, that part would rather be a very small sacrifice for a much greater good.

Many will argue that OILL is only possible with higher level (at least intermediate) learners. However, many more autonomous language learners engage in frequent music listening, watch L2 movies (although perhaps with subtitles in their L1), chat with other L2 speakers, or watch short simple videos. While more difficult, it is possible to find feasible resources for language beginners. Embedding OILL in the instruction does not mean full comprehension of all resources but rather exposure to meaningful (because if interesting, it will have unique meaning for the learner) input to the L2 and to its pronunciation, melody, and cultural background. And understanding even just a few words in a song or movie makes a learner feel excited about the learning experience and more intrinsically motivated. Moreover, combining OILL with class instruction, especially with lower-level learners, fosters an opportunity for learners to have the teacher's support at all times and, thus, develop their L2 abilities and particularly their autonomous learning skills.

### Conclusion

In today's world it may often seem that time and space are fiction and never before, we have such an easy access to the farthest places on earth with just a click of a mouse or tap of a finger. Traditional paper textbooks become less and less popular, teachers are more and more often reaching out to and creating Open Educational Resources to find instructional materials that don't break a student's bank but are also more current, not expiring every few years, and most of all, are available in the digital format. Finally, the Covid-19 pandemic suddenly moved all education online and showed us how much and how fast we need to change. All these changes and the influence of technology changes also the role of the teacher from that of the leader in the know to a guide, facilitator, enabler. Verspoor (2017) suggests that "teacher's job should not be to teach but to create an environment in which an optimal learning path for each individual can be accomplished." But we also need to make sure that our foreign language students are ready for this change and for taking ownership of their learning of also foreign languages.

There are certainly many paths to learn a language, and every student has to find the right one for themselves. The educational changes that have happened in the last few years, for the first time, make it possible to raise truly autonomous learners in a constructivist pedagogy environment. With little help like through domesticating the Virtual Wild environments, they can get there much faster. Exposure, meaningful language use, and cognitive, emotional, and social engagement are essential in learning a new language (Verspoor 2017) and embedding OILL into a formal instruction is an easy, fast, and effective way to ensure creating these circumstances.

## Bibliography

Benson, Phil. 2001. "Teaching and researching learner autonomy." Harlow: Pearson Education.

Blyth, Carl. 2018. "Immersive technologies and language learning." *Foreign Language Annals* 51 (1): 225-232.

Bybee, Joan. 2008. "Usage-based grammar and second language acquisition." In *Handbook of cognitive linguistics and second language acquisition*, edited by Peter Robinson & Nick C. Ellis, 216–236. Routledge.

Bybee, Joan. 2010. *Language, usage and cognition.* Cambridge University Press.

Candy, Philip C. 1991. *Self-Direction for Lifelong Learning. A Comprehensive Guide to Theory and Practice.* Jossey-Bass, 350 Sansome Street, San Francisco, CA 94104-1310.

Clark, Brendon, Johannes Wagner, Karl Lindemalm, and Olof Bendt. 2011. "Språkskap: Supporting Second Language Learning 'In the Wild.'" *Språkskap: Supporting Second Language Learning In 'The Wild'.*

Cohn, Michael A., and Barbara L. Fredrickson. 2009. "Positive emotions." *Oxford handbook of positive psychology* 2, 13-24.

Cole, Jason, and Robert Vanderplank. 2016. "Comparing autonomous and class-based learners in Brazil: Evidence for the present-day advantages of informal, out-of-class learning." *System* 61, 31-42.

Cross, Jay. 2007. *Informal Learning.* San Francisco, CA: Pfeiffer.

Duff, Patricia A., and Steven Talmy. 2011. "Language socialization approaches to second language acquisition." *Alternative approaches to second language acquisition*, 96-116.

Ellis, Nick C. 2003. "Constructions, chunking, and connectionism: The emergence of second language structure." *The Handbook of second language acquisition* 14, 63.

Ellis, Nick C. 2006. "Cognitive perspectives on SLA: The associative-cognitive CREED." *Aila Review* 19 (1): 100-121.

Eskildsen, Søren W. 2009. "Constructing another language—Usage-based linguistics in second language acquisition." *Applied linguistics* 30 (3): 335-357.

Fredrickson, Barbara L. 2001. "The role of positive emotions in positive psychology: The broaden-and-build theory of positive emotions." *American psychologist* 56 (3): 218.

Gettys, Serafima, and Iwona Lech. 2013. "Cognitive perspective in SLA: Pedagogical implications for enhancing oral proficiency in foreign languages." *Journal of the National Council of Less Commonly Taught Languages* 13, 51-69.

Godwin-Jones, Robert. 2019. "In a World of SMART Technology, Why Learn Another Language?" *Journal of Educational Technology & Society* 22 (2): 4-13.

Goldberg, Adele E. 2009. "The nature of generalization in language." *Cognitive Linguistics* 20 (1): 93-127.

Holec, Henri. 1981. *Autonomy and foreign language learning.* Pergamon Press.

Horwitz, Elaine K., Michael B. Horwitz, and Joann Cope. 1986. "Foreign language classroom anxiety." *The Modern language journal* 70 (2): 125-132.

Hutchins, Edwin. 1995. *Cognition in the Wild.* MIT press.

Jiang, Jiahong. 2019. "An Investigation into Chinese College English Teachers' Beliefs of Students' Web-based Informal Language Learning." In *Computer-Assisted Language Learning: Concepts, Methodologies, Tools, and Applications*, 1717-1729. IGI Global.

Kemmer, Suzanne, and Michael Barlow. 2000. "Introduction: A usage-based conception of language." *Usage-based models of language*, 7-28.

Krashen, Stephen D. 1985. *The input hypothesis: Issues and implications.* Addison-Wesley Longman Limited.

Lech, Iwona Barbara. 2018. *Language learning in the virtual wild: The influence of emotions on learning another language in informal virtual environments.* Northern Illinois University.

Lech, Iwona B., and Lindsay N. Harris. 2019. "Language learning in the virtual wild." In *Teaching language and teaching literature in virtual environments*, pp. 39-54. Springer, Singapore.

Little, David. 1994. "Learner autonomy: A theoretical construct and its practical application." *Die Neueren Sprachen* 93 (5): 430-442.

Richards, Jack C., and Theodore S. Rodgers. 2014. *Approaches and methods in language teaching.* Cambridge University Press.

Roed, Jannie. 2003. "Language learner behaviour in a virtual environment." *Computer assisted language learning* 16 (2-3): 155-172.

Schunk, Dale H. 1996. "Learning theories." *Printice Hall Inc., New Jersey* 53.

Sockett, Geoffrey. 2014. *The online informal learning of English.* Springer.

Taylor, John. R. 2008. "Language in the mind." In *33rd International LAUD Symposium, Cognitive Approaches to Second/Foreign Language Processing: Theory and Pedagogy*, 856-882. Prepaper, Series A.

Tomasello, Michael. 2009. "The usage-based theory of language acquisition." In *The Cambridge handbook of child language*, 69-87. Cambridge University Press.

Tyler, Andrea E., Lourdes Ortega, Mariko Uno, and Hae In Park. 2018. *Usage-inspired L2 instruction: Researched pedagogy.* Vol. 49. Amsterdam: John Benjamins Publishing Company.

Versppooor, Marjolijn. 2017. "Complex dynamic systems theory and 12 pedagogy." In *Complexity theory and language development: In celebration of Diane Larsen-Freeman*, edited by L. Orgega and Z. H. Han. Amsterdam: John Benjamins Publishing Company.

Vygotsky, Lev S. 1978. *Mind in society: The development of higher psychological processes.* Cambridge, MA: Harvard University Press.

Wagner, Johannes. 2015. "Designing for language learning in the wild: Creating social infrastructures for second language learning." *Usage-based perspectives on second language learning* 75, 101.

Chapter 9

# The Kubo Project: Content-Language-Technology Integration through Literature

Kim Yong-Taek
*Georgia Institute of Technology*

Shin Seung-hwan
*University of Pittsburgh*

Lee Mina
*Defense Language Institute Foreign Language Center, Monterey*

Yi Hyunkyu[1]
*Columbia University*

**Abstract**: The Kubo project proposes new pedagogical models for advanced Korean language education in response to the growing demand of upper-level courses as a consequence of the steady growth of student registration in Korean language programs. The goal of this project is twofold: integration of both content and technology into language learning. This project understands content and new educational technologies to be not simply supplementary but intrinsic to language education, and seeks to develop a holistic pedagogy where language, content, and technology are all coordinated into an organic relationship. For content, this project turns to literature—more specifically, texts all built on a fictional *flâneur* writer named

---

[1] Korean names follow the East Asian custom where the last name precedes the first name without a comma. For transliteration of Korean words, the Yale Romanization system is used except for proper nouns that already have widely adopted spellings.

Kubo and his observations of Seoul's social and cultural landscapes at different historical junctures from the colonial period to the present. This project also argues that new educational technologies are essential to the learning experience, especially for young learners, and experiments with new forms and platforms of presentation and publication. In doing so, this project aspires to contribute to the ongoing endeavors to readjust language pedagogies for the present environment that becomes ever more multicultural, multilingual, and technologically mediated.

**Keywords**: Korean as a foreign language, technology integration, holistic pedagogy, innovation, language education.

***

## 1. Introduction

Most foreign language programs across the U.S. have witnessed a continuous decline in class registration in the past decade or so. On the other hand, the Korean language programs have shown a steady growth (Looney and Lusin 2019). In tandem with this trend, the demand for upper-level classes has also risen. As a result, fulfilling the mounting demand for advanced Korean language education has now become one of the most pressing issues for Korean language educators. The Kubo project grew out of the endeavors to meet this challenge. To that end, this project experiments with the integration of literature into language learning. Theoretically, it would be inspired by the Content and Language Integrated Learning (CLIL) approach, which is simply for learning the target language through contents (Coyle, Hood, and Marsh 2010; Ball, Kelly, and Clegg 2015). The CLIL theory has been widely studied and put into use all over the world. Yet few efforts have been made to apply it to Korean language education. Furthermore, there has been little discussion on the use of literature for CLIL practices. The Kubo project thus aspires to fill the voids by developing a viable pedagogy for content-integrated Korean language education and by using literary texts as the vehicle for CLIL-oriented practices.

The Kubo project also regards new educational technologies as central to the innovation of language learning. This question becomes even more important when we consider how much our communication is mediated by current technology. New technological tools are proven to be essential to the learning experience, especially for young learners. This project is particularly concerned with how to incorporate new technological tools into some major learning activities, such as presentation and publication. In technology-integrated CLIL, new presentation tools or platforms are not only a means of presentation. As shown in studies like the Substitution Augmentation Modification Redefinition (SAMR) model (Puentedura 2009), they are not supplementary but rather integral to the content, form, and quality of presentation. The Kubo project thus seeks to develop a pedagogical model based on both content and the integration of technology.

Before outlining the Kubo project, however, this paper takes a moment to provide a brief overview of the CLIL method to clarify the theoretical premises of the project. This will be followed by a discussion on content integration: more specifically, how to reconfigure the CLIL approach in order to integrate literature into Korean language courses. The literary works for this project consist of four Kubo texts, which all focus on a fictional *flâneur* novelist character named Kubo and provide a journey through Seoul's social and cultural landscapes at different historical junctures: "Soselka kwupossi-uy ilil" (*A day in the life of Mr. Kubo, the novelist,* Pak Taewon 1934); *Soselka kwupossi-uy ilil* (*A day in the life of Mr. Kubo, the novelist,* Choi In-hoon 1969-1972); *Kemun sangche-uy pullwusu: Soselka kwupossi-uy halwu* (*Blues of the black wound: One day of Novelist Kubo,* Joo In-seok 1991-1995); and *Sewul akheyitu phuloceykthu* (*Seoul arcade project,* Yoo Sin 2013). The following section answers the question of technology integration and discusses its rationale and creative ways of blending new technological tools into CLIL projects. Finally, this paper closes with an explanation of this project's effectiveness and contributions it is expected to make in order to advance language education programs and scholarship on technology-integrated CLIL.

## 2. CLIL: History, theory, and practice

### 2.1 History and theory

The concept of CLIL began to receive serious attention in Europe in the 1990s (Coyle 2007). Given its ties to the multilingual environment in Europe, the concept dates back to the 1960s when Europe began to stress multilingualism. The origin of CLIL reminds us of a truth that is fundamental not only to the concept itself, but also to language education, in general. Language can never be taken independently of the society where it is shaped and reshaped. In other words, language education cannot be separated from the history and culture that is inherent in it. In that sense, CLIL can be held as an endeavor to reverse the institutionalized division of disciplines and return to the historical and cultural origin of language.

Accordingly, CLIL has generally been understood as a dual-focused educational approach, where a second or additional language is used for the learning and teaching of both content and language (Coyle, Hood, and Marsh 2010). More specifically, CLIL underscores four essential elements in language education: *content, cognition, communication,* and *culture.* They are all inextricably connected as a whole. Figure 9.1 (Coyle, Hood, and Marsh 2010) illustrates how they are intertwined with one another.

**Figure 9.1.** The 4C's Framework

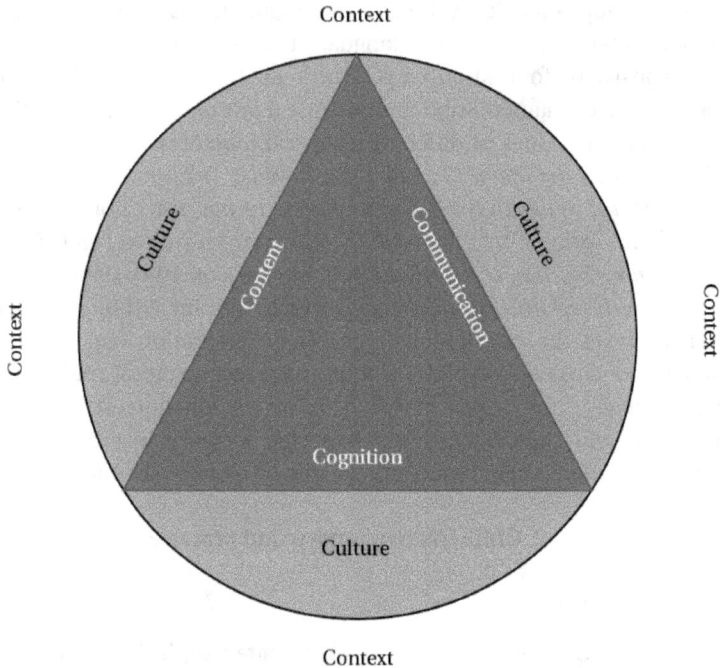

(adapted from Coyle, Hood, and Marsh 2010)

*Content* means the progression in knowledge, skills, and understanding regarding specific elements of a defined curriculum. It is content that determines the learning route. *Communication* refers to the learners' use of language in learning the content, which goes beyond the grammar system. *Cognition* is related to the development of higher-order thinking skills (i.e., analysis, evaluation, and creation) and lower-order thinking skills (i.e., memory, understanding, application). Lastly, *culture* is a thread which weaves its way as a circle throughout the topic. It concerns how exposure to alternative perspectives and understanding of different cultures and languages deepen awareness of both others and oneself.

## 2.2 Comparison with content-based instruction (CBI) and immersion

The Comparison of CLIL with other approaches such as Content-Based Instruction (CBI) and Immersion theory (Thompson and McKinley 2018) may help to enhance our understanding of CLIL's benefits. First, there are some similarities between CLIL and CBI. Above all, both have a dual focus on language and content. However, CLIL aims to advance the skills of cognition and social interaction, while CBI is more geared towards the use of contents to enhance the effectiveness of language learning. In this sense, CLIL also differs from Immersion. Immersion has also been widely adopted to promote multilingual education. At its core, however, this dive-and-swim strategy is largely concerned with greater exposure to contents. CLIL, on the other hand, sees language and content indivisibly intertwined with each other and intends to coordinate them together into the learning process.

**Figure 9.2.** Comparison of CBI, CLIL, and Immersion

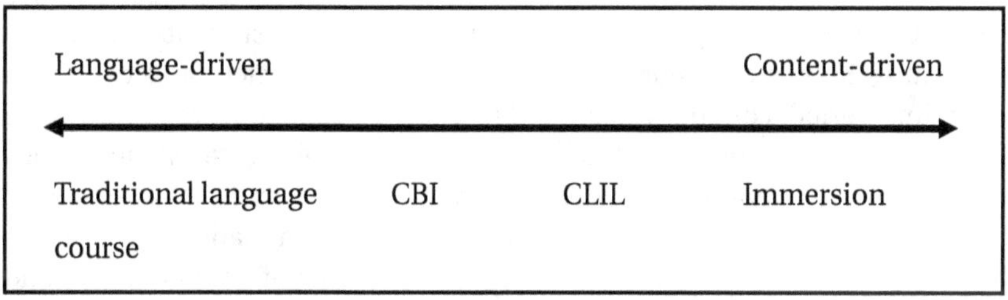

| Language-driven | | | Content-driven |
|---|---|---|---|
| ← | | | → |
| Traditional language course | CBI | CLIL | Immersion |

(adapted from Thompson and McKinley 2018)

Herein lies another justification for the use of CLIL in upper-level language learning. CBI relatively leans towards language, whereas Immersion tilts more towards content. On the other hand, CLIL seeks a balance between content and language. A holistic approach is central to an advanced language course; it requires a setting in which cognition, communication, and social interaction are all intertwined in an organic relationship and complement one another. The Kubo project does not focus on one particular side. It aims to help the language learner to recognize and understand history and culture in language and thereby gain a higher level of competence in the use of the target language.

## 3. The Kubo project and content integration

One of the major goals of the Kubo project is the integration of content into language learning. To that end, it turns to literature, more specifically, Kubo texts. This section is concerned with offering a pedagogical model for the task.

Kubo, a fictional novelist character, was first invented against the backdrop of colonial Kyengseng (old Seoul) by Pak Taewon in "A day in the life of Mr. Kubo, the novelist." This *flâneur* character has repeatedly been summoned to different historical junctures by later-generation writers, such as Choi In-hoon (*A day in the life of Kubo, the novelist*), Joo In-seok (*Blues of the black wound: One day of Novelist Kubo*), and Yoo Sin (*Seoul arcade project*). The central story-building strategy shared by all these four Kubo texts is Kubo's daily drift around Seoul and observation of Seoul's social and cultural landscape. Thus, these texts present a rich archive packed with a wealth of notable political, economic, social, cultural, and linguistic references to urban life and its transformations in Korea. In this respect, this Kubo archive can be put to creative use for an exploration of modern Korean history and society.

Drawing upon Kubo's journeys (and his *flâneur*-like gazes) in and around Seoul in four different time periods (the 1930s, the 1960s-1970s, the 1980s-1990s, and the 2010s), this Kubo project aims to develop a pedagogy for content-integrated language education. In this venture, students are guided to identify Kubo's engaging observations of Korean society and culture in each time period, conduct student-led research by expanding on topics taken from Kubo's reflections, and finally publish their research results in various new forms of presentation. Students, thereby, can acquire both an advanced language skill set—reading, writing, listening, speaking, and even Korean-language research skills—and a deeper understanding of Korean history and culture. In this project, language and content are not only supplementary to each other. In many language classes, historical and cultural materials are randomly chosen, largely to make language learning more interesting. This strategy may appear effective in the short term, but in the long term, it does not bode well because it does not help in sustaining the students' interest in language learning up to the advanced stages. As a language learner moves to upper levels, motivation, or the purpose of learning the language, becomes much more important. In turn, the practical use of language helps the learner gain advanced knowledge of the target language. Thus, in an advanced language class, it becomes imperative to carefully integrate 'things students learn the language for' into language learning. Therefore, at its core, the Kubo project aims to develop a pedagogy that makes creative use of content sources to galvanize students into an enduring endeavor for both a greater understanding of Korean society and a more advanced knowledge of the Korean language. In doing so, this project also seeks to reinforce the symbiotic relations between language and content programs, while enhancing the synergy between them.

Although the Kubo texts can be used in varying manners in different settings, this study suggests four steps as fundamental to any variation: research topic selection, research guidance, student-led research, and publication. Hinging on the four Kubo texts, the model for this study is structured into four sessions. Each session begins with research topic selection, which includes text reading, discussion, and selection of the research topic. The class reads and discusses a chapter, or an excerpt carefully chosen from the original text (each of the four Kubo texts). Reading the entire original text is unnecessary: first, because this project's premise is not literary study; and second, because a chapter or a passage in all the Kubo texts can be read independently. Furthermore, they are built on Kubo's daily journeys, rendered in a stream-of-consciousness manner, and are loosely connected. Nonetheless, text reading requires an effective introduction that would help students be equipped with basic knowledge—such as contextual information, the rationale behind text selection, and the objective of the classwork—and that triggers them into a productive discussion. Text reading and discussion can also include such activities as translation workshop, which can challenge students to enrich both their knowledge of vernacular expressions and understanding of historical and cultural implications in the text. Finally, the discussion will be followed by research topic selection. A research topic can be selected entirely by students, or the instructor can provide suggested topics for them to choose from. A sample topic introduced for the present study is *tapang* (teahouse; 茶房) culture, which includes café (*khaphey*) and coffee shop (*khephisyoph*)— for other possible topics, refer to "Variations."

Once the research topic is determined, the instructor provides students with guidance on their research. The guidance includes both research instruction and information of research resources such as major archives (libraries, museums), popular search engines, special exhibitions, and important locations. This guidance intends to help students gain both foundational knowledge of research resources and Korean language research skills and experiences. As the class moves to the research phase, the instructor monitors research progress and assists students who experience researcher's block. At the final stage, students will present their research results in various modes of presentation—this issue will be discussed in more depth in Section 4.

### 3.1 Research topic selection: History of *tapang* culture

*Tapang*, café, or coffee shop has been a key part of the cultural fabric of modern Korean society. *Tapang* has a special validity for a physiognomic reading of Korean culture and its changes over time—from early to late modernity (Moon et al. 2019; Oh 2017; Woo 2010; Son 2002; Kim 1997). It has been central to social interactions particularly as a space that has mediated much of Korean daily life between home and the workplace. The history of *tapang* culture, thus, offers a fascinating glimpse of sociocultural life in Korea and its transformation as well. *Tapang* indeed occupies an important place in the topology of Kubo's everyday life in all four texts. At the same time, however, it assumes distinct social and cultural meanings in each of them. For Pak's Kubo, it is an indispensable space of his daily drift in the 1930s colonial Kyengseng (old Seoul), as he frequents it to rest his enervated body, to wait for his friends, or to watch the patterns of people's behaviors for his modernology, or archeology of modern society. For Choi's Kubo, too, *tapang* is also a routine part of his daily outing. For a novelist like Kubo who does not belong to any company or organization, it is a place to do business, chat with colleagues, kill time between meetings, or catch some breaking news on TV. In the life of Joo's Kubo, a former political activist struggling with rapid changes after democratization in the early 1990s, *tapang* largely appears in marginal spaces and its imagery is also permeated with negative connotations. Nevertheless, or because of that, his sketch of the *tapang* culture in the 1980s and 1990s presents a valuable glimpse of Korea's social and cultural climate during that period. In the last decade, *tapang* has long given way to large franchise coffee shops such as Tom N Toms Coffee and Starbucks. In these coffee shops, Kubo, conjured up again by Yoo in modern-day Korea, witnesses both the dream of late capitalism or the yearning of Seoul urbanites for a cozy retreat where the accelerated tempo of the heavily populated city can be temporarily suspended.

### 3.2 Text reading and discussion

For reading and discussion, the instructor selects a chapter or a passage with references to *tapang* or coffee shop from each of the Kubo texts. In the case of Pak's text, it is a short story and the entire text is recommended for reading. In Choi's novel, the majority of chapters have one or two scenes set in a *tapang* (Ch. 1, 4, 5, 6, 8, 9, 11, and 13). The instructor can use one of the *tapang* scenes in these chapters. In Joo's novel, there is one remark on Kubo's habit of watching baseball games in a *tabang* and a scene set in a *tapang* both in Chapter 1, and respectively in Section 4 and 10 (pp. 23, 43-45), while Kubo in

Yoo's novel visits Tom N Toms Coffee and Starbucks in Chapter 4 (pp. 161-164, 167-168).

During the discussion, the instructor helps students improve not only their reading skills, but also their recognition of history and culture embedded in language. The instructor challenges them to probe the intricate ways in which *tapang* is depicted—tone, vocabulary, specific references—and reflect on the social and cultural implications embedded in such formal choices. For instance, the instructor encourages students to reflect on questions such as: how *tapang* became a privileged place for intellectuals and their meetings in the 1930s; why Choi's Kubo prefers *kapay* (가배), an outdated term for coffee in the 1970s, to *khephi*, a Korean transliteration of coffee; why the 1990s Kubo portrays *tapang* in a cynical manner; and why Kubo in the 2010s often chooses to work on his writing in a café, with all his deep antipathy toward the capitalist logic in it. In wrestling with questions like these, students can gain a better understanding of the subtle meanings hidden between the lines.

### 3.2.1 Variations

The present model takes *tapang* as the research topic. It is also configured for diachronic research, the evolution of *tapang* culture. However, the Kubo texts are replete with an abundance of intriguing historical and cultural references that can be arranged into various creative research projects. The following table shows possible research topics.

**Table 9.1.** Sample research topics

| Category | Pak's | Choi's | Joo's | Yoo's |
|---|---|---|---|---|
| Politics | Colonial rule | The Cold War order; national division; the thaw between the U.S. and China; the South-North Red Cross Meeting (1971); the Vietnam War | Military Rule; Gwangju Uprising (1980); June Uprising (1987); the end of the Cold War era; incomplete democratization | Post-political era |
| Economy | Great Depression; gold rush; destitute low class | Rapid industrialization | Economic boom; stock market | Late capitalism; consumerism |

| Society | Colonialism; modernization; materialism; unemployed intellectuals; | Cold War paranoia, division ideology, night curfew, hakkwan (hagwon), air pollution (exhaust fumes), counterfeit goods. | Legacy of national division, incomplete democratization, demise of political activism, post-political discourse, postmodernism. | Consumer society; lure of commodities, architectural spectacles; disempowered individuals |
|---|---|---|---|---|
| Architecture/ places | Gwanghwamun; Cong-ro; Hwashin Department Store; Keyngseng Station; Joseon Bank; Joseon Hotel; Hwangkumceng | Gwanghwamun; Gyeongpok Palace; Citizen's Hall; Changgyeongwon (zoo); high-rise buildings; Western-style houses; apartment buildings; *hanok* houses. | Setaymwun Prison; Kicichon; Gyeongpok Palace | 63 Building; Multiplex malls (Yeongdeungpo Time Square, KOEX); department stores; Sewoon Shopping Center; Plaza Hotel; Seoul City Hall; Lotte Hotel; Lotte World |
| Transportation | Streetcar; bicycle | bus; taxi | Bus; taxi; subway | Subway; KTX (high-speed train) |
| Culture (fashion, food, arts, etc.) | New women; romantic love; crisis of marriage customs; phonograph; dandyism; gold watch; jewelry ring | Mini skirt; high heels; Lee Jung-seob (a painter) | Professional baseball; soap operas; Burberry coats; instant coffee (Maxim, Choice) | Arcade; smart phone; multiplex theater; fast food chain; plastic surgery; convenience store |

With these themes and references, students can develop a variety of different research plans. For instance, students can create a project on the developments of the public transportation system in Korea as a way of tracking the change in Seoul's landscape. Yet the research does not have to be on one topic, nor does it have to be diachronic. Choosing a distinct topic in each Kubo text or in each time period will allow students a wider range of options—for instance, a new woman in the 1930s, a mini skirt in the 1970s, instant coffee in the 1980s, and multiplex malls in the 2010s.

### 3.3 Student-led research

The text reading and discussion are followed by group research. Taking their cues from the four Kubo texts, students research the *tapang* culture of each time period when each of the Kubo texts was written: the 1930s, the 1960s-1970s, the 1980s-1990s, and the 2010s. Prior to research, the instructor provides research guidance and primary resources for Korean language research to help students: first, develop valid and practical research plans; and second, gain the skills and knowledge required for research on Korean language materials. Over the course of research, the instructor regularly meets with each research group to monitor their progress and assists students to successfully work through challenges in their way. The major sites for Korean language research include:

- Academic databases: KISS (http://kiss.kstudy.com); RISS (http://www.riss.kr/index.do); DBpia (http://www.dbpia.co.kr).

- Public libraries and archives: National Library of Korea (https://www.nl.go.kr); National Museum of Korean Contemporary History (http://www.much.go.kr); National Archives of Korea (http://www.archives.go.kr/next/viewMain.do); Encyclopedia of Korean Culture (http://encykorea.aks.ac.kr).

- Special archives: Korean National Commission for UNESCO (https://heritage.unesco.or.kr); Seoul History Institute (https://history.seoul.go.kr); 5.18 Archives (https://www.518archives.go.kr); The Seoul Institute (https://www.si.re.kr/); KTV National Broadcasting (https://www.youtube.com/channel/UC8_LPVE4Yuc6KF0opF6uS_w).

- Media archives: KBS, MBC, SBS, and EBS.

- Popular news portals and search engines: Naver, Daum, Google, and YouTube.

### 4. Technology-Integrated CLIL

The final stage of the Kubo project is demonstrating research results with various new technological tools of presentation. In this project, presentation does not only include a report on findings. Students of the new generation often become more engaged in classwork when they can relate it to what they experience in their everyday lives. In other words, new techniques or platforms of presentation are just as important as research is. These elements complement each other. Thus, this project allows students to experiment with various new technological tools such as video essays, vlogs, virtual museums, timeline creators and e-book publishers, rather than relying on conventional methods such as written essays and oral presentations. As students publish their research outcomes through such new technological forms of expression or communication, they not only enhance their new media literacy, but also engage in their research with a greater sense of ownership and responsibility.

## 4.1 Technology integration pedagogy

Over the past decade or so, learning technology has developed rapidly, and the educational environments have also changed significantly. Many new web-based educational tools or programs have been invented and language educators have been particularly keen to embrace these new tools and programs in order to renovate their teaching strategies. However, technology-integrated pedagogy is still new to many due to a dearth of serious research on the issue, and many language instructors continue to struggle to figure out how to successfully integrate such new technologies into their teaching practices. In many cases, they end up using new tools for old content or old approaches. Technology integration does not just include putting it in the service of content. Integration refers to the coordination of content and technology, which are reciprocally engaged with each other. Here, the SAMR model (Puentedura 2009) may help to further clarify the meaning of integration.

**Figure 9.3.** SAMR model

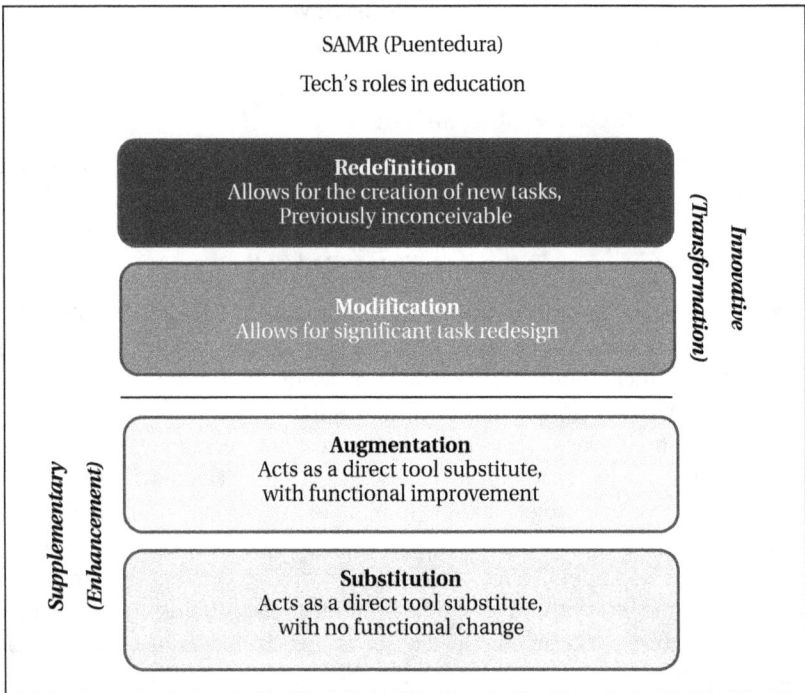

(adapted from Puentedura)

SAMR refers to four roles that technology can play in an educational setting: substitution, augmentation, modification, and redefinition. The upshot of this theory is the transformative functions technology has in education: Modification and Redefinition. Here, technology is no longer just a medium to be employed at the final stage of a task to wrap, decorate, and deliver an end product that is already completed. Rather, it involves the entire process of the task; it can lead to the reconfiguration of the task or the creation of new tasks that were previously inconceivable. Written essays, oral presentations with PPT, or Prezi slides are still widely used in language classes. Yet they can seldom reach beyond enhancement; they largely remain as tools that can be used as a substitute for the original choice or can enhance the delivery of what is to be presented, but without affecting the presented material. On the other hand, new technological tools can modify or redefine the task plan and design.

New technology by itself, however, would not guarantee transformation. Its transformative potential becomes a reality only through its effective use. In order to maximize the benefits of the integration of technology into a CLIL project, the instructor and students need to carefully review both the nature of the project and the features of technological tools to determine how to successfully blend these elements together. Examples of such technology-integrated pedagogy include collaborative research published through an e-book tool equipped with multimedia components that allow the user to employ various useful applications and multimodal elements such as map application, 360-degree street views and YouTube videos to make the presentation informative and effective. These forms of technology-integrated publication or presentation, such as e-book and video, often require different sensibility and approaches to the task itself. In other words, they can result in *modification* during the process of completing the task. On the other hand, online platforms of presentation or publication (blogs, vlogs, videos, e-books), unlike conventional formats such as paper and oral presentations that are limited in terms of both time and space, allow for more durability and availability, which invites more response from the audience. This increased interaction and communication encourages students to continue to *redefine* their work, even beyond the class and the term, instead of simply brushing it aside once the work is finished. It is also worth noting that these technology-integrated learning practices often galvanize students into active independent learning.

## 4.2 Practice

### 4.2.1 Timeline project and Sutori

Timeline project is suitable for all levels of content and language classes, but particularly preferable for an advanced class with a particular focus on diachronic study or understanding of historical transformations. This formula is indeed useful for the Kubo project. It is conducive to creating the history of *tapang* from the colonial era to the present. As noted above, *tapang* as a space between home and work and between public and private life is imbued with varying historical and cultural meanings. Drawing on references in the four Kubo texts, a *tapang* timeline allows students to examine distinct values *tapang* assumes in each different time period and compares them to create a history of *tapang* in modern Korea. Through this *tapang* timeline project, students can learn Seoul's geography and understand historical meanings of spatial and architectural landmarks in the city. For a timeline project, several popular online presentation tools are available. Yet this study opts for Sutori[2] because it is easier to use than other tools, especially for non-professional users.

As with other online educational tools, Sutori is equipped with various interactive and collaborative functions. Yet these functions are not simply built to enhance the task. They often encourage students' independent learning, creative engagement in their project, and also collaboration with peers during the project. To borrow from Puentedura's terminology, they make Sutori *transformative*. With Sutori, students can create a roll of pictures with texts and videos that highlight the characteristics of the *tapang* culture and their social connotations in each major time period between the 1930s and the present. Besides, unlike other tools, Sutori also allows students to incorporate forum discussions and quizzes to promote student engagement and collaboration. Students tend to be better motivated when they participate in a creative and collaborative project and when they know that their work will be reviewed and receive feedback, not only by their instructor but also by their peers. They also find their work more meaningful when they produce it not only as an assignment, but also as a way to communicate with others, which attests to Sutori's transformative potential.

---

[2] See Sutori, https://www.sutori.com.

**Figure 9.4.** History of *tapang* in Seoul, a Sutori timeline project with a forum and a quiz added along with a YouTube video

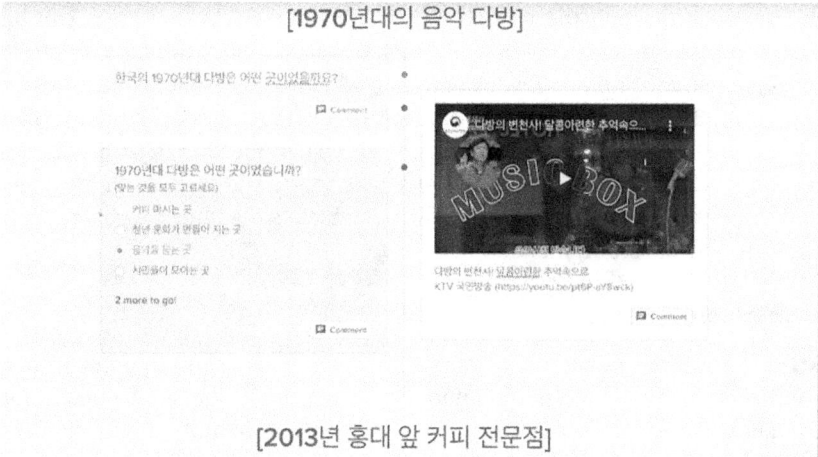

**4.2.2 Storytelling with Artsteps**

**Figure 9.5.** Tapang in Seoul: Old and new, a virtual exhibition that shows *tapang*'s old and new faces

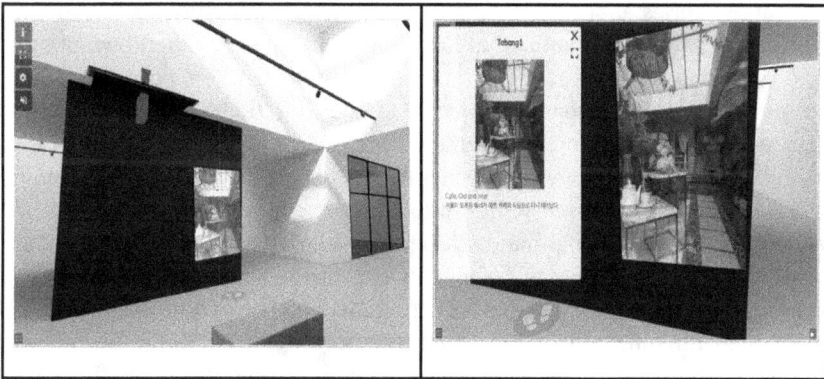

Artsteps[3] is another interesting tool that incorporates multimedia elements and narrations into a 3D virtual exhibition hall. Students can curate photos and videos of the *tapang* culture from different time periods and add written

---

[3] See Artsteps, https://www.artsteps.com

and audio commentary to highlight historically varying qualities of the *tapang* culture so that the audience can watch and learn the history of *tapang* as they walk through the virtual exhibition rooms. All virtual areas can be easily shared on social media, personal websites, and students can share ideas and exchange opinions through chat, which is an embedded function in this tool. By allowing students to "follow" other creators, students can participate in a community that shares similar interests. These works can inspire students to further explore a specific topic, and learn both language and content on their own in the real world, which is the ultimate goal of both the CLIL and the SAMR model.

### 4.2.3 Travelogues through Book Creator

Kubo is an urban *flâneur* who wanders and observes Seoul. In other words, drifting is a central motif in the Kubo texts. Thus, a travelogue is a good fit for the Kubo project. The instructor guides students to identify descriptions of places and architecture in Kubo texts such as *Namdaemun, Kyengseng* Station, *Cong-ro* Intersection, *Myeong-dong,* and research their historical and cultural meanings. When students are able to visit these sites, a field trip can be a great strategy for students to enrich their project. Through this kind of research, students can understand Korean geography, history, and culture more effectively. Furthermore, they can improve Korean proficiency by recreating stories about Seoul with literary devices. For students who are in Korea, taking the same paths that Kubo took and collecting their own photos and video clips would be ideal. Those who cannot visit Korea can use online resources for their research project. Methods for their final presentation include blog-style writing, vlogs, and e-books. For a travelogue or a field trip report, an e-book is especially popular for publishing research results. Among the more commonly used online publishing programs is Book Creator.[4] It allows for direct drawing, handwriting, and recording as well as image and video attachment. Figure 9.6 shows a page with hand-written notes and drawings with a recording of narration embedded in it and a page with an embedded YouTube video. These features encourage the users to be creative in making their e-book more personal and unique. Its collaboration functions help students find their work more meaningful and thus motivates them to engage more deeply in their project.

---

[4] See Book Creator https://bookcreator.com

**Figure 9.6.** Myeong-dong Arcade: Lotte Department Store to Sewoon Shopping Center, a Book Creator project

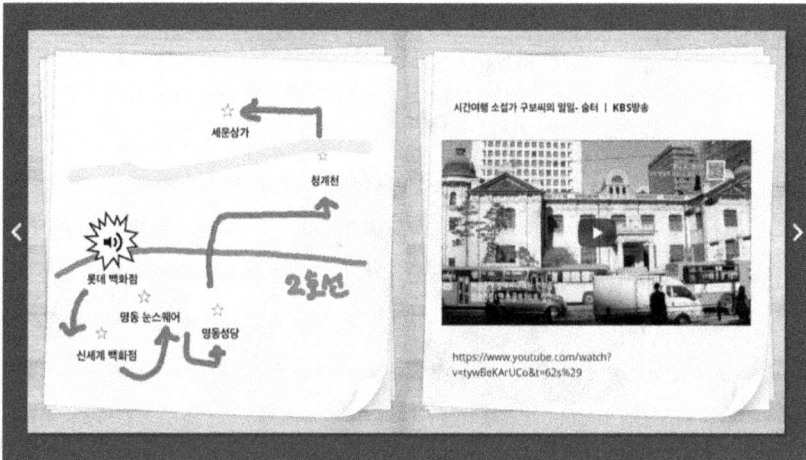

## 5. Conclusion

The Kubo project has not yet been fully tested and its practicality and impact on language learning are yet to be verified through its full-scale application to language courses and thorough assessments of students' performances and responses. However, some of the key elements such as translation, student-led research, and research showcase through new forms of presentation have been experimented with, and students' feedback to those practices has also been collected, if not yet systematically, through surveys. The survey results have been overwhelmingly positive, which conforms to the expectations set up for this project. For instance, fourteen students who took Korean Culture: Old and New (KOR 3410) at the Georgia Institute of Technology during the Summer 2020 semester were asked if the class stimulated their interest in Korean courses, language or content-based, to which the vast majority of students showed positive responses as below.

Regarding whether students were now willing to take more content-based Korean courses, almost 80% of the students expressed their eagerness to do so as shown in Figure 9.8 below, which proves the Kubo project's effectiveness in inspiring students to pursue greater knowledge of Korean society and culture.

**Figure 9.7.** Q. Did the class stimulate more interest in Korean courses?

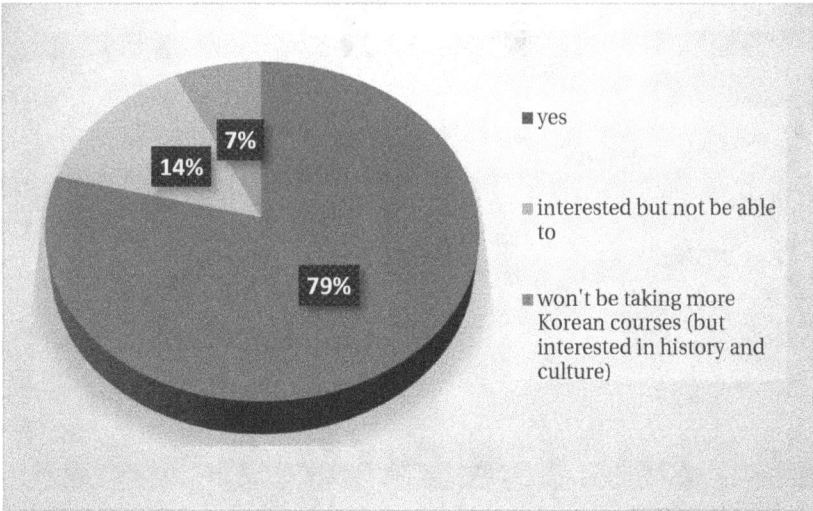

**Figure 9.8.** Q. Do you feel like taking more content-based Korean courses after this course?

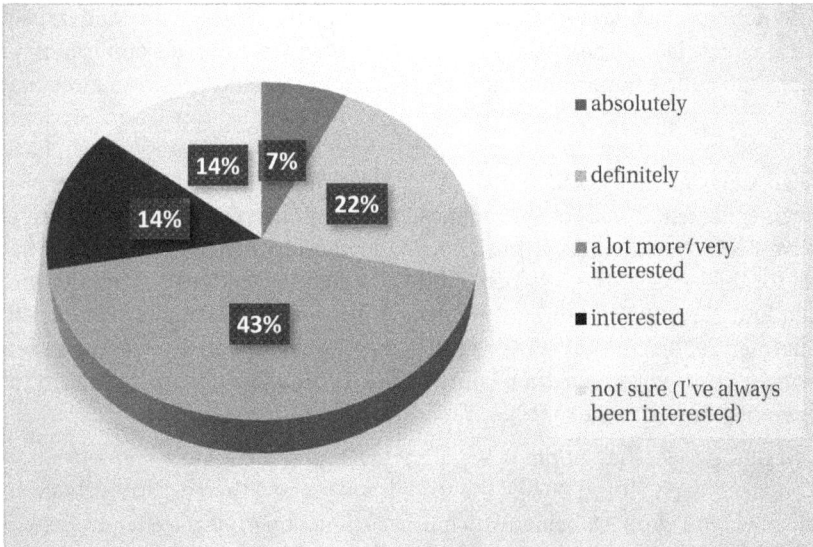

As shown in the feedback from students, the Kubo project, although still in progress, is expected to make significant contributions to the continuing endeavors in developing a viable pedagogy for advanced Korean language education. Its prospect also includes a constructive engagement with the scholarship on content and technology integration into language learning. Educational environments are rapidly changing as our society becomes ever more multicultural and multilingual and learning technologies also continue to evolve. It is thus imperative to recalibrate our thinking to successfully adapt to or make productive use of these changes and develop new pedagogical ideas for language learning. At its core, the Kubo project aims to offer fresh input to the ongoing efforts to meet this challenge.

## Bibliography

Ball, Phil, Keith Kelly, and John Clegg. 2015. *Putting CLIL into Practice*. Oxford: Oxford University Press.

Choi, In-hun. 1976. *Soselka Kupossi-uy ilil* (*One day in the life of Novelist Kubo*). Seoul: Mwunhakkwa cisengsa.

Choi, In-hun. 1985. *The Daily Life of Ku-Poh the Novelist*. Translated by Ki-Chang Hong. New York: Fremont Publications.

Coyle, Dorothy. 2007. "Content and language integrated learning: Towards a connected research agenda for CLIL pedagogies." *International Journal of Bilingual Education and Bilingualism* 10 (5): 543-562. https://doi.org/10.2167/beb459.0.

Coyle, Dorothy, Phillip Hood, and David Marsh. 2010. *CLIL: Content and Language Integrated Learning*. Cambridge: Cambridge University Press.

Joo, In-seok. 1995. *Kemun sangche-uy pullwusu-soselka kupossi-uy halu* (*Blues of the black wound: One day of Novelist Kubo*). Seoul: Mwunhakkwa cisengsa.

Kim, Suk-Su. 1997. "Hankwuk tapangmwunhwau-uy pyenchen-ey kwanhan yenkwu" (A study on the history of Korean da-bang culture). *Hankwung sillayticain hakhoy nonmwuncip* (*Journal of the Korean Institute of Interior Design*) 13: 37-44.

Krathwohl, David. 2002. "A revision of Bloom's taxonomy: An overview." *Theory Into Practice*, 41 (4): 212-218. https://doi.org/10.1207/s15430421tip4104.

Looney, Dennis and Natalia Lusin. 2019. "Enrollments in Languages Other Than English in United States Institutions of Higher Education, Fall 2016." *Modern Language Association*, last modified June 14, 2019. https://www.mla.org/content/download/110154/2406932/2016-Enrollments-Final-Report.pdf

Moon, Ji Hye., June Young Lee, Sunna La, Giho Kim, and So Yeon. Kim. 2019. "Sopi kongkan-ulose khaphey-uy uymi pwunsek yenkwu" (Coffee shops as a consumption space: Analysis of the meaning). *Sopimwunhwayenkwu* (*Journal of Consumption Culture Studies*) 22 (4): 153-174.

Oh, Younjung. 2017. "1930 nyentay kyengseng motenisuthutul-kwa tapang naklangphala" (Korean modernists and the cafe 'Nangnang Parlour' in 1930s colonial Seoul). *Hankwung kunhyentay miswulsahak* (*Journal of Korean Modern & Contemporary Art History*) 33: 33-56.

Pak, Taewon. 1934. *Soselka Kupossi-uy ilil* (A day in the life of Mr. Kubo, the novelist). *Cosencwungangilpo*, August 1-September 19.

Pak, Taewon. 2015. *A Day in the Life of Kubo the Novelist.* Translated by Sunyoung Park in collaboration with Jefferson Gatrall and Kevin O'Rourke. Seoul: ASIA.

Puentedura, Ruben. 2009. "Technology, Change, and Process." *Hippasus,* last modified October 19, 2009. http://hippasus.com/resources/actem2009/TechnologyChangeProcess.pdf.

Puentedura, Ruben. 2013. "SAMR: Moving from enhancement to transformation." *Hippasus,* last modified May 21, 2013. http://www.hippasus.com/rrpweblog/archives/000095.html.

Son, You-kyung. 2002. "1930 nyentay tapang-kwa mwunsa-uy cauysik" (Cafes in the 1930s and self-consciousness of literary men). *Hankwung hyentaymwunhang yenkwu (The Journal of Korean Modern Literature)* 12: 93-123.

Thompson, Gene and Jim Mckinley. 2018. "Integration of Content and Language Learning." In *The TESOL Encyclopedia of English Language Teaching,* edited by J. I. Liontas, 1–13. New Jersey: Wiley.

Woo, Jeong-gueon. 2010. "1930 nyentay kyengseng khaphey mwunhwa-uy sutholi mayp-ey kwanhan yenkwu" (A study on story map of Kyungsung's café culture in the 1930s). *Hankwung hyentaymwunhang yenkwu (The Journal of Korean Modern Literature)* 32: 343-370.

Yoo, Sin. 2013. *Sewul akheyitu phuloceykthu (Seoul arcade project).* Seoul: Minumsa.

Chapter 10

# Assimilation of Web 2.0 Tools in a Language Classroom for Authentic Novel Learning Experience in India

Divekar Neha

*Symbiosis Institute of Technology, Symbiosis International University, Pune*

**Abstract:** The objective of this study is to explore how authentic language learning experiences can effectively take place by integrating technology and Web 2.0 tools. Technology widens the horizon of a teacher as diverse pedagogical modes can be incorporated to promote learning; lending full scope to explore creativity at its best. To this end, the present research was an effort to discern the varied tech-based pedagogy tools implemented by the ELT teachers, teaching undergraduate University students in India; in face-to-face as well as virtual mode in a language classroom with emphasis on their application in the class. A qualitative research was carried out by administering a questionnaire to ELT teachers. Findings stated a comparison among the varied tools employed to engage learners with emphasis on the effectiveness, selection criterion of tools. Practical pedagogical recommendations and suggestions on proper selection and effective application of Web 2.0 tools are provided in this study.

**Keywords:** Web 2.0 Tools, Technology, ICT, Pedagogy, Language Learning, ELT, English Language Teaching, Ted Talks, Movies, YouTube, Short Films, Documentaries, Apps.

\*\*\*

## Introduction

English language teachers have a huge responsibility on their shoulders to facilitate language development and enhance the proficiency of the students in English. Language pedagogy is expected to have eminent approaches and incorporating them in teaching is regarded as a stimulating mission for the teachers; when teaching students who are learning English as a second language. With the advent of ever-changing technology and disruption in the tech-based world; its effects are noticed strongly even in the educational field. Today, education is undergoing a drastic change as disruption is also taking place in the teaching and learning process. Growth and development happen due to experimentation and assimilation of novel techniques in the pedagogy to bring about positive results.

Contemporary learners are engulfed in the labyrinth of digital media. Therefore, making use of Web 2.0 as teaching tools, materials, learning sources facilitates better learning. Technology enables speedy absorption of knowledge as it satiates educational demands. There is a plethora of Web 2.0 tools available on the web, and shortlisting and selecting from the digital media ocean is a herculean and daunting task before academicians. English language teaching (ELT) teachers need to make knowledgeable choices by considering frameworks and tenacities which will be beneficial to the learners.

English is a global language (Dorner and Cervantes-Soon 2020) and in India it is the language of instruction in education (Sheth 2018). Even employability is dependent on possessing good command over the English language, as it is the chosen language in business houses, companies and organizations (Erkan 2020).

Language learning ecology is undergoing an optimistic transformation by catering to the changing educational needs. Technology has become indispensable in the twenty-first century with the arrival of globalization (Mai 2020).

### English language teaching and technology amalgamation

Technology has become an integral part of our routine lives and has even entered the world of the education (Taher 2020). In contemporary times there is a pressing need to incorporate Web 2.0 interactive tools to improve the language proficiency of the students. Web 2.0 tools help retain learning excitement in the class (Mai 2020). ELT can be taken to the next level by discovering and adapting tech-based tools, blogging technologies and using mobile applications; so that lexical skills of the learners can be upgraded. Although using Web 2.0 tools in teaching has become the norm, ELT teachers face some challenges such as paucity of time in selecting, designing and implementing technology-based instruction within the stipulated class time. Furthermore, students sometimes use mobile application for entertainment or casual interaction purpose and not for building their language competency.

Thus, a teacher faces a dilemma whether to use mobile technologies or not. On the other hand, it cannot be denied that technology has become an indispensable part of our lives; it is impossible to discard their supreme presence in ELT (Kazhan et al. 2020).

It is important to be flexible when it comes to embracing digital upheaval in today's ever-changing scenario. Language learning media is undergoing a massive change along with the arrival of industry 4.0. The digital disruption in technology can be used with advantage in a language classroom by incorporating Web 2.0 tools, skillfully. Appropriate tasks, activities, assignments must be designed keeping the goal in mind to increase learner engagement in as well as outside the class. If the right kind of activities are selected then, it will help sustaining the interest of the students in the subject and also help in their subject advancement (Viera and Sanchez 2020).

A teacher has to understand the diverse nature and attitudes of the students and accordingly construct knowledge to cater to the explicit requirements of the learners. Students can monitor their performance when the teacher builds a perfect learner-oriented atmosphere (Mai 2020). Web tools can be explored in numerous ways and collaborative learning is stimulated. Web 2.0 tools make the personalization of information feasible, as many interactive activities and exercises can be designed, and content can be formed in collaboration. Interactive learning media is always beneficial as it creates an aura encouraging knowledge integration with reference to a specific topic or context. Every class begins with some teaching and learning objectives and by the end of the class, those goals must be attained. Similarly, it is important to note whether these tech-based tools are fulfilling those objectives.

It is advantageous to use Web 2.0 tools which are considered higher order skills according to Bloom's taxonomy in the pedagogy process such as application, analysis, evaluation and creation (Marshall and Kostka 2020).

## ICT in ELT

ICT integration in the teaching and learning of the English language comes up with its own incentives. Firstly, a teacher has access to a colossal repository of web-based study resources. Secondly, greater collaboration and numerous opportunities for communication develop. Thirdly, the drive to learn is at its peak.

## Web 2.0 tools in ELT

Customized teaching strategies must be evolved as one size does not fit all. Teachers have to be sensitive towards the learners and emphasize on bringing translingualism in English Language teaching. Teaching and learning process must come out of text-based material shell. Web 2.0 tools support linguistic, audio, visual, gestural, tactile and digital modalities to fit in ELT. Inclusive and equitable teaching practices must be advocated by teachers to raise the contextual learning stakes of the students. Teachers have the onus to produce transformative literati by juxtaposing serious and participatory teaching systems (Vinogradova 2021).

After going through studies conducted on this subject, there were a few studies which shared a negative perspective and reported that students were not very optimistic about learning a language with the aid of tech tools (Genc and Aydin 2011) and faced technical glitches which led to poor experiences.

Tech tools and internet connectivity allows perpetual learning to take place without any obstruction. Holistic language development will take place when teachers select and design sustainable Web 2.0 tools and collaborate them efficiently in an ELT classroom (Taher 2020). Technology has transformed ELT as teachers become facilitators emphasizing on student-centered approach in language instruction (Erkan 2020).

## Research questions

The following research questions will be addressed in this study:

i.     How authentic language learning experiences can effectively take place by integrating technology and Web 2.0 tools in an ELT class?

ii.    What kind of Web 2.0 tools are used by ELT teachers in virtual as well as traditional classroom?

iii.   Which Web 2.0 tool is effective according to ELT teachers with reference to effectiveness and selection criteria?

## Research design

The chief aim of this study was to reconnoiter how authentic language learning experiences can effectually take place by incorporating technology and Web 2.0 tools in undergraduate ELT classes in Maharashtra, India. Teaching and learning process has undergone a tremendous change with the advent of technology. Varied pedagogical tools are served by ICT on the teaching platter to teachers; from which materials and ICT tools; can be carved into a new masterpiece to cater to the contemporary teaching demands and student expectations. The prime objective of this research was to comprehend the wide-ranging Web 2.0 tools implemented by the ELT teachers in conventional as well as virtual classrooms, teaching undergraduate University students in Maharashtra region,

India. This small study was conducted in 2020 in Maharashtra region, India to gain insights from ELT teachers about their perceptions of using Web 2.0 as pedagogy tools.

A wide range of ICT and Web 2.0 tools are available to ELT teachers since the inception of the internet. There is a lot of information overload and teachers get perplexed at times and find it difficult to select an effective tool to elicit language proficiency in students. This study is an effort to simplify teacher's tool selection job to a certain extent as this study would reveal varied tools currently used by ELT teachers; followed by suggestions and inputs from them as well as the researcher; thereby simplifying the pedagogy process. To execute this research, a qualitative research design was adopted to extract exhaustive discernments of the respondents. Detailed perceptions and practices of the participants are obtained by employing qualitative research design.

### Research instrument and data collection method

A survey was carried out by administering a questionnaire prepared via the medium of google form, to ELT teachers in Maharashtra region, India followed by qualitative analysis. The participants in this study were ELT teachers from Mumbai, Thane and Pune region in Maharashtra, India. The consent of the participants was obtained before sending the questionnaire and they were informed that the data collected will be used for research purpose only. The participants were briefed about the purpose of the study before taking their consent and sending the Google forms. They were given a span of a week to fill the questionnaire.

The questionnaire encompasses of two parts where the teachers' demographic information was collected in the first part; whereas their technological knowledge and experience with reference to Web 2.0 tools containing their inputs was collected in the second part. The questionnaire consisted of both open-ended as well as closed-ended questions; which provided ample of scope to the researcher to get exhaustive responses from the participants. Elasticity and autonomy in research design are crucial to get meticulous responses; thereby facilitating effective data analysis. The questionnaire consisted of 37 questions and was administered in the English language.

The first part of the questionnaire collected the demographic details of the participants such as age, gender, place of teaching, area of work, teaching experience, designation, classes taught by them and their contact details. Whereas, the second part of the questionnaire focused on seeking answers to the above-mentioned research questions. The survey helped the researcher understand digital-pedagogical competence development of the ELT teachers in Maharashtra, India.

## Data analysis

To analyze the data collected from the survey questionnaire, Qualitative Content Analysis (QCA) was adopted and applied to the data. This research data analysis method facilitates effective construal of the content of the data and helps in detecting themes or patterns followed by their orderly cataloging through codes (Wildemuth 2016, 318-329). The data was sorted into pre-decided themes methodically by espousing descriptive coding method. It was easy to bifurcate patterns and differences between data by using analytical coding. Data was investigated after classifying the data as follows:

a.  Types of Web 2.0 tools used by ELT teachers

b.  Advantages of Web 2.0 tools

c.  Limitations of using Web 2.0 Tools

d.  Comparison between tools

e.  Pedagogical recommendations on Web 2.0 tools

## Results and discussion

The participants in this study were 14 ELT teachers from Maharashtra region, India. Their work experience ranged from 6 months to more than 15 years. The following information related to ELT teachers was collected from the questions focusing on the demographic data such as age, gender, contact details, length of teaching experience, area of work, classes taught, designation, organizations where they work.

There were 7.1% of teachers aged 25 to 30, 21.4% of teachers aged 30 to 35, 42.9% of teachers aged 35 to 40 and 28.6% of teachers aged 40+. It was observed that there were no teachers from 20 to 25 age group and majority of the ELT teachers were in the age range from 35 to 40. The participants comprised of six females and eight males. The collected data indicated that 14.3 % of participants taught in rural areas, 35.7% taught in urban areas and 42.9% of teachers taught in metro areas.

The data revealed that maximum ELT teachers were from Pune region followed by Mumbai, Jambhul Taluka, Kalyan District Thane, Loni Kalbhor, Pune. It was observed that the participants taught English to the students enrolled for the courses ranging from BE, B. Tech, M.A., BBA, BCA, B.A., B. Com, Diploma undergraduate courses (engineering), LLB and few delivered trainings as a consultant to working professionals. Except two courses all ELT teachers taught undergraduate university students whereas one teacher taught at post graduate level and the other taught working professionals. It was worth noting that 100 % teachers incorporated Web 2.0 tools while teaching English. The teaching experience of the participants is computed in Table one.

**Table 10.1.** Teaching experience of ELT teachers

| Teaching Experience | Frequency | Percentages |
|---|---|---|
| 1-5 years | 1 | 7.1% |
| 5-10 years | 3 | 21.4% |
| 10-15 years | 6 | 42.9% |
| More than15 years | 4 | 28.6% |

## Type of Web 2.0 tools used by ELT teachers

The researcher provided a list of some pre-determined Web 2.0 tools from which the participants had to select ICT tools which were used by them in the teaching and learning process. The analyzed data is enumerated below:

**Figure 10.1.** % of teachers using tech tools

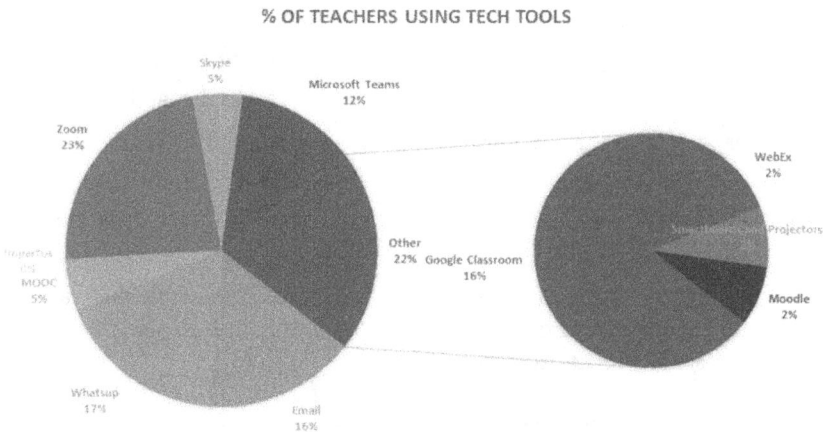

% OF TEACHERS USING TECH TOOLS

Zoom platform was at the pinnacle of the ICT tools as 92.9 % of ELT teachers made use of it. The next in line was Whatsup followed by email and Google classroom. 50 % of the participants made use of Microsoft teams and 21.4 % used MOOC and Skype as a pedagogy tool. WebEx, Smart boards, projectors and Moodle stood last in the list of the arrays of Web 2.0 tools with 7.1%. Not even a single participant used Impartus as a technical tool to teach students.

The next question in the survey form was an open-ended question where the participants were asked to mention the Web 2.0 tools integrated by them in their pedagogy process. Firstly, it was eminent that all teachers used technology in ELT teaching; out of which 10 teachers used all Google tools such as Google Classroom, Google forms and Google Meet. Secondly, YouTube was extensively used by eight participants. Thirdly, only two participants used TED Talks and fourthly, only two teachers used short videos to teach. It was observed that only 1 % of faculty used tools such as Twitter, Facebook, Instagram, movies, Voxvote, LMS, ESL lab, MOOC, Blogs, Apps such as Memrise, Kinemaster, Filmora, ESL websites, Wikipedia, Whatsup, Zoom, etc. Interestingly, there was one participant who had designed and created a self-faculty website exclusively dedicated to the respective students enrolled for that course under the faculty to cater to the educational demands of the budding ELT learners.

### Web 2.0 tools used in a virtual class

Teachers cited that they favor to use tools such as Zoom, online quizzes, short videos, Google Meet, YouTube, Osha videos, Google forms, Kahoot, Edmodo in a virtual class.

With reference to a virtual class Teacher two stated that: "I prefer to use online quizzes and videos; as it helps to retain student's interest in virtual class."

Teacher three said that: "We use Google classroom as it is user friendly and provided by the college."

Teacher six mentioned that: "In a virtual class I favor to use YouTube and Zoom as it is fast and convenient to use."

Teacher nine advocated for Zoom as its features were likeable and easy to use. Teacher eight recommended short videos as it helped in simplifying the comprehension levels at students end.

### Web 2.0 tools used in a traditional class

It can also be inferred from the survey questionnaire that Web 2.0 tools were used even in a traditional class. Teachers stated that technology effect could be noticed in a class, as it was observed that students were motivated and enjoyed a session when Web 2.0 tool was amalgamated with the topic. The survey conveyed that ELT teachers preferred to use the following tools in a conventional classroom:

**Table 10.2.** Tools used in conventional class

| Tools | Reason to Use |
|---|---|
| TED Talks and short videos | Help to retain students' interest and make them think |
| Educom | As many CDs are available according to the class level and topic. In addition to that even Syllabus related information is provided. It can be incorporated as authentic information is available. |
| Documentaries | Documentaries captivate the attention of the learners and can be used to improve speaking skills as group discussion can be conducted after watching the video. |
| Mentimeter | It helps in creating and building an interactive PPT. |
| YouTube | Encourages autonomous learning and offers enriching learning flavor |
| Podcasts | It is time-efficient and user-friendly |
| Audios | Rich accessible content is available which helps in conveying the intended meanings, thoughts precisely. |

Based on the survey it can also be inferred that teachers were comfortable in using Web 2.0 tools in a virtual as well as a traditional classroom to augment English language learning. 92.9% of respondents felt that using tech-based tools in an ELT class helps students learn the English language better; whereas 7.1% of respondents did not share the same perspective. Majority of the teachers also agreed that using web-based tools in ELT has proved to be successful in the current COVID scenario which led to elasticity in pedagogical domain but was also challenging. It was worth noting that respondents observed improvement in the performance of the students with the advent of tech-based tools.

## Pedagogical recommendations on Web 2.0 tools

All the ELT teachers were keen to use web tools to provide authentic language learning experiences to their learners and were quite enthusiastic about it. Effective implementation of Web 2.0 tools is a challenge and promotes novelty in a class as monotony doesn't creep in. The prime goal of ELT is to improve communication skills and promote better interaction; with this intention in mind language teachers can explore tech-based tools to encourage authentic learning experience.

The teachers highlighted that the engagement level of students and drive to learn was high when Web 2.0 tools were used in an ELT class. Authentic language learning experiences can be catered to students with apt planning, selection, implementation and follow-up of the ICT tool in enhancing proficiency in language. Teacher one insisted on using Memrise app to promote learning as this helps in improving the fluency of the students:

> I definitely recommend teachers to use app such as Memrise as basic membership is free so it can be used easily. In addition to that it promotes healthy competition amongst students and learning becomes fun. Memrise helps in conditioning the brain of the learners and leads to word retention. It is a wonderful tool for developing vocabulary of the learners. I use it in my class and have received good results; even my students are happy with it. It has been designed in such a way that beginners, intermediate and even advanced level of students can use it. I plan and conduct activities incorporating web-based tools and keep it learner centered.

Teacher two believed that social media should be used to provide authentic learning experiences as it is a wonderful platform to share thoughts, feelings, views, ideas and first-person perspectives with the world around you. Students can have hands on experience of writing and reading in a social setting. Twitter, Facebook, blogs, news channels can be explored in myriad ways to explore language learning. Inculcating social media in language instruction offers free interaction with native speakers and thus facilitate better learning. Teacher two advised that an ELT teacher can record and create own videos and then share them with students. Specially videos can be created to improve pronunciation skills of the learners as limited resources are available on this topic.

Teacher three emphasized that students must be provided with self-study kits to practice speaking and writing skills. As this will assist self-learning and will bring in guided autonomy in language learning. Teachers can design and develop apt, novel rich study material and make it accessible to students. Students would get an added benefit of studying the material at their own pace as per their convenience.

Teacher four stated that Web 2.0 tools bring diversity to a language class. An ELT teacher must understand learners needs and their culture so that they can engage the class more effectually.

Teacher five advised that controlled web-based activities should be a part of the pedagogy plan as they would provide a language experience. The stoic presence of Web tools helps an ELT teacher integrate all the four skills of the English language such as listening, speaking, reading and writing.

Teacher eight highlighted the benefits of using the ZOOM platform in ELT teaching: "I have created Zoom classes with breakout room for presentations, group discussions, email writing, small report writing etc. This practice was indeed fruitful for both the teachers as well as the students." An interesting technique was shared by ELT teacher 11 in the survey form as follows: "I enjoy using smartboard as good modules can be designed on it."

To sum up the inputs from all the ELT teachers, authentic Web 2.0 tools help students in sharpening their grip and command over the English language as adequate practice can be provided with the help of an internet connection. Internet facilitates better, reliable and assorted receptive language skills. Plenty of language games can be incorporated to charge up the classroom; as students like to compete with each other and victory plays the role of an added incentive to study and practice hard. There is a lot of pedagogical potential in using Web tools which must be explored to the fullest. The data analysis revealed a colossal plethora of tools and techniques which can provide an enriching experience to learners. The following recommendations were stated by the respondents such as skill specific Web tools must be selected to help students interact with native speakers. Furthermore, activities promoting experiential learning may help in providing authentic language learning experience. Quality well-studied Web 2.0 resources must be used effectively to cater to varied language related skills and types of learners which includes authentic texts, videos, documentaries, video lectures etc. Adequate practice must be provided to learners by conducting group discussions and presentations. A teacher must provide the necessary exposure to the students by making them use the language concepts in real life situations.

## Tips to engage students with Web 2.0 tools

All the ELT teachers shared several tips to engage the learners in an ELT class:

1.  ELT teacher one mentioned that Web 2.0 tools must be included in the teaching-learning process in the form of an activity to motivate and engage students. Activities provide students real practical exposure in implementing the language hands-on.

2.  Respondent two shared an interesting observation, "My college students are more interested to learn online than face to face. They enjoy learning and participate enthusiastically in all activities and exercises given to them since teaching involves ICT."

3.  Teacher three asserted that it is crucial to give an opportunity to students to participate actively in the class and contribute as required.

4.  Respondent four said that Presentations provide good experience to students and contributes in improving their speaking and delivery skills. This builds confidence in the learners and they learn by trial and error.

5.  ELT teacher five found the experience of incorporating mock interview practice and group activities beneficial; as students became more positive towards such tasks and it also helped in catching the attention of the learners and their involvement accelerated.

6.  Teacher six commented that asking questions surely encourages student involvement and they must be accompanied with presentations and group discussions.

7.  Respondent 10 indicated that students can be engaged in the class if an opportunity is provided to them to present their own assignments in front of the class followed by a question-and-answer session. This aids in making the class interactive.

8.  The respondent 11 believed that adequate practice must be provided to students to practice their pronunciation. To enhance their pronunciation audios must be included in the classes; so that students hear the accents of the word; thereby improving their accurate pronunciation.

### Advantages of Web 2.0 tools

Academic and professional growth becomes a blissful reality by integrating tech-based tools in language assimilation, and in the twenty-first century, this has become indispensable. The art and skill lie in making apt pedagogical decisions; teachers must have adequate knowledge about technology and its integration in teaching. Furthermore, teachers must possess abilities to select and use varied tools in their teaching activities (Mulyadi et al. 2020).

Digital resources would help in simplifying genuine problems faced by the students in learning the language. Such authentic glitches can be reduced by taking maximum advantage of Web 2.0 tools. ELT teachers must focus on reconnoitering accurate learning resources and create communication opportunities in class. Another benefit of using Web tools in teaching is that students get a chance to communicate with global partners and practice the language with native as well as foreign speakers (Mulyadi et al. 2020).

ICT's unification with education helps in keeping monotony at bay and has proved to be effective due to its user-friendly nature. It is convenient and can be assimilated easily by the learners in the twenty-first century. Furthermore, if compared with traditional pedagogical methods, ELT teachers get an added benefit in using Web 2.0 tools as it provides authentication and adds variety in the teaching and learning process. The study findings indicated that tech-based tools are an excellent source to make learning successful. It was commonly indicated by the respondents that very good content is available in every form for all types of English learning and teaching. Plenty of wonderful materials are a click away; which can lead to drastic developments in terms of honing a learner's miscellaneous language skills. One teacher emphasized that live interactions are better as compared to passive recordings as doubts can be clarified and customized inputs can be given after categorizing students into advanced, medium and slow learners. Using ICT based resources definitely endorse a learner-friendly atmosphere and offer more student talk-time. Application based learning accentuates the learning drive and raises the learning curve; thus, giving birth to smart efficient learning. Web 2.0 tools help in managing time as well as accelerates the momentum and enthusiasm to nurture a budding learners' liking for language adaptation.

### Limitations of using Web 2.0 tools

Seven ELT teachers stated that using Web 2.0 tools come up with some challenges related to internet service, connectivity and internet speed. Sometimes reaching to students who do not have access to internet is not feasible. Another limitation is the unavailability of necessary hardware especially in rural or semi-rural regions. Quality of internet service is also sacrificed in some regions due to which effective, focused and dedicated learning does not take place.

Teacher six drew attention to problems related to student engagement:

When you make use of ICT tools; at times learners may get distracted as it is very difficult to keep the attention span especially if there are technical issues, also it becomes challenging when class topic is related to reading skills, where focus is required to comprehend the content. Sometimes effective learning is affected due to student's passive involvement and at times students are just not interested in learning.

Web 2.0 tools incorporation also poses potential health hazards as screen time increases and eyesight is affected according to teacher two: "Prolonged use of ICT tools may affect eyes if proper care is not taken." Teacher 11 pointed out another probable downside concerning the diversity in a class: "Student diversity in an ELT class can be a boon as well as a bane. At times the biggest challenge in front of a teacher is to match the varied levels of the students and their mother tongue influence."

Another pitfall was mentioned by teacher three:

> In case of large classes where the student strength is quite high; conducting virtual presentations is a challenge as there is a possibility of the class getting distracted. Whereas in a traditional class playing a video is a limitation as the teacher has to make technical arrangements prior to a class such as arrange for a projector, a speaker, download a video with subtiles in case there is no internet connection in a classroom.

Teacher eight referred to evaluation and examinations as potential disadvantages:

> I feel a teacher must possess adequate content, technical as well as pedagogical knowledge to design effective tests to conduct evaluation via Web 2.0 tools. This is a time-consuming process as a teacher has to spend a great deal of time in researching, selecting, finalizing and implementing a tool to measure the progress of the students. In rare cases students can take help of Web tools and clear a test which makes keeping check on students difficult. It is hard to distinguish whether a student has written the exam or the assignment sincerely or has copied from someone or taken external help.

As a noteworthy point on feedback mechanism, teacher 13 remarked that: "Although there is a gigantic potential in using Web 2.0 tools in an ELT class; the downfall is that they lack human presence and the teacher may not be available at times to solve the problems. Sometimes teacher may not get immediate feedback from students and it will be difficult to gauge whether students content comprehension has taken place or not."

Finally, it is worth noting that five ELT teachers were absolutely comfortable and confident about using Web 2.0 tools in their teaching and learning process. They shared the opinion that Tech-based tools can cater to varied students' learning needs and expectations. A vast sea of rich sources is available to an ELT teacher as well as a student.

### Comparison between Web 2.0 tools

The researcher found that the three effective Web 2.0 tools recommended by all the ELT teachers were YouTube, Zoom platform and Google tools. According to respondents one, seven, nine and 11 YouTube is an effective tool as students find it catchy, engrossing, interesting and they are well aware of it. YouTube can be selected as a teaching tool when the teacher wants to enhance speaking skills, listening skills, writing skills, develop vocabulary, grammar or pronunciation. It is indeed a multi-dimensional tool. Students really enjoy watching different videos on YouTube followed by an activity in a class. In order to develop speaking skills, YouTube videos which are easily available can be shown to students; followed by group discussions or impromptu speaking based on the video. Videos in English language from movies or documentaries can be shown to students to help them practice their pronunciation. Context-based vocabulary can also be taught with the help of this versatile visual and auditory tool.

Nearly, all ELT teachers shared their perception towards Google tools and considered them beneficial as they were user-friendly. Secondly, Google forms can be used for continuous assessments for updating learners' skills and knowledge. Objective type of questions can be designed to enhance grammar, vocabulary and comprehension abilities of the students with the help of Google forms or quiz. It is easy to create a quiz with the help of Google forms and an added benefit is that students too can get immediate feedback. To add another feather in the cap of Google tools, study material, resources can be stored on Google drive and can be accessed from anywhere if internet connection is available. Google Meet too is a wonderful tool as it can be used to conduct virtual discussions on novels, poetry, short stories or simply to hone communication skills in general. Google classroom too is wonderful platform where all records can be maintained, assignments can be posted and evaluated, progress can be measured, rubrics can be applied to an assignment, etc. In addition to Google tools Zoom too is a good platform to practice the above-mentioned skills. It was observed that only one ELT teacher suggested Microsoft Teams as an effective tool as teachers felt Google Meet was more user friendly as compared to Zoom or Microsoft Teams.

Surprisingly, there was only one ELT teacher who was not sure as to which tool was effective and expressed the need to search for more tools. The sessions can be recorded in Zoom as well as in Google Meet so that students can watch how they perform by watching the video of the class and get immediate self-feedback. A teacher can also watch their video later on and give personalized inputs to students via email.

### Incorporating Web 2.0 tools in pedagogy Vs traditional pedagogy

Eight ELT teachers expressed a similar opinion that it is better to use Web 2.0 tools in teaching as compared to conventional teaching. With time teachers should change and adapt to the advancement of technology. Students enjoy learning with Web tools, it gives teacher an opportunity to experiment, and come up with innovative activities and provide an enriching learning experience. ICT tools not only help teachers in making variations in teaching styles but even provides better avenues to learners. They can be implemented with ease and create avenues for meaningful learning. The student generation is growing up with technology and is already advanced, so it is crucial for a teacher to raise the bar by incorporating Technological Pedagogical and Content knowledge (TPACK) model in teaching and learning process. Adapting will help the teachers as well as the students sail smoothly in the language acquisition process.

Teacher three mentioned that occasionally it is better, whereas teacher eight stressed on the usage, "Effectiveness depends upon how it is used." One participant staunchly denied by stating, "No, I would not agree as context, age, topic decide the use and effectiveness of web tools. The traditional and conventional teaching have their own benefits." To partially support this viewpoint another participant said that, "Not really! There can be a blend of the two methods to reap fruits."

### Inputs from the researcher

I feel that varied factors must be considered before integrating diverse digital literacy approaches to empower ELT teachers in incorporating Web 2.0 tools to teach English. Varied intrinsic factors have to be taken into consideration like attitudes, self-efficacy and training which come under teaching approach before implementing technology in pedagogy. Intrinsic factors are followed by extrinsic factors such as subject curriculum, time, funding, national technology policy and infrastructure to ensure effective teaching learning process (Erkan 2020).

I would like to recommend ELT teachers to customize Web 2.0 tools according to diverse learning aptitudes and styles with a motive to encourage student involvement and language enhancement. Teaching has become multi-faceted with the arrival of Web 2.0 tools in the field of English. Constructivism as a learning theory is a game changer and can facilitate language development in its true sense. It can help students to create charts, maps, multimedia presentations, digital stories cartoons, incorporate animation, include images thereby making the learning aura intricate, conversational, collaborative, dynamic, intended and generating the pathway for reflective education. Multiple perspectives can be brought in a language classroom by embracing Constructivism as an educational concept (Okumus 2020). ELT teachers must explore and embrace multiliteracies in teaching English (Warner, Chantelle and Dupuy 2018).

This research found out that ELT teachers must not focus on using limited tools but must explore varied avenues which are easily available online. In spite of a great deal of advancement in technology and pedagogy; there is a dearth of teachers using smartboards, but it cannot be denied that 100% respondents were aware of and had knowledge about combining technology with pedagogy in an ELT class. The data gathered from the survey questionnaire supports the claim that teachers are using technology to teach but still some avenues are left unexplored.

TPCK framework can be adopted for better language teaching and developing language literacy. This will help in understanding concepts which are easy to implement and likeable. However, only knowing and incorporating varied types of Web 2.0 tools is not sufficient but teachers need to understand how to explain the content with the help of technology. In short, pedagogy skills must synchronize with digital classroom practices, and this in itself is a mammoth endeavor to enrich ELT classrooms (Viera and Sanchez 2020).

ELT teachers have a massive accountability in inculcating knowledge, innovation, ICT in the students to help them confront the twenty-first century challenges successfully. ELT pedagogy must emphasize not only on language literacy skills but also on inculcating information, communication, media literacy. In addition to these points, inculcating social, cross-cultural skills is also essential. Leadership skills too demand high language literacy; creativity, communication, collaboration and problem-solving skills which can be combined with ELT to provide an enriching authentic learning experience to students. ELT curriculum must take care of dual aspects comprising of knowledge and skills. Teachers must leverage technology in indoctrinating language competency where tool selection is quite significant. Web 2.0 tools must be designed, selected and used in such a way that students learn to identify problems, solve them, employ varied techniques to comprehend to achieve class objectives. ELT teachers can curate a variety of resources to make meaningful experiences for the learners, allow students to demonstrate competency in achieving their language learning.

Creativity in communication must be encouraged and adequate practice must be provided to the learners so that they express themselves clearly and communicate confidently. Navigating online platforms in an organized manner will help maintain orientation. Informed decisions must be made after completing an ideal pedagogy cycle like searching online platforms, selecting apt materials, organizing the collected content and discard irrelevant unprofitable materials (Vinogradova 2021).

Openness, flexibility in learning duration, independence of location, validity, diversity in programs and websites, continuous interaction among students in the class, self-content creation, clearly structured lesson plan, variety in pedagogy methods and cognizant administration are some of the beneficial characteristics of incorporating Web technologies in an ELT class.

## Conclusion

Ripe learning opportunities must be seized by the teachers as well as shared and introduced to the students. Indeed, it is advantageous to use Web 2.0 tools due to their perpetual availability. They can be reviewed and arbitrated as per learner's learning requirement. Web 2.0 tools are multi-functional as with their presence students can connect, compare, interact, sift data, exchange and collaboratively build knowledge.

Any Web 2.0 tool will provide authentic learning experience only after due guidance from a teacher. No matter what type of tool is used, apt feedback must be given individually after completing the activities or exercises. English language input must be delivered to the students appropriately as per their level. Resources will be authentic only when they suit students' requirements. Methodology too must be chalked out well in advance keeping the topic objectives in mind. There should not be any delay in addressing the varied types of linguistic problems faced by the learners. Authentic learning experiences can be provided when technology, language concepts and pedagogical approaches are combined. A combination of all the above elements piques students' curiosity and leads to their active involvement in language learning. It is necessary that more resources be explored by ELT teachers.

## Bibliography

Dorner, Lisa M., and Claudia G. Cervantes-Soon. 2020. "Equity for Students Learning English in Dual Language Bilingual Education: Persistent Challenges and Promising Practices." *TESOL Quarterly* 54 (3): 535-547. https://doi.org/10.1002/tesq.599

Erkan, Hatice Ceren. 2020. "Digitalization of English Language Teaching in Higher Education: Insights from English Preparatory Classes in Turkish Universities." 1-39. http://urn.fi/URN:NBN:fi:hulib-202006223344

Genç, Gülten, and Selami Aydin. 2011. "Students' motivation toward computer-based language learning." *International Journal of Educational Reform* 20 (2): 171-189.

Kazhan, Yuliya M., Vita A. Hamaniuk, Svitlana M. Amelina, Rostyslav O. Tarasenko, and Stanislav T. Tolmachev. 2020. "The use of mobile applications and Web 2.0 interactive tools for students' German-language lexical competence improvement." 392-413. http://ceur-ws.org/Vol-2643/paper23.pdf

Mai, Nguyen Thanh. 2020. "Integrating Information and Communication Technologies into Second and Foreign Language Teaching: Pedagogical Benefits and Considerations." *VNU Journal of Science: Education Research* 36 (4): 1-7. https://doi.org/10.25073/2588-1159/vnuer.4401

Marshall, Helaine W., and Ilka Kostka. 2020. "Fostering Teaching Presence through the Synchronous Online Flipped Learning Approach." *TESL-EJ* 24 (2): 1-14.

Mulyadi, Dodi, Testiana Wijayatingsih, Riana Budiastuti, Muhimatul Ifadah, and Siti Aimah. 2020. "Technological Pedagogical and Content Knowledge of ESP Teachers in Blended Learning Format." *International Journal of Emerging Technologies in Learning (iJET)* 15 (6): 124-139. https://doi.org/10.3991/ijet.v15i06.11490

Okumus, Aysegül. 2020. "The Perceptions and Preferences of 8th Grade Students in Digital Storytelling in English." *International Online Journal of Education and Teaching* 7 (2): 585-604. http://iojet.org/index.php/IOJET/article/view/654

Sheth, Dhirubhai L. 2018. "The great language debate: Politics of metropolitan versus vernacular India." In *At Home with Democracy*, 169-195. Palgrave Macmillan, Singapore. https://doi.org/10.1007/978-981-10-6412-8_10

Taher, Zeenat. 2020. "Amalgamating Technology into Teaching the English Language." *Journal of Xi'an University of Architecture and Technology*, 12(5), 1247-1264.

Viera, Rodrigo Tovar, and Diego Ismael Velasco Sánchez. 2020. "Research on Technology Competencies in EFL Language Instructors: Technology-Pedagogy-Content in Language Teaching." *SCRIPT Journal of Linguistics and English Teaching* 5(1): 32-43. http://jurnal.fkip-uwgm.ac.id/index.php/Script

Vinogradova, Polina, and Joan Kang Shin, eds. 2020. *Contemporary Foundations for Teaching English as an Additional Language: Pedagogical Approaches and Classroom Applications.* Routledge, 277-287.

Warner, Chantelle, and Beatrice Dupuy. 2018. "Moving toward multiliteracies in foreign language teaching: Past and present perspectives... and beyond." *Foreign Language Annals* 51 (1): 116-128. https://doi.org/10.1111/flan.12316

Wildemuth, Barbara M., ed. 2016. *Applications of social research methods to questions in information and library science.* ABC-CLIO, 318-329.

# List of Acronyms

| | |
|---|---|
| B.A. | Bachelor of Arts |
| BBA | Bachelor of Business Administration |
| BCA | Bachelor of Computer Application |
| B. Com | Bachelor of Commerce |
| BE | Bachelor of Engineering |
| B. Tech | Bachelor of Technology |
| ELT | English Language Teaching |
| ESL | English as a Second Language |
| ICT | Information Communication Technologies |
| LLB | Bachelor of Laws |
| LMS | Learning Management System |
| M.A. | Master of Arts |
| MOOC | Massive Open Online Courses |
| QCA | Qualitative Content Analysis |
| TPACK | Technological Pedagogical and Content Knowledge |
| TPCK | Technological Pedagogical Content Knowledge |

# List of Contributors

**EDITOR BIO**

**Carmela Bernadetta Scala** received her Ph.D. in Comparative Literature from the City University of New York. Her main field of research is Baroque literature, fairytales, folklore, and dialect literature. She is also interested in contemporary literature and has published a book on contemporary cinema, "New Trends in Italian Cinema: "New" Neorealism." She has also published a book on Basile's Lo cunto de li cunti titled "Fairytales- A world between the Imaginary. Metaphors at Play in Lo cunto de li cunti by Giambattista Basile" and an Italian reader "Un viaggio fantastico nella lingua e nella cultura italiana." Her last article, "Matteo Garrone's The Tale of Tales-Visual Metaphors and Transmedial Storytelling," was published in the book entitled "The Body of Naples: Corporality and Performativity in Baroque Naples" (Lexington Books, 2017). She has published articles on language acquisition in the NEMLA Italian Studies journal. She is the Director of the Italian Language Program at Rutgers University and the study Abroad Program Director. She is the founder and chief editor of the Language Teaching and Technology (LTT). She has won an entrepreneurial grant to develop a Professional Development workshop entirely online for Italian teachers and many other small grants to create innovative online language courses. She received the Rutgers prestigious Ernest E. McMahon Class of 1930 Award for the academic year 2019-2020. She has recently published a book *From Design to Teaching: Granting Our Students An Engaging Learning Experience Online* (Cambridge Scholar Publishing, 2021); an article *How to Foster Equality in The Language Classroom,* in "Rhetoric and Sociolinguistics in Times of Global Crisis," (IGI Global, 2021.); and *Replacing the 'melting pot' with a 'colorful mixed salad' in the language classroom,* in "Global and Transformative Approaches Toward Linguistic Diversity" (IGI,2022.)

**CONTRIBUTORS BIO**

**Jon Bakos** is an Associate Professor of TESL and Linguistics at Indiana State University, and studies sociolinguistics with a focus on the regional dialects of Indiana. He is also focused on developing innovative writing materials for ESL.

**Valentina Ornaghi** is currently a PhD student at the Italian Institute of Oriental Studies (ISO), University "La Sapienza" (Rome), Curriculum "East Asia". She graduated in 2009 with a Master's degree in the Chinese language from the University of Milan and has since been teaching Chinese in high schools, universities and the Confucius Institute. Her research fields are Chinese language teaching, Chinese as a second language (CSL) acquisition and the use of technology in teaching.

**Ching-yi Amy JUAN**, from Taiwan, is a native speaker of Mandarin. She obtained her PhD degree in Environmental Sciences from Lancaster University UK. Living and working in different countries stimulated an interest in languages which inspired her to study "teaching Chinese as a second language" at Beijing Language and Culture University. She has been teaching Chinese as a foreign language at various universities in Lombardy, Italy since 2006.

**Silvia Tiboni-Craft** is an Associate Teaching Professor of Italian at Wake Forest University. She obtained both a B.A. and M.A. in Italian Literature from the Università degli Studi di Urbino Carlo Bo and a Ph.D. in Italian from Rutgers University. Her research and teaching interests include 19th and 20th-century Italian women writers, 20th-century Italian poetry, domestic space, feminist theory, Mad Studies and pedagogy. Silvia published articles and book reviews on Italian Women Writers and Italian Literature.

**Qiaona Yu, PhD** is an Associate Professor of Chinese at Wake Forest University. Her research specializes in the intersection between Chinese linguistics and second language acquisition by defining, assessing, and developing Chinese syntactic complexity. She is also passionate about language for specific purposes, task-based language education, cognitive linguistics, and psycholinguistics.

**Jasmine Yu-Hsing Chen** is an Assistant Professor of Chinese and Asian Studies at Utah State University. She specializes in Chinese theater, media, and literature and has been teaching Chinese as a foreign language for numerous years.

**B. Eda Hancı-Azizoglu** gained her Ph.D. in English Language from Indiana University of Pennsylvania with a double major in Composition/Rhetoric and Applied Linguistics/TESOL. Her knowledge and experience lie in the areas of English language, literacy, culture, and writing. She is an expert on global perspectives on language and literacy policies, practices and English language learning and writing programs. She has extensive English Language teaching experience in American public schools and universities. She served as a chair in English Departments, where she developed English language programs depending on her students' unique and diverse needs. She has given master's level courses to certified American school teachers to provide them leadership and skills on language teaching methods for multicultural students. Her research interests are artificial linguistic intelligence, linguistic analysis, the poetic and creative function of English as an additional language.

**Dr. Maha Alawdat** holds a Ph.D. in Composition and TESOL from Indiana University of Pennsylvania and Master's Degree in foreign English Literature from Ben Gurion University in Israel. Currently, she teaches at the English Department of Kaye Academic College of Education and Ort Abu Rabe'a Multidisciplinary School. She is also a member of the national English Advisory Committee of the Ministry of Education in Israel. Previously, she taught at Indiana University of PA and the Language Centre in the United States. During her career, she got a number of awards like Fulbright Scholarship from the American Embassy, Teaching Excellence Award from IUP, Graduate Women's Leadership, Dissertation Completion, and Exceptional English Teacher Award from the Israeli Ministry of Education. She has also published a number of articles, poems, and books. Her interest is digital media, Distance learning/Online Education, English as a foreign language, Multiculturalism and intercultural communications, Professional development, Digital Writing, and storytelling.

**Stefano Maranzana** is Lecturer of Italian and French in the Department of World Languages and Literatures at the Southern Methodist University in Dallas, Texas. His research interests focus on the acquisition of Italian grammatical gender, captioned video in listening comprehension, virtual reality in language learning and Italian American ethnicity and immigration. His latest research centers on the use of French language variations (argot and verlan) in contemporary TV shows and its implications for learners of French language.

**Elena De Costa** is Associate Professor of Spanish at Carroll University. She teaches Spanish language, Hispanic literature, history, and politics, edits the student magazine *El Coloso,* and directs the annual bilingual theater production. She is the author of a book on contemporary Latin American theater (*Collaborative Latin American Popular Theater*) and numerous articles in scholarly journals and book chapters on the literature and politics of Latin America. Her areas of research include the contemporary literature and politics of Spain, Latin America, and the Caribbean and second language acquisition.

**Iwona B. Lech** is a foreign language educator and course designer. She has recently served as a Digital Humanities postdoctoral research associate at the Language and Culture Learning Center. Her research focuses on learning languages in informal online spaces and the psychology of language learning with a special attention to positive emotions. She is a published author of peer-reviewed articles and book chapters and an avid presenter at national and international conferences.

**Yong-Taek Kim** is Associate Professor of Korean in the School of Modern Languages at the Georgia Institute of Technology. His research focuses on the interrelation between perception, cognition, and language, contrastive linguistics between Korean and Japanese, and application of cognitive linguistics to foreign language teaching.

**Seung-hwan Shin** lectures in the Department of East Asian Languages and Literatures at the University of Pittsburgh. He specializes in Korean cinema and popular culture. He is currently working on a monograph on the film renaissance of South Korea in the 1990s and 2000s.

**Mina Lee** is Professor and Associate Provost for the Educational Technology and Development Directorate, Defense Language Institute Foreign Language Center, Monterey, CA.

**Hyunkyu Yi** lectures in the Department of East Asian Languages and Cultures at Columbia University.

**Dr. Neha Divekar** is an Assistant Professor working at Symbiosis Institute of Technology, a constituent of Symbiosis International (Deemed) University, Pune with Ph.D. in English Literature. She is the faculty head for Literary Club and also runs students and faculty TED Club at SIT. In addition to that, Dr. Neha facilitates GDPI training to students as well as conducts corporate training and is Convener for TEDx.

www.ingramcontent.com/pod-product-compliance
Lightning Source LLC
Chambersburg PA
CBHW050442280326
41932CB00013BA/2216

* 9 7 8 1 6 4 8 8 9 7 0 2 3 *